The Life of the Creative Spirit

5901-ROME

The Life of the Creative Spirit

H. Charles Romesburg

901-ROME

To order additional copies of this book, contact:
Xlibris Corporation
1-888-795-4274
www.Xlibris.com
Orders@Xlibris.com

Contents

PART ONE

The Nature Of Creative Work

PART TWO

Examples Of Creators At Work

PART THREE

The Responsibilities Of Creators

PART FOUR

Credos Of Creative Workers
167

Preface

Something hidden. Go and find it. Go and look behind the Ranges–
Something lost behind the Ranges. Lost and waiting for you. Go!
[From Rudyard Kipling's poem, *The Explorer*]

With this book I have expanded the geographic reach of a seminar I teach on creative work. On the far side of the Ranges lying beyond this page, you will find hundreds of ideas useful to work and life. I recommend that you cross the Ranges three times. First, to learn the lay of the land, read the book through. Second, carefully go over every inch of the land by copying out the quoted remarks of creators, 400 or so words each day. Several times during the day, think about and reread the copied remarks. It will take you about eighteen weeks to copy the 50,000 words. Third, when you finish this, reread the book through, reinterpreting the lay of the land.

I have a request for professors. Please consider giving a course on the book's ideas. They have links to, and among, every area of university learning: the arts, the humanities, the physical sciences, the social sciences, engineering, business, ecology, and even the rock-climbing gym. Such a course will help students choose their majors, choose their courses, and make connections among subjects. The classes will be interesting and lively. Most of the ideas will extend what students already believe or suspect is so. Other ideas will have the effect of a cold front coming through, a clash of beliefs producing a storm of instructive debate.

The last thing to say is that the proceeds from the book's sale go to nonprofit charitable organizations whose missions are to promote either the humane treatment of animals or the preservation of wilderness. As to why this is, you will find the reasons behind the Ranges.

Chapter One

Introduction To Important Matters

The October cover was very nice. So are many of the covers, but this one pleases me more than most because it is of a painting.

The *Journal [of Forestry]* is interesting but as I approach age 65 I reflect again that it devotes no thought or space to the matter which must surely concern most other foresters as it has me for many years. The matter of which I speak is the life goal, reality, achievement, philosophy—in short, the spiritual thrust which no amount of mensuration, dendrology, increments, fire plans, or ethics can address, guide, explain, satisfy. Foresters are not just workers and technicians, but sensitive people in need of discussion, essays, shared experiences, and comfort from mature minds in and out of the Society [of American Foresters].

I don't think most of us have made it, are making it, or are going to make it through to a satisfying conclusion by just being good foresters. I do think we might by striving with some guidance to understand ourselves (and others) as we pursue the annual allowable cut. Like some cities which set aside 1 percent of new construction budgets for art, the *Journal* should set aside an issue each year, or at least every five years, in which important matters are treated.

Edgar J. Murnen, Jr.

[Letter to the *Journal of Forestry*]

To those who look to science for answers to a better life, it is irritating that it has nothing to say of the spirit, particularly of its substance and role in creative work. Neurologists, after all, have good success in understanding the brain. Brains of cadavers are routinely deposited into stainless pans and weighed, sketched, magnified, snipped, centrifuged, chemically analyzed, and possibly desiccated, at all stages of slicing them down, yet the creative spirit is nowhere to be found.

It is just as well. For suppose scientists did get their hands on the creative spirit, perhaps a softly lit vaporous thing. Confining it in a bell jar, they would proceed to determine its specific gravity, its index of refraction, its viscosity, its electrical properties, and to locate its variables and quantify their relations. Although perfectly objective and sure to make scientists beam, the knowledge has no pulse.

But then, where the approach of the objective scientific assay is closed, the approach of the subjective meditative essay is open. Such is the essay of this book. It aims to answer Mr. Murnen, not only for foresters but for teachers, computer programmers, soldiers, entrepreneurs, doctors, financial planners, merchants, managers, engineers, preachers, and all.

The answer lies in understanding the universal artist. To be a universal artist, approach your work imaginatively. Bring to fullest productive being the artist within you, creating use, beauty, or both, of rare note. Take it from Robert Henri: ". . . Become an inventive, searching, daring, self-expressing creature. . . . [You do] not have to be a painter or sculptor to be an artist. [You] can work in any medium. [You simply have] to find the gain in the work itself, not outside it."

With a view to making the universal artist understandable, Part One of this book explains the nature of creative work. Among the ideas are: what goodness is—why goodness is not arbitrary—why goodness is not always what feels good—what excellence is—what quality is, and how it is not excellence—what the function of quality is—what the creative spirit is—how creative work may be collaborative—what motivates creative workers.

The chapters of Part Two look at the universal artist in action, through seven kinds of work, that of artist, scientist, mathematician, mechanic, entrepreneur, rock climber, and collector. These span the range of kinds, and creators in other kinds will know which of the seven theirs is closest to. Among the ideas are: how the work of the artist and the work of the scientist are essentially alike—how the work of the entrepreneur is closer to the work of the scientist than to that of the artist—how the work of the rock climber is most like the work of the mathematician—and in general, how every creative vocation and avocation has much the same artistic life and soul, and how creators, apart from their outward differences in temperaments and abilities, education and training, and tools and equipment, are much the same.

Our responsibility to creative work dictates supporting responsibilities. Covered in Part Three, they are the responsibility to guard ourselves against falling into a life of seeking sensual gratifications; the responsibility to raise our children to appreciate excellent works, that they may grow up to create their own; and the responsibility to raise ourselves to put great goodness into the world. Two seldom-discussed responsibilities round out the list, yet with every step of climbing to meet them we become better creators. They are the responsibility to revere every form of life, and the responsibility to learn about and preserve nature.

Last, Part Four presents the whole of these matters from another standpoint, through an anthology of credos extracted from diaries, letters, journals, and autobiographical literature of creators whose ideas affirm and extend those of the three preceding parts. Treated as a data base, the anthology amounts to a grand credo of our species, declaring that the ultimate orienting direction is to be forever trying to create great goodness; that this and only this fully unites people into humanity; and that this is the gist of one's identity, the origin of spiritual satisfaction, the answer to the meaning-of-work question and, by that, an indispensable part of the answer to the meaning-of-life question. When so many creators of esteemed worth believe the same, their convictions reinforcing one another's and fitting neatly into a logical and emotional whole, there must be something to it.

The above-mentioned material will serve those wanting to understand their creative and spiritual possibilities, their work, and their professions.

The same material may offer hope to those with jobs that deter their need to think. They feel their employers pull too often and hard on the reins, limit their choice of projects, or require their steps to fit another's, smothering the spirit. A far-reaching view of creative work may encourage them to discover and move to vocations with increased creative license.

The material also has a part to play in everyday life. Millions welcome having a job with little or no freedom in the harness, taking comfort in the regularity of the tasks, in the schmoozing with fellow workers, and in the justifiably proud feeling of contributing to the running of society. For them, the door remains open to having a creative life in the after-hours. For every formally recognized creative vocation, there are any number of creative avocations beneficial to others. A case, mentioned only to illustrate what is meant, is to do creative projects of perceiving the critical facts bearing on problems in one's town or city, of thinking up and analyzing solutions, and of presenting them clearly through letters to the editor, or a column, in the local newspaper, enlightening citizens more than they think possible.

Finally, it would be good for the world if those in their formative years, looking for guidance to their next five or six decades, unsure about which fields of study are right for them, found in these pages the alternative to letting romantic or fashionable career dreams, embraced by them largely without regard to their potential creative talents, sway their choices.

PART ONE

The Nature Of Creative Work

Chapter Two

What A Project Is

There is a word that Shakespeare's *Tempest* uses three times, Melville's *Moby Dick* once, and F. Scott Fitzgerald's *The Great Gatsby* not at all—statistics belying its importance, for its concept is central to the motives, actions, results, and joys of being spiritually alive. The major Western languages have it nearly the same. The Spanish say proyecto; the French, projet; the German, projekt; and the English, project.

A project is the fundamental unit of creative work. The noun pro*ject* is better understood through the verb *pro*ject. The base "ject" indicates the action, "to throw"; the prefix "pro," the direction, "forth." The purpose of a project is to throw forth—to project—extraordinary goodness into being.

The human spirit decides whether a project does well enough. Does its product send a surge of sublime beauty into the hearts of people, for which they have no phrase? Are they unwilling to exchange this for a score of lesser delights? Is it as if a shared aurora borealis is present in the creator at the creation, and later in the receivers at the re-creation?

Six types of products are recognized, and it helps to think of them as containers for carrying goodness; this reminds us to consider them unfinished and unworthy of presenting to others until we have packed them full. Three are things made: material products, as vacuum cleaners and toothbrushes; knowledge, as scholarly and scientific research; and fine arts, as painting, poetry, and music. And three are things done: services, as teaching; feats, as climbs of the Matterhorn; and performing arts, as theater and dance.

For a project that appears to produce two or more products, the primary one is the type. The dentist makes a filling, a material product, but primarily to produce a service, fixing a cavity. High jumpers are watched primarily for the feats they attempt, and less for their coincidental artistic moves.

A project is composed of five parts. Here is a diagram:

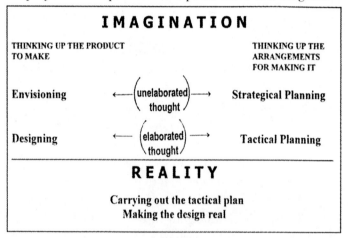

We imagine what to make before we imagine the arrangements for making it; hence the diagram's left to right arrangement of ends before means. And we imagine in principle before we imagine in detail; hence the top to bottom order, where envisioning prefigures designing, and strategical planning prefigures tactical planning.

To illustrate, pretend that your project is to conceive and build a fine path through your garden:

(1) Out of the blue, the vision arrives, the commanding idea of what to make, the first mental traces of the intended path, your thoughts in roughcast and unsketchable form. It is a dim scene

of where the path goes, and of its materials and dimensions, yet its hold on you is brilliant. It is your prenatal creation, and your parental instinct refuses to let go of it, insisting you further its creation, bearing it into the world.

(2) Within the frame of the vision's airy ideas, you conceive hardened ideas of the design, ridding the vision of questions and styling its perceptions, clarifying it to the senses, displaying its details. You think up and compare possibilities of materials—bricks, tiles, and flagstone—and decide. You compose prospects of patterns, textures, and colors, and decide. With safety and appearance in mind, you arrive at its width. With views of flowers, grasses, and shrubs considered, you locate its route. And with durability a concern, you mull over kinds and amounts of ballast, and positions of drainage tubes, choosing which should be. When finished you have graphically displayed the path to its least parts, with perspective drawings from various locations. It is of premium flagstone, except fairyland flagstone, incapable of being walked on.

(3) Having projected the design into your imagination, you go on to project a strategical plan. As with the vision, the strategy is a barely digested notion, a frame with its interior unfashioned, like a silhouette. Broadly it outlines where and how you will obtain the materials—the sand, gravel, flagstones, wood forms, and the money to pay for them—as well as the steps of building and the tools to use.

(4) Within the latitude the strategy grants, you conceive the tactical plan that fills out and pins down the particular preparations. You exactly determine where to buy the materials, and pencil in on the calendar the dates they are to arrive. You exactly list the steps of construction and the required tools. You exactly figure the costs and how you will pay them. Upon completing the design you thought, "This is how I want the path to look"; upon finishing the tactics you think, "I know what it will take to produce that look."

At this point, everything is ready in imagination. Now it is time to get out in the garden and make the path appear:

(5) You put the tactical plan into practice. By its dictates, you lay out tools: spade, pick, tamper, tape measure, chalk line, carpenter's square, claw hammer, nails, level, saw, mason's hammer, trowels, and more. Trucks deliver the calculated amounts of sand, gravel, flagstone, lumber, concrete mix, and so.

Laying the path brings information which you use to enlarge the tactics and better the design. Unexpectedly running into underground rocks, you extemporaneously devise a plan to remove them, involving a crowbar. Mixing and matching textures and colors of flagstone, paring down pieces, and joining their shapes, you add improvements to the design.

The path bodies forth. Internally in vision and design, you had glimpsed and felt its pregnant goodness; now you are sensing and feeling it from the outside. You have brought into reality a thing that you and your guests and neighbors would have to look around a long time before finding an equal.

For the sake of directness, this illustration omits some points:

First: As used here, the word plan means the arrangements and preparations for materializing the design, the blueprint of the product. It is not used to mean the design, although this usage exists. What an architect calls a floor plan is really a floor design. And a company that announces, "Our strategical plan is to sell our products over the Internet," means that its vision is to sell its products over the Internet. The strategical plan for achieving its vision is another thing.

Second: There is a method of determining which is which, design or tactics. Examining the finished product shows the design behind it, but usually the tactics are hidden. In the case of the garden path, the gravel is tamped and leveled, parts of its design, though it is anybody's guess of the tools that were used, and for how long.

Similarly for services, feats, and performing arts, this method can be used on a completed project to separate the wanted doings from the doings to get the wanted doings. At a performance of *Macbeth*, you see the realization of Shakespeare's, the director's, and the actors' parts in the design, but none of the planning that went to making the design real, such as hiring and dealing with the actors, scheduling rehearsals, and obtaining stage props, for instance a convincing cauldron.

Third: Unless from stem to stern a project is everywhere error-tight, it is sunk. Unlike arithmetic, errors in two or more of a project's five parts never cancel. For a listless vision, no design can compensate. With a feeble strategy, the tactics can do no better than carry forth the feebleness. Mistakes in implementing the tactical plan, or in transferring the design to reality, kill the vision's promise of moving the passions. The product arrives stillborn.

Fourth: Plans cannot be too flush with preventive measures and fallback remedies against unanticipated difficulties, conditional safety nets of the essence, "While implementing, if I find these steps unworkable or ineffective, or these materials run out, or these tools break, here are the counter steps I will take."

In projects where time is important, troubles may become emergencies. What is more, numerous possibilities of improbable emergencies add up to likely having a real emergency in some way. Success rests on being alert to the first sign of trouble, and on having a large and practiced variety of solutions to draw upon and improvise from. Eddie Rickenbacker had this in mind when he warned his son to "never forget than an airplane is like a rattlesnake, [and] you must keep your mind and eye on it constantly or it will bite you when you least expect it which could prove fatal."

Fifth: Projects divide into three types according to where creativity mostly enters. Creativity may be concentrated in the vision and the design, with the plans tried and true, stock in trade, requiring little or no attention. A project to create a poem is like this, almost wholly envisioning and designing. Once the poet gets the design down on paper, that is the poem. How complicated the poet's searches for strategy and tactics would be if a poem had to be carved out on a Mount Rushmore.

Or it may be that the vision and the design are off the shelf, with the plans created to order. The project that produced the Great Pyramid is an instance–derivative in what to make, original in creating the arrangements for making it.

Or creativity may enter a project throughout, in envisioning and in composing its design, and in strategically and tactically managing its building. The Empire State Building was unprecedented all around.

The implications of these divisions bear upon choosing one's profession. Often, people who creatively shine at one of a project's five parts tend to be unremarkable or do poorly at the rest.

Abraham Maslow, impressively cut out to be an imaginative visionary, wisely decided to be a university professor. Weak were his skills and interests for designing, and nearly absent were those for planning to put his ideas into practice. Woe to passengers of a city's bus system with him in charge of the maintenance.

Sixth: Happily, no product, even Kenneth Grahame's *The Wind and the Willows*, agrees with everybody. Subjectivity, rendering us each unique, is to be treasured.

If creators and consumers were all objectively standardized like electrons, the mass and charge of which are identical around the universe, the range of creations would be narrow, and only a few creators could succeed. That creators come in diverse talents and interests, and consumers in a spectrum of tastes, means successes occur in pockets, with many to go around.

Simply create what turns your spirit on, and your product will find those spirits that marvel over the same thing, and in time you will possibly win converts, people's tastes shifting to yours.

Seventh: Of the imaginative parts of projects, visions are most prized. Besides guiding projects, visions radiate charm to the point of getting the upper hand of their creators. They are grand dream-wishes. They beckon. They tease. They promise. They appeal to sentiment, to the glands. They are bait, luring us to make the future happen. This they do most effectively by being vague, indistinct, wispy, sparse. Too many details would spoil the mood, which is perhaps why our nature has designing and planning as separate mental processes, to be performed when romance has run its course, and our attention is sober, our thinking rational.

What fascinates us so about visions and envisioning? Perhaps we are instinctively taken with ideas of pre-existence, of first glimmers of light, of causes unattributable to previous causes. Coming out of the subliminal headwaters of mind, casting the prospect of wonderful value into the near future, visions get projects off to flying starts, and our reverence for this induces fascination.

Eighth and last: Specifying common ground for communicating with aliens from distant planets has occupied cosmologists, and mathematics seems to be it. But what is the common ground for communicating with aliens from the distant past, our ancestors of thirty thousand years, as those in the Chauvet Cave, going about their projects of painting bears and rhinoceroses on the walls? Not mathematics. It would have to be something infinitely seated in both of us. Let us try the nature of projects, five recognized acts to them and to us, humanizing constants of all time.

Chapter Three

How Projects Are Recursive

If there is one book that most encompasses the realities of human nature, it is the dictionary. And if, among word prefixes, there is one set given to a particularly extensive side of this nature, it is those owing their existence to our changing our minds. The list includes "after," as in front of "thought." "Mis," as in front of "take." "Back," as in front of "track." "Up," as before "date." "A," as before "new." "Un," as before "learn" and "do." And the largest group of such words begins with "re," Latin for "again." Appraise, yet be prepared to reappraise. Examine, then reexamine. View and review.

With the root "cur" meaning "to run," to recur is to rerun, and a recursion is a rerunning. Throughout the course of a project, we run and rerun with our thoughts, creating recursively. To coin a word, we "recurse" goodness into being. It follows that only in the broadest view is a project one, two, three, four, five, finished—create directly and in order, the vision, the design, the strategy, and the tactics, then implement and go home. Revising and adapting, back-and-forth shaping and reshaping, wheel always in forming the design and the tactics, and this now and again brings amendments to the vision and the strategy.

The repeating stroke of a recursion pairs intuition and intellect. Intuition, a reflex whisper of the subconscious, discovers ideas and casts the preliminary decision of whether to use them or not. Intellect, armed with reason and experience, scrutinizes intuition's suggestion, determining if the preliminary merits stand up to close examination. Ingmar Bergman explained it this way:

> I make all my decisions on intuition. But then, I must know why I made that decision. I throw a spear into the darkness. That is intuition. Then I must send an army into the darkness to find the spear. That is intellect.

Tens of thousands of recursions crowd into a project, with the creator generating and selecting ideas piecemeal, little by little composing them into a running design of a product, and tactics for making it real. At every turn, intellect may reject an intuited idea, or tentatively accept it. Or intuition and intellect, widening their purview, may raise second thoughts about the work of the past days, decide to abandon ideas that previously looked good, set the project back to an earlier point, and begin searching anew.

A sketch of Ingmar Bergman creating his film *The Seventh Seal* illustrates. Getting him under way, a vision surfaced into awareness, the leading theme and mood of the film's substance and form. After examining it for several weeks, still it prepossessed him. He had to give it specific impression. He began designing the screenplay, surmising details, testing them with reason, rejecting most, adopting some–the particulars of the plot, the historical period, the scenes, the costumes, stage settings, lines of dialogue, postures and attitudes, tenor and voice, rhetorical devices, inflections and emphases of speech, and who the actors would be.

His trail was a mess of windings, false starts and restarts, dead ends and withdrawals from once-gained grounds. At times, fresh ideas rendered prior promising ideas worthless. Other times, ideas that two days before had warmed him and seemed entrenched, inexplicably turned cold from sitting in his mind, growing familiar. Disheartened, he cast them out, unsuspecting that in his depths he was already back at work, nosing around far afield, researching for lasting replacements.

A third of the way into the work, nearly every idea he had generated for the design he had come to think better of and let go, and few of the remaining ones would last the course. The bubbles and their bursting–groups of ideas that had looked good, only to go to pieces–played the educating role, positioning him to rally with the excellent ideas that belonged in the finished film.

With the design nearly complete, he drew upon his experience of making films and conjured up a strategy. Within its frame, he recursively created the tactical answers to lining up financial backing, and to settling where and how the film would be shot, who would be the costume makers, the make-up specialists, the movers, the electricians, the cameramen, the accountants, the expediters, and so forth, not to mention dealing with fickle actors. Once more, stumbling-blocks, standstills, wild-goose chases, and sourings confronted him. Managing to quiet one trouble spot, another would erupt. Yet prized ideas surfaced too. While stalled in difficulties, reworking his plans, he spied openings to rework the design, inching it past what had seemed as good as he could expect. Infrequently, too, nature intruded with a gift, as when a fortuitous dark cloud approached during the filming, which to wonderful advantage he fitted into the Dance of Death scene.

No one should be surprised that recursion is the agent of creative work. It is the agent of everything:

Recursion is the agent of biology. How, unless by replicating DNA and protein, iterating the instructions of its genetic plan, is the barely noticeable Sequoia seed, the diameter of this o, able to command the growth of a three-thousand ton tree?

Recursion is the agent of patterns. See it as it was long ago, along the chalk cliffs of southern England, in the ribbed spiral shells of 200-million-year-old fossilized ammonites. See it as it is today in the tiling designs of mosques, and in the budding petals of the wild rose.

Recursion is the agent of foot travel. When John Muir walked a thousand miles to the Gulf of Mexico, his basic stride of left foot, right foot took tiny bites out of the distance. He recursed his way there, whittling away the miles.

Recursion is the agent of mammal life. The elephant, by repeating the elemental sequence of wrapping stalks of grass with its trunk, pulling them out, shaking soil off, and putting them into its mouth, instructions which occupy little space in its mind, eats enormously.

Recursion is the agent of arithmetic. Children quickly learn the elemental steps of longhand addition, summing a column and carrying the amount greater than nine. Iterating the steps, they total long lists of large numbers. Given another day or two to learn the steps of subtraction, multiplication, and division, they are equipped to solve practical problems of everyday calculation.

Recursion, it follows, is the agent of computer programs. A program is a set of instructions, executed recursively. With thirty or so lines of interconnected computing steps, do-this's and go-here's, a program for computing pi levers a huge effect, delivering millions of its digits to their pen.

Recursion is the agent of the cowboy, whose recursive program, marked by whoops and shouts, reining and spurring his horse this way and that, rounds up and delivers cattle to their pen.

And recursion is the agent of plant growth. Watching a speeded-up movie of a climbing vine is like watching a computer program or a cowboy or a rock climber. The lead tendril feels its way along, exploring for holds, threading an aerial maze, recursively drawing upon a small repertoire of moves. Mimicking this repertoire, a computer program can be devised to simulate the vine's climb.

Turbulent inventing, it appears, fathers orderly inventions. Although recursive machines execute beeline routes to their objectives, recursive creators of the machines do anything but. Examine the beaver, an efficient machine at recursively felling birch trees. Chaotically did evolution recurse about in begetting the beaver. Or examine a computer program that speeds right to its job of corralling pi; the programmer who devised it shot thousands of blanks in creating its commands. Or examine Henry Ford's first production line, assembling cars on a timetable; in his guesswork of designing it, it was necessary that he forget about finishing on a timetable. Or examine any art. At the end is produced a beautifully ordered sight, but the recursions leading to it are an ugly disordered sight. What more fitting example is there than Johann Strauss, countlessly imagining and testing variations to arrive at his design, a clockwork waltz?

This calls into question the meaning of wasting time, which is to say it bears persuasively on keeping efficiency experts from trying to shape up creators. The stopwatch is the bane of the inquisitive. It bars them from roving to and along faraway side paths of curiosity, essential for ultimately stumbling upon orienting glimpses of excellence that can be sighted in no other way.

Called into question, as well, is the undecidedness among philosophers about free will. Our recursive nature confirms we have it. For if God is pulling our strings that take us on all these groping trials, through scores of alternatives to reach decisions He insists we make, He is cruelly abusing us. As our designer, one expects better of Him.

But then, are we not a stroke of His genius and charity? By a brain the size and weight of two containers of cottage cheese, ours can hold a mind capable of creating fine works. So much potential from so small a thing, its recursions applied to where best to go and how best to get there, is God's astounding gift to us.

Chapter Four

How Projects Use Modeling

By the scope and variety of our creations, we deserve to be called the iterative species–the heuristic species–the recursive species–or more precisely, the species whose participating members run and rerun with their creative thoughts, bit by bit probing for goodness, until the final retained bits make a product that is unlikely to be bettered for some time to come. In turn, this reflects a further distinction, less acknowledged but as true, that we are the modeling species.

It is scarcely our making or using models of existing things that justifies this. A boy plays with a model airplane, a scaled-down copy of the actual, sweeping it through the air, now low, now high, a miniature of real flight. Still, if this is the only kind of modeling he does, he is sure to grow up well entertained but incompetent to the complicated challenges of creating excellent works.

It is modeling in a second vein that is the one. Like the first, it involves make-believe and is occupying. Unlike the first, it reverses the roles of the model and the real thing. Rather than the model coming afterwards, it is created first, a basis for making the real thing.

Why model in the arts? By going on in front of the senses, recursive modeling excites the artist's imagination, invigorates the finer intricacies of creating, brings intenser clarity and illumination to designing.

Sculptors, before ever touching a block of marble, dream their way through iterations, top to bottom, front to back, playing out imaginary trial-and-error arrangements, exploring variations, adjusting and readjusting ideas. Yet pure dreaming, going on in isolation behind the eyes, is insensible of much, finding its best creation short of better ones capturing sublime effects of form, and of light and shadow. Thus the sculptor recurses in the media of pencil sketching, and wax or clay—convenient for trying out decisions, easy to ball up and start over with. Under the guidance of direct seeing, fingers dart recursively around the model statuette, probing and reprobing for beauty's principal reliefs, lines, and shadings, searching for the elements of harmony and rightness that will stand the erosion of time.

When the modeling is finished, the statue ready for carving, the sculptor casts the clay statuette in plaster, measures it point to point, scales up its proportions, transfers them to the marble block, and with pointed tools roughs out the main protuberances and hollows, and with dented chisels chips away bits of stone. In due course, further and finer measurements are transferred to the emerging figure, and the cutting continues, converging on the final form.

The particular art sets the media of modeling. Frank Lloyd Wright recursively modeled his designs with drawings and miniature buildings. Ingmar Bergman recursively modeled with pen and typewriter, storyboards, and experiments at rehearsals. And Beethoven, while composing his works, tirelessly sketched and resketched on music manuscript paper, six or eight bars at a time, playing and judging the trials at the piano, exploring for those delicate changes of the kind that, borrowing Antoine de Saint-Exupéry's words, ". . . involve something that I can't define, which concerns the lasting quality of what I say."

A thousand sketches and resketches, and Beethoven had a rough draft; a thousand more, a refined draft; another thousand, a refinement of the refined draft. And it ended not there. First performances were his concluding medium for modeling, stimulating his imagination as sketching and listening at the piano could not. Hearing his Fifth Symphony on opening night, he changed its beginning, inserting bar four, the last touch of what came to be its lasting quality.

To artists, the design is everything. Typical is Ingmar Bergman. His rule: don't stint on the design. His reason: the creation of beauty rides on it, because the design made real is what satisfies or not the human spirit. A production of masterly design, though average plan, has a heart to it. But one of average design, regardless of how superior the plan, is a waste of life. Therefore, much the most of his interest and time he spent designing. The least of himself he gave to putting together decent plans, content to have them do acceptably well, to not spoil the realizations of his designs. As should be expected then, modeling is central to artists in their designing, and peripheral or nonexistent in their planning.

Opposite to artists are manufacturers. Their rule: don't stint on efficiency. Their reason: profits depend on it. A project with an average plan, though masterly design, risks tipping the balance sheet into the red. A project with a highly efficient plan, though a design that scrapes by, might fill the coffers.

Almost always then, the chief interest of manufacturers is to compete on price. Because if it was to create excellent designs, they would have pursued careers in the arts.

The managers and industrial engineers of a brickyard are representative. Their question is not, "Are our bricks marketable?" Past sales figures answer that; the designs were set years ago, with millions sold. Their question is, "How can we devise more efficient, less expensive means of manufacturing our bricks?" Naturally their use of modeling is more for planning than for designing.

First, in the time-honored way, with hands clasped behind their heads, leaning back in their chairs, beating their brains for ideas, they conceive a strategy. But conceiving close tactical detail is largely outside this inner approach. Ideally for that, they should run and rerun pilot experiments. At the same time, they cannot buy on approval five million pounds of machines, haul them about in trial layouts, investigate alternative routings of materials among them, and physically do all else, down to the last questions of production, to see by direct examination what best trims costs.

Instead they do as their predecessors of up to the middle of the Twentieth Century did. They turn to recursive modeling to stimulate their planning, to glean further improving possibilities. In brainstorming sessions they configure and reconfigure miniature layouts of plant and equipment. But as their predecessors could not, they recursively run computer simulation models for courses of action they hypothesize, predicting how much each pares down manufacturing time and wasted raw materials. In other words, "If we purchase such and such machines and arrange them in this or that way, the computer calculates the cost savings to be the following, and is it an improvement or not?" By this they overcome some of their blind spots, hit upon prosperous insights which thought alone might miss, and eventually settle on what they should do.

Monthly the articles in management science journals propose fresh modeling techniques for economizing production, and the best of these are taught in management courses. Put into practice, factory efficiency rises, new plans besting old. The manufacturer or businessperson of today, modeling with the techniques of a decade ago, risks being driven out of business.

Two general remarks remain:

Up to a point, the more pliable the medium for modeling, the more rapid the progress, speeding the rounds of intuitive spear throwing and intellectual judging. Advantageously changing our minds more often, getting our misjudgments behind us faster, our work reaches heights that modeling in a less adaptable medium is unable to. But there is a limit. Intuition does not speak until ready; we think just so rapidly; a point exists beyond which increased pliability affords small gain.

Second, along with the bright side of modeling is a darker one: that modeling, a liberating tool of thinking, invites overreliance on its use, and chances becoming an enslaving tool. Modeling is liable to tempt creativity to take paths of least resistance. Racking one's mind and accumulating large stores of failed trails to mull over are necessary for precipitating select ideas. If modeling is allowed to substitute for hard thinking, the creator's genius underdevelops, and power of envisioning and designing suffers. Equally unacceptable, like a coddled child sheltered from work's arduous trials and disappointments, the creator's skin does not grow so thick, nor resolve as firm, and confidence is more easily punctured, compared to what might have been.

Regarding the arts, a fictional Leonardo da Vinci, able to sketch and to try out colors on a computer screen, might never come up to the talents of the real Leonardo. Or to put it differently, was lack of a word processor all that stood in Homer's way to a less perfect version of the *Odyssey*, as well as of himself?

Not necessarily. The trick is to embrace modeling's liberating advantages while shunning its siren qualities that ease the rigor and narrow the range of thinking.

Chapter Five

How Creators Collaborate

A team of creators is assembled or bands together, chips off dissimilar blocks, filling out a wider range of knowledge, instructive experience, and lines of thinking than a single person can have. Still, regardless of how mutually complementing their intuitive and intellectual powers are, an effective super-mind is unable to form unless the team's members speak freely. For this nothing so completely topples the fences of polite reserve as the members' restless interests and enthusiasms to accomplish the project. Then the creative power of the group compounds that of its members, bringing into reach stubborn products that individuals have no chance at.

Collaborative projects divide into four types. In the first, each member participates in envisioning, designing, planning, implementing the plan, and executing the design. An example is James Watson and Francis Crick's project to envision and design the picture of DNA, showing what it must look like if magnified trillions of times.

Watson and Crick were counterparts, attacking problems from angles quite apart. Watson was expert in biology and thought qualitatively, but knew little of the mathematics of crystallographic structures. Crick was well versed in this mathematics, but weak in biology. Determination to reveal DNA's nature led each to hold nothing back from the other. To the point of rudeness, theirs was an open, undefensive, let's-be-absolutely-frank attitude to scrutinizing ideas.

The supporting plans for their project included scheduling times to get together, arranging meetings with outside researchers to gather information, and obtaining permission to use a vacant laboratory. Casual luck, as it often does, filled in the holes, as when Crick, stumped by a crucial problem, accidently bumped into an acquaintance who put him onto finding the solution.

The course of their iterations was to guess the rough picture of DNA, the vision of it, and deductively work out the fine picture, the design of it. Anytime this failed to match any experimentally-known fact of DNA, they made changes and tried again. Gradually their design grew less objectionable, until nothing of it seemed wrong.

In collaborative work as this, modeling promotes common understanding, which aids the unambiguous exchange of ideas. Early in their modeling work, Watson and Crick cut out cardboard profiles of the nucleotides known to be in DNA, and played at arranging and rearranging them. By this they discovered the unique pairings of nucleotides that could be stacked in a way that agreed with relevant rules of chemistry and known properties of DNA. From there they went on to model with balls connected by rods, supported on jigs, stacking the paired nucleotides and companion molecules in a helical line. From this, staring them in the face was a likely truth they had not consciously designed into the model—a replicating mechanism for DNA to convey genetic information—convincing them they had it right.

That every profession is distinctly grooved in its thinking can at times blind its members to the obvious which an outsider might plainly notice. The historical account of the DNA project rejects the view that Watson worked out only the biological and qualitative parts of the picture, his speciality, and Crick only the crystallographic and quantitative parts, his speciality. To mention two instances, Watson spotted the answer to a key crystallographic puzzle that was defeating Crick, and Crick solved a key biological puzzle whose solution Watson had missed.

Alone, neither Watson nor Crick had any chance of getting far enough. Paired up, each was a sounding board and clue-giver for releasing the other from what baffled him, advancing the course of discoveries. Moreover, this contagiously magnified their pleasures. How often does a hermit give three hearty cheers? Celebrating breakthrough insights in company beats celebrating them alone.

Science goes to prove that absence of born genius rarely stands in the way of gaining notable or incomparable success. Of major scientific problems, a tiny fraction will yield only to a mental giant, an Einstein. Most are like researching DNA, manageable by ordinarily bright, well-schooled and complementary allies, who put pretense away and run their minds as a unit, a super-mind.

Turning to the second type of collaboration, usually one person or group conceives what to build, and another conceives how and builds it. Just so, the designs of the stained glass windows at Coventry Cathedral are of the artist John Piper, and the craftsmanship of Patrick Reyntiens. Similarly, the artist Mark Chagall and the artisan Charles Marq are responsible for windows in Chichester Cathedral.

The details of this type of collaboration stand out clearly in Frank Lloyd Wright's work. Hating the idea of having his ideas, his soul, and his destiny fused with anyone else's, he single-handedly envisioned and designed the house *Fallingwater*, casting its blueprints almost into the utopian realm. Responding to the complications this raised, the builder and its construction workers extended their techniques and skills to devise strategical and tactical steps.

Following their plan, they evacuated the foundation, ordered and sawed the redwood, made forms for the concrete work, quarried flagstone and cut it to size, erected the house's shell, plumbed and wired it, sealed its frameless windows, hauled every bit of scrape away, and handled all else, down to the grading and landscaping. In one instance, contrary to their pact to speak openly, they went behind Wright's back and boosted his dangerously thin safety factor by installing twice the concrete reinforcing rods he had specified.

The third type of collaboration, which may include in its parts either or both of the first two types, is familiar in projects made of component projects. It is a case of "I'll (or we'll) do all five parts of our project, my (or our) speciality, you do all of your project, your speciality, and we'll assemble our products into the desired one." Think of the project to conceive and build a prototype jet engine. There is a project for the engine's shaft, a project for its blades, another for its bearings, another for its case, and so on for the rest. Each component project has the fundamental five parts, complete with recursive modeling, with responsibilities entrusted to the project's engineers, metallurgists, machinists, and foundry specialists. Out of the partnerships within component projects, and partnerships among, the products are made and joined, the jet engine born.

In the graphic arts this type of collaboration occasionally occurs on large works. Joan Miró once united with a group of artists to design and make a ceramic mural. Responsible for his project to do his section according to his creative desires, but subject to the overall motif, and with others responsible for their sections, a satisfying whole resulted. He explains:

> Mural art is the opposite of solitary creation; but although you must not give up your individual personality as an artist, you must engage it deeply in a collective effort. It is a fascinating experience, but one filled with risks— one that takes place on a construction site rather than in the solitude of a studio. I therefore looked for my ideas on the site itself; it was there that I conceived and developed my project . . . And so I drew and painted

small models at 1/100th scale and submitted them to the committee in charge, which accepted them.

These first compositions underwent considerable changes when I worked on larger models. As a matter of fact, there were changes at every step along the way. Like going from paper to clay, each move to greater dimensions necessitated important alterations of form and color.

A variant of this type of collaboration has two creators practicing different branches of art, interlacing their designs, aiming by combined action for a synergy in the aesthetics. Ansel Adams called this "synaesthetics," saying that in a single work "two creative elements join to produce a third form of communication." Synaesthetics is common in song writing. For instance, Lorenz Hart created lyrics, and Richard Rogers created melodies befitting Hart's lyrics.

It is worth mentioning an extension of this which, although it stretches the meaning of collaboration, has its powerful effect. It is the creator who is a polymath, having a mongrel mind of disparate knowledge, as if several creators in partnership work within one body. Cole Porter was a polymath, creating the lyrics and the music of his songs. Rockwell Kent was a polymath, writing books about his adventures and creating illustrative engravings of their scenes, the two mutually-reinforcing arts producing synaesthetic impression. And Linus Pauling was a polymath, creating chemical knowledge by his skillfulness in drawing on mathematics, physics, and chemistry.

Finally, the fourth type of collaborative project is one that Isaac Newton recognized when he said, "If I have seen further [than others] it is by standing on ye sholders of Giants." Even lone creators in the fine arts lose sight of their reliance on those who have created before. Perhaps the thought never crossed Thomas Hardy's mind when he composed his poem *The Convergence of the Twain*, but he was standing on the shoulders of poets he had read, William Blake's among them. Hardy's poem, in its theme and treatment, is a variation on Blake's *The Sick Rose.*

A lesson can be gathered from this. From our earliest student days onward, we should be recruiting into ourselves a diverse association of high-shouldered collaborators, studying and absorbing their works and approaches, that we may enlist them in our work. They will contribute to rounding out our intuitions and intellect, to toughening our resolve, and to inspiring us to do great good.

Chapter Six

What Goodness And Quality Are

The first thing that needs to be said is that there is goodness of use, and there is goodness of beauty.

Goodness of use pleases by its practical function. Creators put it into products to settle problems, to ease or speed unpleasant tasks, to relieve discomfort, or to add comfort where none or little exists. If we had no bodies, there would be no such thing as goodness of use.

And if we had no souls, there would be no such thing as goodness of beauty. Goodness of beauty pleases to please. It derives from the likes of artistic lines, textures, hues, shadings, shapes, arrangements, balance, timbre, tones, harmonies, and rhythms. As well it derives from things apart from art. Efficiency is beautiful, wasteful excesses are not. Purity is beautiful, pollution is not. Vitality is beautiful, sluggishness is not. Expression of cherished themes of life and universe, which speak to the roots of humanness, is beautiful; petty, insincere, counterfeit expression is not. Determination to do a job with originality is beautiful; perfunctorily wishing to get through a thing is not. And rounding out a longer list than this, acts of kindness are beautiful, while standing selfishly by as people or animals are distressed is the ugliest of ugly sights.

The second thing to be said is that excellence is great goodness: goodness singled out for its superiority.

It follows that there are creations valued for their excellence of use, such as the latest passenger airplane. Secondly there are creations valued for their excellence of beauty, such as the *Mona Lisa*, a solo climb of Everest, and a heroic rescue at considerable personal danger. Finally there are creations valued for excellently combining use and beauty. The 1947 Studebaker Starlight Coupe, styled by the industrial designer Raymond Loewy, allies function and form, a car not merely for transporting the body but the soul.

Time usually numbers a product's years on the stage of excellence. The tide of goodness rises, and new products push the old off into the wings. The goodness of the average modern pocket calculator has submerged that of the slide rule. The prized geological hypothesis in 1950 of how the continents formed has become a superseded idea. Still, endurance can be immeasurably long where the creator has addressed ageless matters in a seemingly matchless way. Homer's *Odyssey*, a happy anomaly, has stood for thirty centuries.

Every little while something of the reverse happens. Excellence is created before its time. People, perhaps put off by a new product's radicalness, are unprepared to recognize its value, and it is slow to move onto center stage. The world leisurely warmed to Blake's poetry and to van Gogh's painting. Certain revolutionary scientific theories, initially ridiculed, have had later opinion swing their way. And even with nostalgia subtracted out, the 1934 Chrysler Airflow car, meeting little favor then, has gotten into the blood of an audience today.

Much as the words excellence and quality are used interchangeably in everyday language, this doesn't do for understanding creative work. The two are distinct. Quality is the goodness of great goodness. But excellence is another name for great goodness. Quality, therefore, is the goodness of excellence.

Quality is virtually synonymous with the creative spirit. Just as there is a part of the brain for rational thought, and a part for intuition, there is a part for the creative spirit. The creative spirit is the detector of excellence, and the issuer of quality.

Anytime we meet products whose goodness is below the creative spirit's standard, the spirit sleeps. Anytime their goodness is above, it leaps to life and celebrates, suffusing us with spiritual goodness, quality. The two kinds of goodness—the excellence that sets the spirit going, and the quality due to the spirit going—exist side by side, superimposed.

To illustrate, imagine a visit to an art museum, where paintings are successively placed before you, beginning with one from a thriftshop, each afterward improving on those before, progressing toward goodness in the first degree, toward excellence. This doesn't mean going through a quantitative continuum, like turning up a rheostat strengthens an electric current. Each painting with the next higher degree of goodness is unexampled and unrecognizable from the last. It better interprets the great themes of life and human being, better reaches the enduring human cares, better makes our individual experiences universal, better raises our thoughts to the condition of poetry—in other words, approaches the terms of a masterpiece given by the art critic Kenneth Clark. At some point in the approach, well above the common run of goodness, the unexpected happens. A threshold is crossed. All heaven breaks loose. A second goodness, a sublime kind, appears—quality.

Returning to the 1947 Studebaker Starlight Coupe, to automobile enthusiasts it prompts a great worldly sensation, and out of this excellence breathes quality, spirituality, otherworldly sensation, which neither its usefulness nor its beauty alone might evoke. Similarly, *Fallingwater* evokes quality. Functional for living in, and free of dead lines and showiness, its goodness is a harmony of use and beauty, the sum of which is to many people sufficient to wake their spirit.

The same is true of products whose excellence is all in their use. Long wanted and worked toward, the first polio vaccine kept company with the influential works of history. To look coolly on it, the spirit would have had to look coolly on such creations as Holland's invention of a practical submarine, Watt's of a steam engine, McCormick's of a reaper, as well as Bernard Baruch's work in finance, Lavoisier's in chemistry, and the Curies' in physics.

Culture and ordinary upbringing fit the creative spirit to work with things like watching a rocket climb heavenward or, as Odysseus did, the rosy fingers of dawn climb the eastern sky. But for most things, unless we have educated the spirit by gaining experience and knowledge of the intricacies of the things, we are blind to detecting and delighting in their excellence. Science is a case in point; it takes learning and acquaintance for the spirit to know which technical ideas are outstandingly good. Lay people are at a loss to see the promise of a novel theory implicating an esoteric gene with cancer. If quality is felt, only medical experts feel it.

It is the same with mundane products. Consider a certain garden trowel. Relative to alternative designs, its creators intended it to serve suitably well across a range of features—retaining its sharpness, resisting bending at the handle, inhibiting rust, neither fatiguing nor raising blisters, while costing less than other trowels. Excellent feats went to solving its interrelated mechanical and economic problems, and to maintaining tolerances while manufacturing it. Most of us miss this; our spirits sleep. If we learned to grasp and respect the complications of its creation, our spirits might leap.

Chapter Seven

Where Quality Comes From

What it comes down to is that quality is as much or more about creators than about the things they create. Hear Barbara Tuchman on this:

> . . . As I understand it, [quality] means investment of the best skill and effort possible to produce the finest and most admirable result possible. Its presence or absence in some degree characterizes every man-made object, service, skilled or unskilled labor—laying bricks, painting a picture, ironing shirts, practicing medicine, shoemaking, scholarship, writing a book. You do it well or you do it half-well. Materials are sound and durable or they are sleazy; method is painstaking or whatever is easiest. Quality is achieving or reaching for the highest standard as against being satisfied with the sloppy or fraudulent. It is honesty of purpose as against catering to cheap or sensational sentiment. It does not allow compromise with the second-rate.

Going on, she describes Michelangelo's project of painting the ceiling of the Sistine Chapel. Intolerant of the lesser standards of his five assistants, he dismissed them and for four years worked alone to shape the masterpiece. She concludes, "That is what makes for quality—and its costs—and what helped to make Michelangelo one of the greatest artists, if not, as some think, the greatest, of all time. Creating quality is self-nourishing."

Examine the words she uses to explain quality. They are about a human, a creator, not about a painting: "investment of the best skill and effort possible"—"you do it well or you do it half-well"—"reaching for the highest standard"—"honesty of purpose."

Holding the ceiling of the Sistine Chapel in view is like watching a fresh comet render those that came before it less fit to dwell in the heavens. Michelangelo's painting, the outer excellence he produced, delights our aesthetic sensibilities. But the fresh comet that gives the spirit life is not so much this immaculate object of our outward-looking eyes, but is what must have been Michelangelo's inner excellence, his immaculately engaged self which we catch through our inward-looking spiritual eyes, his place in the enshrined constellation of great creators, turning on in us respect for what may be called "creator-hood."

Michelangelo's excellence astonishes the spirit into thinking, "What a great representative of our species he is. How he brought himself to create unexampled goodness. Here is responsibility in its highest sense of becoming as masterful as one can be." Automatic and instinctive is the detective work, based on no more than that when a piece of work is exceedingly fine, its source must have dedicated its life to making exceeding fine things, with itself growing in reaction to become exceedingly fine.

That quality is due to the inner excellence of the creator is easy to prove. Think of a juggling machine that makes child's play of the feats of the most accomplished jugglers. Although the graceful sight of the machine circulating twelve rings in the air intrigues people, their spirits are blind to the event. Twelve beats seven, the best humans can do, yet no one applauds. The condition for touching a spiritual nerve transcends the face of things, the number of rings.

Only if people recognize that twelve rings pushes an absolute limit, that the feat was gained against impressive odds, will the thought of the inner excellence of the machine's creator blanket them with spiritual goodness, the wonder of quality.

To show how the spirit imputes inner excellence from outer excellence, suppose there is a week-long contest among a hundred cooks to conceive new meals, where each day they receive like packages of a surprise selection of vegetables, fruits, nuts, grains, mushrooms, and spices. They work in identical kitchens, for equal time, and their conceptions are judged by a panel. At the end of the week, the daily rankings are averaged to balance out chance variations, and the five cooks of the best meals are awarded stars.

The material resources and working conditions are the same, but the delectableness of the meals is not. Something else must be entering the top recipes, an intangible ingredient, an efficacy for creating excellent meals. It is excellence of mind, compounded of intelligence, values, imagination, creativity, standards, dedication, effort, tenacity, sincerity, courage, curiosity, attentiveness, assertiveness, and an attitude that rejects the best that has been done as not good enough.

In every walk of life, the spirit's respect for inner excellence goes less to the creator's inborn talents and more for the creator's made talents. Katherine Mansfield created extraordinarily fine stories; it can only be concluded she was extraordinarily responsible to her education and work. Igor Sikorsky invented the first practical helicopter, a height of goodness previously unreached; we must say he was wonderful for making himself be this wonderful engineer.

Finally, inner excellence is more widespread than we are aware of. Although the names that come to mind are of those whose works stand high in the public eye—Paul Robeson, Wernher von Braun, Christian Doppler, Goethe, Martha Graham, Geoffrey Chaucer, Roger Tory Peterson, Louis Armstrong, Barbara Tuchman, and the like—we overlook the legions of un-quoteworthy creators whose respect and eminence is local: librarians, family doctors, blacksmiths, homemakers, luthiers, mechanics, and all manner of inconspicuous fighters for mattering causes. Nor should we overlook serious hobbyists, many with livelihood vocations consisting of humdrum tasks, as the steelworker who, after working by the book from eight to five, with little chance for originality and independence, goes into the garage on evenings and weekends, aiming to conceive and build an uncommonly good experimental airplane.

Likewise not to be forgotten is the Creator of nature. A breeze shapes and whitens a geyser's plume against the blue Yellowstone sky, and the quality felt derives from where? That is easy—from the responsible agent, God.

Chapter Eight

How Inner And Outer Excellence Run Each Other

Many are the ways of expressing the interplay between the maker and what is made:

One's skills hone the job, and the job hones one's skills.

Or equivalently:

Improvements made on products make improvements on the improver.

Or equivalently:

Inventing the invention invents the inventor.

Or equivalently:

Inner excellence begets outer excellence, and outer excellence begets inner excellence.

Inherent in these expressions are two modes of creation: creation by projection and, in response to this, creation by transformation. Michelangelo, by his excellence, projected the excellence of the Sistine Chapel's frescoes. Wrestling with the problems of his project transformed him into a more capable projector.

By following in each project the compass of your creative spirit, a guiding hand will unnoticeably operate across projects. You head toward nearby outer horizons, trying to create much goodness, days or weeks away, and somehow this inches you toward the best of all inner horizons, a lifetime away. No matter that you can barely see beyond the current project to the next, you have only to ply squarely into the steepest gradient of increasing outer goodness that you can manage, and the response is the just-right transformation of your inner goodness, boosting your skills and determination, fitting your mind to do the next and best most difficult projects. No amount of playing, schooling, and book learning can by themselves so thoroughly search out and correct your weaknesses, nor so sustain your intent.

Now and again the above is challenged with this claim: "Goodness is whatever I make it, and I can make it be anything I want." And this: "Life has no purpose. It's all a meaningless game." Such claims are untrue. Goodness is absolute, not whatever one personally declares it to be. First, nothing but goodness is the basis for lighting the creative spirit. Make anything else great, and the spirit refuses to recognize it. And second, only goodness has a future and gives its creator a future. If as a substitute for creating good things we create trivial things, or perverted things, or evil things, we curb the expansion of our development. The guiding hand forsakes us.

To illustrate, imagine you have the taxing project whose vision is to sit in more seats of an empty football stadium in eight hours than anyone has before. You have to devise an efficient route for moving around, and a way to avoid getting weary and sore. Then at the scheduled time, adhering to plan, you do it, sitting in 18,773 seats. You have gone up against a mass of resistance, and some people came to watch. On the action-reaction principle it has changed you. But if ever there is a meaningless game it is this. The project is trivial, its basis other than goodness. How do you know? First, your spirit failed to light up; it can't for stunt work. Second, if you continue over the years creating stunts, you will look back and see that your mind grew into a freakish, limited affair, unable to create anything of great worth to people.

Types of stunts outnumber what they seem. Though we naturally think of physical daredevils, a stunt is anything that concentrates on inventing and carrying out difficult means to unworthwhile visions, visions which if achieved could not possibly light the spirit. Solving a hard but useless scientific problem is a stunt. So is developing a complex device to do a job no one might ever want done. So is writing an essay that struggles with a small idea in a big way. Whatever the stunts, gone by middle age is the stunt-maker's desire to conquer frivolous complexities. And worse, the potential for imagining fine visions atrophies for lack of use.

If stunt making kills the guiding hand, a quicker way to its death is to take pains to create perverted products, making them as poorly as one can. Although no sane person does this, the possibility is instructive. In pursuing the more perverse, almost immediately the direction to it is lost, not to mention interest. Imagine a perverted scientist who seeks to make the falsest claims imaginable. Soon the scientist is without a criterion, as it is uncertain to say which in a large collection of falsehoods is falser, as falseness can be evaluated only in the region near truth. Or take perverted art. Trying to write down the least-moving poem reaches a point where, among a thousand nominees, it is impossible to tell which doggerel is worse. Or take perverted mountaineering. In a topsy-turvy world where climbers start from peaks and lower themselves down, soon no one knows which route to try, or much cares.

As for the evil-minded given to malignant aims, to producing fiendish tricks, the antithesis of goodness, they lack inclination to perceive what is more damnable beyond the unfeeling cruelties they have done. Once a good thing is blown to smithereens, there is little depraved gratification in going to finer bits.

Goodness is boundless, evilness has a nearby limit. Goodness attracts constructors, those who believe in union among people. Evilness attracts levelers, those who believe in estrangement. The leveler is quick to arrive at where all alternatives go to equally black states of disfigurement and ill emotion. The competence of the leveler at leveling is unable to grow on and on.

It is in the best interest of evil people to realize that being evil perpetrates its destruction on themselves. It denies them the guiding hand, denies them keeping company with quality, denies them the evolution and renewal of themselves. In place of this it deals them an existence like boulders, cold and static, hidebound and lonely.

None of this—creating the trivial, the perverted, or the evil—is a match for creating goodness. By creating goodness, the guiding hand operates, deepening and widening mind so that mind can more deeply and widely create, the mutually sustaining and spiritually vitalizing circle that, uniquely among alternatives, deserves to be called life. Life that is always with prospects of better ahead. Life that gathers the ingredients for its future advances as it goes. Life that responsibly emanates from creativity, goodness, excellence, and quality. Life that scraps banal values and engages sublime ones. Life that is unfailing in curiosity and fresh ideas. Life in which most every day is the time of one's life.

Chapter Nine

How The Creative Spirit
And Quality Humanize Us

Desires and urges of our animal side lure us to food, warmth, shelter, and safety, vital to maintain and grow our bodies, without which we would not exist to be lured. Concerning food, its essential calories, vitamins, and minerals are dispersed among chemical flavors whose role is to tempt our mouths to water, inducing us to eat. At dinner we sit down to feast on the flavors, unaware of the tasteless nutrients entering us. Evolution invented the Trojan Horse.

But of our spiritual side, what is there about dining on excellence that we have trouble putting a finger on, but apparently must have? Why is great goodness by itself not enough? Why this higher goodness—the goodness of great goodness—quality? What are its ethereal calories, vitamins, and minerals, and what are they for?

The answers begin with the comparative anatomy of our brain and the brains of other mammals. Common to both is the cerebellum which runs the instincts, from maintaining balance, breathing, and digestion, to moving around. The fact is that as cerebellums go, ours is the least polished of the lot. In running, jumping, leaping, and pouncing, the cat is the artist and we are the klutz. It seamlessly blends its moves; we stitch ours together.

And the cat is no set-up subject to clinch the point. On grace and coordination, rating the basketball player alongside the kangaroo, the scuba diver alongside the marlin, and the t'ai chi ch'uan master alongside the caterpillar, we fare poorly.

Our redeeming possibility is the cerebrum. Located above the cerebellum in the front of the cranium, it singles us out. It is able to hold an imaginative, creating mind with a spirit that feasts on excellence and digests it into quality. And it will, provided we are loyal to developing its potentials. Then the cerebrum becomes insatiable.

With only a cerebellum, enough is enough, but with a cerebrum, enough is never enough. Contrast how the sparrow builds and how we build. The sparrow gathers twigs and grass for a nest, relying on a cerebellum weighing a fraction of an ounce. That so little a thing does so much attests to its having no use for "What if . . . ?" deliberations, instead deferring to tried-and-true policies, carrying out its programmed duties indistinguishably from its predecessors' of a thousand generations ago.

Why are sparrows unconcerned with advancing the goodness of sparrow nests? Why do they not glance across at neighboring sparrows and determine to outdo them? Because survival is a threshold phenomenon. Biology runs on the law, "Be within tolerance or die." Work to go beyond the threshold of adequacy buys little extra protection against death. It is inconsequential to natural selection whether survival occurs in damp straw or in a warm bed. Survival is survival, apart from how painful or enjoyable the experience may be. There is a point of design at which a nest acceptably promises existence for baby sparrows, and existence does not admit a superlative.

As for us, we are malcontents unless we are bounding past the point of merely getting by. Our quest for excellence, the heaviest of undertakings, biggest of all jobs, is ruled by a lightweight, an otherworldly, airy thing, the creative spirit. It equalizes opportunity. It makes a mockery of brute force and machismo. It puts men and women on a par.

And it keeps us above our computers. Much as chess-playing algorithms run rings around us, we can breathe easily. An objective test sets the standard for judging whether an artificial mind can make us obsolete. Leave it by itself for some years and come back. Has it conceived great projects? Has it contributed to the organic substance that underlies visions, and taken to shaping designs beyond compare? Is it steadily transforming itself into a more competent and determined creator?

The future holds none of this. Computers can neither be given nor acquire a creative spirit, so they cannot sense excellence and quality. They have no qualms about accepting any aims we assign them. They will do atrocities and damn civilization to misery if instructed.

Finally, there is an additional way in which quality humanizes us. Quality is a medium of communication. Without television and the telephone we'll get by, but not without quality.

First of all, quality is our most classic medium of communication. It abolishes time and space, ties us together, sustains our spiritual heritage, makes us function as a human colony bound throughout the ages. Quality echoes of what is genuinely laudable in human being—the universal artist of all places and times and occupations. Though divided by language, could somehow Frank Lloyd Wright and the creators of the Parthenon have met, tacitly and exactly they would have understood one another by the quality of their work.

Second, quality is our most truthful medium of communication. We cannot tell lies with it. Sham excellence and sham human being cannot be put past the spirit; it refuses to go into rapture at anything but the genuine.

Last, quality is our most magical medium of communication. It overrides every theory of information, all of which have it that the more states that can be transmitted, the more that can be said in a message. Well, the medium of quality can transmit but two, Q and non-Q, and when the on-state of quality is sent it says everything about who we are and what our species is.

Chapter Ten

What Motivates Creators

Dabblers aside, creators may be divided into three kinds according to their commanding motive. Those of one kind need to create purely for the sake of creating; creating is, in and of itself, their reward. Those of a second kind need to create products that serve human welfare; creating is a means to altruistic ends. Those of a third kind need to create to feed their egotism. They create products to make themselves important in the eyes of others.

THE MOTIVE OF CREATING FOR THE SAKE OF CREATING. This motive is typical of painters, literary writers, poets, dancers, mathematicians, philosophers, photographers, potters, rock climbers, mountaineers, and more. An obsession pushes them, and a labor of love pulls them.

The obsession is this. A vision, a beautiful seed of knowledge or achievement, flashes into them on its own accord. The vision is personal, uniquely theirs. If they had never been born, it would not be. Left alone, it will wither and die, an unbearable thought. An insistent urge possesses them to rescue it, make it bear its latent fruit.

This pushing obsession to project the vision is helped along by a pulling labor of love. This has been variously phrased: "Work is about voyaging, not about landings"–"The hunt is everything,

the trophy nothing"–"The allure is in the game, not in the stakes."
To Robert Louis Stevenson it was, "To travel hopefully is a better
thing than to have arrived." To Emerson it was, "Everything good
is on the highway." To Montaigne, "The journey not the arrival
matters." And to Shakespeare, "Things won are done, joy's soul
lies in the doing."

Joy's soul derives from pleasures enlivening the creator's
projects, and satisfactions the creator's career. The pleasures make
up in height what they lack in length; the satisfactions make up
in length what they lack in height.

Projects have their most alluring pleasure at the start. There
you are, unaware of exciting times ahead, and a really good idea
of something to create comes along. Even if you must wait until
you have time to deal with it, it ignites an impulse you cannot
back off from, to take the idea, weakly in focus, the sense without
the form, and create its definite shape.

Eventually you get on the way to creating its design. As the
main journey recursively wends into miniature journeys, and
miniatures within those miniatures, and within their miniatures,
curiosities and suspenses of "What next?" surge at every level.
Thousands of times you are stuck for what to do, and thousands
of times relieved with spurts of pleasure in finding out.

Other sorts of pleasures lie in the last lap of the journey.
Reflecting back on the course of your work, you pleasantly
meditate on the difficulties you have overcome, the risks you
have handled with skill. Then turning your attention around,
you look forward to the coming pleasures of completing the project,
and thinking of them brings forefelt pleasures. Mountaineers get
plenty of this in the closing hours of their expedition. The sky
around them drawn almost to a sphere, success assured, they
pause and review their efforts that have brought them thus far,
and anticipate their steps to the summit.

The final pleasure occurs soon after the project is finished.
Success is wearing out its welcome. Giving yourself a lift, you
fantasize over projects to come, dreaming of their visions which

you have kept in warm storage. Staying with the mountaineering example—yesterday high on a peak in oxygen debt, today the climbers come down into "pleasure debt," and on the ride home get out of it by passing time in happy reverie over the climb they will make tomorrow bring.

If the pleasures are like short-lived flames, the satisfactions endure like a bed of glowing coals, living long upon the mind, tranquilly felt at work and away. From time to time your spirit turns its gaze on how your creative life has been going. Seeing what it likes, it rejoices.

It is satisfying when your spirit takes in the enormity of your accomplishments. Each project has been the result of your generating a multitude of ideas, and making a multitude of decisions about them. Easily a thousand days and a thousand decisions a day go into, for instance, writing a book: Virginia Woolf, by rough calculation, made more than ten million in her lifetime (in turn, making Virginia Woolf). Hence when you stand before one of your works, its fineness towering over your abilities of the moment to reproduce its equal, with satisfaction you sense the leveraging power of the concerted efforts of your prior selves who day by day duteously went about creating it.

And it is satisfying when your spirit sees you are staving off staleness and world-weariness with imaginative work, the adult version of children's play, which gives you new eyes for old, freshens your outlook on life, and perpetuates your youth.

And it is satisfying when your spirit gazes over your career and sees you have cheated the hollow life, that you are earning what the writer Jack London called ultimate happiness. Ultimate happiness is of the spirit; it accumulates through creative work.

At any point in your career, as you are earning ultimate happiness, the sequence of your project-journeys on the outside are inside you creating the grand journey of bringing yourself into being. It is the one justifiable branch of escapism. Your work grows into a wonderful personal tradition. You join with the great creators of all times and subjects. This afterglow of your happy and prosperous past sets you looking to years hence, and basking in the fore-glow of more to come.

Those who create purely for the sake of creating usually work alone. A labor of love can't stand a killjoy. The artist's fences are always cantankerously up against meddling interference. If somehow another poet had played the backseat driver with William Blake, whispering the lines he was about to think of, the intruder would have deprived him of his animating joys.

The motive of creating products that serve human welfare. The difference between the scientist Richard Feynman and the humanitarian Florence Nightingale is the difference between a commanding motive to envision and project theories and a commanding motive to improve human welfare. Feynman was essentially an artist who used equations to "paint" pictures of the subatomic world. To him the journey of creating mattered above the arrival; to her it was the reverse. More pointedly, devising theories gripped him in inescapable thrall; her ardor was to make society better off. He was self-centered and worked alone; she was other-centered and collaborated. To him, envisioning and designing were foremost; to her, it was planning and putting into practice.

Those driven to improve human welfare will gladly give up their work for being handed the result. Conservationists who undertake an imaginative project to preserve a species must be delighted on hearing that safeguarding regulations have just been enacted, and their efforts can be called off. Rescue teams at avalanches feel similarly at seeing the buried somehow crawl out on their own. And in the event of a genie bequeathing a cure for cancer, it is hard to imagine medical researchers refusing to hear of it, preferring the chance to discover it themselves.

The motive of creating to feed one's egotism. Despite their differences, in one sense Richard Feynman and Florence Nightingale were alike. No prospect of fame, pride, position, personal gain, bettering one's station, feeling important in the eyes of others, or cashing in on the work could have bought off his compulsion to paint the subatomic landscape, or her altruistic zeal for eradicating the poor sanitary practices of hospitals.

The impression and probably the truth is that creators with a commanding motive to feed their egotism are mostly men. They may create under the stimulus of amassing riches and luxuries. Or perhaps the thought of being second-in-command galls unbearably, and they must issue orders and pull levers of control. Or perhaps they need to be in charge for the sake of vanity, status, applause, radiating importance, being envied, or getting the better of rivals, under the logic of "I accomplish hugely, therefore I hugely am." Or perhaps it is a means of paying off old scores, a There-I've-shown-you! resentment directed to someone who long ago loosed meanspirited remarks which saddled them with feeling inferior. Or perhaps they aspire to escape anonymity after death, erecting monuments and public works in their names. Any or several of these may operate in them.

Something good is to be said of them. Along with the charitably driven, they are society's mundane lifeblood. How else can complex projects of uninteresting necessity and great tonnage be accomplished? How else can food be counted on to be delivered to supermarkets, and electricity and water come affordably into homes? To staff the positions with people overcome with their private dreams, many ill-suited for working cooperatively and to timetables, is useless. Those with the temperament of van Gogh will not get the practical work done.

WILL POWER. Whichever of the three motives is commanding, having inexhaustible will power at one's beck and call can make all the difference when complications mire progress. Hence to the rescue we order another type of push to come, an unwavering force to trudge, to lug, to haul, to shove the work forward.

A leading example of the extent to which will power can help accomplish matters is P. N. T. Barbellion. Barbellion was a cogged locomotive. Born under a sentence of impending death, his heart dropped beats, throwing him into faints, and his doctor doubted he would see his thirtieth birthday (he didn't).

Scattered through Barbellion's *The Journal of a Disappointed Man* are his angry complaints to God about being cheated of time to create consequential works. But cheated or not, he refused to capitulate. Into his foreshortened years he ordered himself to squeeze progress that would count. On almost nothing but resolve he raced his life's work against his body's deadline, to accomplish in zoology and in writing what we are unaccustomed to seeing from those granted twice and longer his time.

MIXED MOTIVES. Whichever of the three motives is commanding, the remaining two may add supplementary force. Françoise Jacob exemplifies. He was head over heels into projecting visions, specifically to conceive and test important theories of microbiological science, and he swam in the joys of the work. Still, he was keen on his discoveries benefitting science, and on making them before competing scientists could. Also to his liking, his work incidently fattened his paycheck, put his name on the lips of microbiologists everywhere, and even soothed his long-ago injured vanity, offering a measure of boastful revenge by holding up his extraordinary accomplishments to a former girlfriend who once had spurned him.

CHOOSE YOUR CAREER ACCORDING TO YOUR COMMANDING MOTIVE. The young Françoise Jacob did this to guide himself to microbiology. The method is to first decide on the kind of sea you need to sail on—the sea of creating purely for the sake of creating, as artists do; the sea of creating products to improve human welfare, as humanitarians do; or the sea of creating products to feed your egotism, as empire builders do. Once you decide your main motive, you have decided your element.

It remains then to guess your boat, your combination of skills that you can grow and make great. Here you can be surer of excluding than including. Guess which of your skills you cannot grow far, boats you could probably never raise to the level of the best boats sailing, and forget about them. From the remaining, go with the skills that seem to fit your interests and job opportunities well, and launch your career. If later this proves a mistake, go back and launch again—perhaps into the same sea with a new boat or, realizing you misjudged your inherent element, into a new sea. Keep in mind that sailing on a given sea with a given boat may bring out latent boats—hidden combinations of skills—you had no idea were in you, as well as bring out a need to do your sailing on another sea.

Chapter Eleven

How To Be A Universal Artist

Robert Henri's idea bears repeating and elaborating: ". . . Become an inventive, searching, daring, self-expressing creature. . . . [You do] not have to be a painter or sculptor to be an artist. [You] can work in any medium." He is speaking of being a universal artist; one who, most anywhere in the universe of vocations and avocations, works as artists do.

How to be this?

First of all, go after making your dream products, for that is what artists do. Forget about audiences and canvassing them about their tastes. If what you create is any good, it will find its audience. Take it from Thornton Wilder: his aim was to write plays that he himself would love to attend. And take it from J. R. R. Tolkien whose hobby was reading epic myths—Rudyard Kipling's *Puck of Pook's Hill*, the stories of George MacDonald, and more. After Tolkien exhausted the supply, he determined to create his own. About *The Lord of the Rings* he said, "I wrote [it] as a personal satisfaction, driven to it by the scarcity of literature of the sort I wanted to read."

And take it from Ferdinand Porsche who, concerning the first Porsche automobile, said, "We did no market research, we had no sales forecasts, nor return-on-investment calculations.

None of that. I very simply built my dream car and figured that there would be other people who share that dream."

Second, become a polymath, developing and yoking together two or three areas of knowledge and skill. Part of the power of the polymath mind derives from its diverse areas feeding and feeding off of each other. Another part derives from its many-sided makeup and versatility which are able to detect value in ideas that narrower minds dismiss.

To single out several of the better-known polymaths, Linus Pauling grew his mind in three areas—physics, mathematics, and chemistry. It is safe to say that strictly as a physicist, or a mathematician, or a chemist he would have been ordinary, but the combination made him extraordinary. J.R.R. Tolkien forged his abilities in old dead languages and in epic myths into an ultra-talent. Herbert Simon's genius issued from a combination of skills in psychology, computers, economics, chess, and literature. W. H. Auden brought together interests in philosophy, psychology, and versifying, to invent poems unlike any other. And with a mind that studied rhythms of the ocean, Oriental art, and folk dances, Martha Graham originated ballets of every description.

With any number of intellectual areas to select from, the possible combinations of specialities reaches astronomical figures. The result is made genius of one-of-a-kind proficiency. Thus a polymath mind has no rivals.

That the "riv" in rivalry is the "riv" in river repays study. Originally, rivalry referred to conflicts on a river or a stream. If you were a farmer drawing water, and farmers upriver siphoned off a portion you wanted, they were your rivals.

Not having enough to go around causes rivalries. Two armies vie to occupy a hill—they are rivals. Two or more boys vie for a girl's love—they are rivals. Two or more workers vie for the same job opening—they are rivals. There is only this particular hill, this particular girl, this particular job opening. Equally, rivalries may exist where the object is divisible. Companies in an industry vie for a market share, seeking more than they have.

With excellence, however, there is always enough to go around. The creative spirit has no quota. The polymath mind is free to dream up products of novel substance and form. Countless are its subjects, and countless its insights into expressing them. Whatever it is working on, no one else is likely to be.

H.M. Tomlinson, Loren Eiseley, and Rachel Carson are cases in point. Tomlinson's polymath mind was compounded of interests in poetically descriptive writing and in ships, seas, and faraway travels; Eiseley's, of interests in poetically descriptive writing and in archeology; and Carson's, of interests in poetically descriptive writing, in polemics, and in wildlife and dangers to its existence. How could they be rivals? They transcended their sameness, their interest in poetically descriptive writing, by joining it with other interests that made each of them unique, and their essays and books without the slightest overlap.

Rather than regard rivalry as promoting excellence, see it as reinforcing mediocrity. A polymath mind, by freeing you from rivals, frees you of the temptation to create a thing of little account that can be produced relatively quickly, lest another gets to it first. Able to envision and design uniquely, what is your hurry? Patiently spend however many years and months it takes to make your projects please yourself perfectly.

Of course, compete—but in the original 16th century view of the word, where competition meant to strive together, to join in seeking for the benefit of the world, with none of the gladiatorial beat-or-be-beaten connotation. Artists, actual or universal, in individually striving to create excellence are striving together; the excellence achieved in the group broadcasts fresh standards, outdistancing the old.

This is Isaac Newton's cooperative approach that raises shoulders to stand on and see further. Reading H. M. Tomlinson raised Rachel Carson and Loren Eiseley onto Tomlinson's shoulders. Subsequently their works set a new mark, enabling others to see and reach even further.

The opposite way of looking at this is where everybody creates in isolated unawareness of each other, producing according to their sheltered standards. Too easily will they be satisfied they have done a splendid job, and have created up close to their ultimate capacities. Complacently will they underestimate the extent they and the species can and ought to go.

A good way to remember this is Charles Lawes. In 1864 he set the world record for the mile run, four minutes and fifty-six seconds, an average speed of 1,070 feet per minute. His side in stitches, he must have felt he was near the very top of human performance. Truth is, a hundred years later Derek Clayton ran a marathon at a faster pace, 1,076 feet per minute.

One idea remains. If you work for a company (or university, institution, or government), you can work as a universal artist, enriching yourself, customers, and society. "This is impossible," you may say. "My company fills my day with required tasks." The answer to that is, no harness is so tight it doesn't have infinite artistic freedom within it. "But my company has deadlines, and creating takes time." Yet if you are truly a universal artist, you will find yourself obsessively creating for hours beyond what your company expects, time enough to reach excellence.

Nor must you necessarily like your customers. What matters is that you love the spirit of your profession, its goals, its nature, its discipline, its history, its devoted workers whose common purpose is making excellence. After all, great patriots feel passionately for their country, though possibly not for its people.

"I am not inordinately fond of or interested in children," A.A. Milne, author of Christopher Robin and Winnie-the-Pooh stories, wrote in his autobiography. He was in love with childhood, not children.

PART TWO

Examples Of Creators At Work

Chapter Twelve

The Work Of The Artist

In all the fine arts, as writing, dancing, music, acting, painting, and sculpture, the artist's approach is the same. John Ciardi explains it in terms of the writer: ". . . The writing process is a groping one. There is no end to that groping process, but in time the good writer will acquire not only a sense of *groping for* but a sense of having *groped to*: he begins to know when he has finally reached whatever he was reaching for."

Ciardi goes on to explain the purpose of art, again in terms of the writer: "Writing selects from the unknown reality of things, and, by selecting, it makes known. Writing is a heightening, an excerption, an organic digression from its own beginning, an ordering, perhaps only a moment's ordering; whatever it is, it remains that glimpse through a frame that no man may live in but that the best of men must live toward."

While groping for beauty, there are extended spells in which the artist endures indefinitely long periods of no progress. The artist's stoic persistence comes from knowing that the groping is increasing the chance of striking a step toward essential beauty. The artist with sound sense and faith in hidden progress, at times when little or none is actually appearing, has patience and confidence to go on.

This faith is most needed after bringing a piece of work in progress to where it is average, inert to the spirit. Then begins the really arduous phase. The artist prospects fifty times longer than in the first phase, searching for the almost-invisible changes to the design that abruptly lift beauty and make it rapt to the spirit.

In the case of Rodin, before he cast a bronze bust he shaped a model to portray the person's recognizable mask. From there he had no firm idea or formula for how to reconcile the critical changes toward making the bust be that frame through which select virtues may be glimpsed. For weeks he felt about with his fingers and heart, delicately arranging and disarranging, with two consequences at odds: beauty falling off with one microscopic change and, less often, sharply scaling higher with another. Out of an infinite number of distinctions without a difference, he was able to grope to those that exerted a dazzling difference.

No one who watched him at work ever took home the indefinables of his craft. He himself knew little of the finely decisive hows, except that probing for beauty brings hidden steps toward a successful search, and that this time-tried heuristic approach is the one and only way of hitting upon landmark beauty.

The following story of a painter enlarges upon this.

Set in the 1930s, one minute the painter is walking to the drug store for coffee, just another morning in the exterior world of car horns, street talk, and chewing gum wrappers. The next, a sublimely raw idea for a painting has flashed into him, a special time in his interior world. Conventionally called a vision, negligibly is it visual. It is a prepossessing, crudely comprehended suggestion, providing a centering effect for groping toward beauty of design. His is of a painting through which may be glimpsed something of our essence as the species that projects excellence.

No one envisions without ideas for a design waiting to surface, and soon he has sketched connected scenes of creating and driving an automobile. He tapes them to the wall, a strip of images winding down: engineers huddled around drafting tables, slide rules in hand . . . white-coated technicians sculpting a model car . . . steam shovels at an open pit mine, loading iron ore . . . red-hot steel slabs on rollers, men in undershirts standing by . . . a speeding test-car rounding a banked motordrome . . . a view down the factory's assembly line, hundreds being built . . . a showroom, the car on a platform, sparkling crosses of light, and a man, woman, and two children dreamily gazing on.

Over the next several days he refines his sketches until the usual thing happens. Under his mind's eye, his vision is fascinatingly alive; under his real eyes, his design is stillborn. Here we are, this great projecting species, and his projection of the idea trivializes the fact. The longer he stares at it, the odder it seems, an embarrassment if painted. He shoves the work aside. Yet naturally, the next morning he is back into it, thinking, "That's the trouble. Too much to take in at once. The sparest scene possible, of course! An outright release of the gist, like a dam breaking."

Out of the dumps and into hope again, he pares the strip of sketches down as far as intelligibility allows, trying this and that, to arrive at three connected images: a disembodied luminosity intimating a bright idea; a mockup of a convertible car in the design studio, and a family riding in the real car in the autumn countryside, hair streaming.

Still, for some reason the magic he expects refuses to be. He slaps his pencil down; he will give up. The next hour—no, he will go on, reanalyze the difficulty and sleep on it. A few days afterwards sees him fiddling with scenes of building a house, then of an airplane. Days more, and it is with views of artisans blowing glass. It is a tribute to his will that by the tenth change of subject he is trying another. It is during one of these seemingly hopeless trials that the unheralded windfall appears, precipitated by his prior work which appeared to accomplish nothing, yet was bringing him to beauty's location. It is the notion of a sailboat.

This minor change of subject is anything but minor to the heart. Partly this is because both sailing and creating are rooted in our earliest ancestry; partly because both bring journeying to mind; and partly because both are haphazardly spotted with doldrums and squalls, with yawing about toward their destinations, with running aground on unseen shoals, and with fighting to get clear. And topping this off, the sailboat theme sets the ideal complementary color scheme: orange-gold is the traditional choice for envisioning's impulsive and fervid nature, blue the choice for designing's studied nature, and blue leads naturally into the blue of the sea. When in art a single decision, as "let it be a sailboat," puts so many things emblematically right, it has to be right.

With further sketching until the design seems settled, and with planning the order of painting the parts and scheduling time to do it, the morning arrives when he mixes paints, readies his airbrush, points his dry brushes, faces the blank canvas, poises his hand, blocks out areas, and makes the first lines and shadings. But as the picture begins peeping forth, changes of mind occur, prompting projects incidental to the main project, and projects incidental to the incidental projects. Groping at finer levels of detail, he generates ideas, intuits their promise, and chases them up with analysis, and by the more forward than rearward laying of colors and whiting over, the fragile magic of quality comes haltingly into being. The painting, finished at last, unshielded by distance or illusion, insinuates a grander expression than his first notion.

As a print, the painting actually appeared on the cover of the September 1934 issue of Fortune magazine, giving readers a beautiful look into the nature of creatively imaginative projects, and into human beings as the projecting species. The artist's signed name is Wood, and in the painting's upper right corner he (?) has gone beyond the layers of anatomical drawings into the very core of the human head. Stripped away are nose and mouth, hair and skin, muscle, tongue and teeth, with skull and brain discarded altogether. Not a cell remains, nor strand of DNA, simply the colorful energy of a mind envisioning. We see the orange-gold burst of vision, the genesis of a project. Under pressure like a gas, the spattered glow streams down and across the page into the part of mind where designing goes on, the warm tone diffusing into the objective blue of calculated precision. A little lower is pictured the result: a blueprint of thin white lines defining hull, keel, mast and rigging: a mold of excellence, ready for casting. And to its side below, where blueprint merges into blue sea, sails the completed product, the boat made real.

This story holds a final point of beauty. Out of the door of the artist's studio went the finished painting, while inside remained his more-capable self, beautifully transformed by the recursive work of painting it, to be used in his projects to come.

Chapter Thirteen

The Work Of The Scientist

Ask any number of people, then, "What distinguishes art?" and the answers will have a regularity about them:

Art expresses the higher, less visible realities of being. Artists delve into the unknowns of self, and of self relating to other selves, and to animals, plants, and the inanimate.

Art is subjective, free of regulations, a haven for nonconformists.

Artists are irreplaceable. No Homer, no *Odyssey*.

Some art endures. The classics are indelible delights. Free of diminution by the ages, lastingly current, their excellence keeps. Five centuries later, the *Mona Lisa* still takes our breath away.

Then ask around, "Name art's antithesis." By and large it will be science, perhaps for these reasons:

Science delves into the what and why of nature. At the center of scientists' conversations are data and explanations, topics artists never speak of.

Science is objective and communal, with governing bodies hemming scientists into compliance. Break the conventions of scientific method, act the independent, and be excommunicated, barred from publishing.

Scientists are replaceable. What one discovers, another may as well. Without Kepler, somebody in time would have exposed the laws of planetary motion.

And to round out the list, scientific discoveries are temporarily held, stations on the way to broader, more accurate, more useful discoveries. Mendel's knowledge of biological inheritance superseded Lamarck's. Newton's views overthrew Aristotle's, and Einstein's subsumed Newton's.

Despite these differences, and despite a common belief of a deep division of mind between scientists and artists, and despite the two sometimes sniffing disrespectfully at one another, science and art are fundamentally alike. Scientists and artists are in the business of creating knowledge. Scientists conceive theories, revealing knowledge of physical nature, letting us see snatches of how the material world is. Artists conceive paintings, novels, plays, and more, revealing knowledge of human nature, letting us see snatches of how we profoundly are.

Empirical science is also like art. To show this, consider the research of two marine scientists (reported in the 24 April 1992 issue of the journal *Science*). Octopuses, it was known, sometimes become good at solving problems, such as removing a cork from a jar to get at food inside. The puzzle was, how do they learn? Not from their parents, for they die shortly after their young are born. Nor from neighbor octopuses deliberately acting as teachers, for octopuses are asocial. The researchers hypothesized that octopuses spy on each other and learn from those who have accidentally hit upon solutions.

The scientists' project was to create an experiment to test this idea. They envisioned training octopuses to do an unnatural act in the laboratory, afterwards have untrained octopuses watch the trained ones perform, and note whether the watchers learned to do the same. Upon this vision, they designed a specific experiment. Passing over the recursive details, it ended with this: condition an octopus by placing it some distance in front of a red ball and a white ball, rewarding it with food whenever it attacks the red one. Once it is accustomed to this, arrange two glass aquariums side by side, the performing octopus in the first, a watching octopus in the second. Have the performer attack the red ball a number of times. Wait then for several days, and set the watcher down to face the balls. If the hypothesis is true, the watcher will go for the red ball in many more than half the trials. Replicate the experiment using numerous performers and watchers, and to rule out a possible born preference for red, repeat the experiment with performers conditioned to attack the white ball.

The designed experiment is an imagined situation, and making it real calls for planning. The scientists devised strategy and tactics dealing with the likes of procuring funds for the experiments, scheduling laboratory space and time, fishing small octopuses from the Bay of Naples, and rounding up aquariums and technicians. At length the plan was followed out, projecting into being the apparatus, the materials, and the procedures.

The findings did not disappoint. When a performing octopus went into action, an observing octopus followed it with head and eye movements, in close attention. Then given its chance to perform, it almost invariably attacked the correct ball. This confirmed the hypothesis, eventful for understanding how animals learn, as well as for overturning the prejudice that octopuses are low-class beings.

In general then, empirical scientists create machines called experiments, which consist of apparatuses and procedures for running them. The experiments are run, revealing facts of nature.

Artists may do the same. Suppose a painter envisions and designs a machine intended to create an insightful painting. Dropping in on a van Gogh who does this, we see him groping to compose and position mounds of painters' oils on a canvas which, apart from their colors, are little more attractive than grease droppings on a garage floor. And we see him fabricating a plywood sheet to cover the affair, windows cut in predetermined places, fitted with magnifying glasses of calculated powers, and with a maze of channels fixed to the cover's underside, designed to command the movement of air in specified rates and quantities. At two in the afternoon, on a waited-for day of right weather, he takes the apparatus outside, adjusts its angle to the sun's longitude as the design prescribes, and allows the allotted time for the treatment to act, the oils to flow, curious to know if the intended beauty will develop, and what will be its form. By evening, his uncertainty is resolved with a painting suggesting facets of inner reality.

Fantastic as this is, it obeys workable principles. In one branch of art, artists program computers with artistic rules to create paintings and music.

Otherwise, art and empirical science are quite alike as they are. The artist gropes to create a finished work, a painting or poem or musical composition. This is the artist's experiment, run as it is being created, bit by bit, day by day, revealing to the artist evolving glimpses into latent human nature, ending with a finished look into it. This is followed by a second experiment which is run by presenting the finished work to audiences and critics, for them to judge, confirming or not its worth.

Parallel to this, the scientist gropes to create an experiment, and when it is run it reveals to the scientist not evolving glimpses of latent physical nature but a finished look. This is followed by the experiment of publishing the revelations, for readers and critics to judge.

As to uniqueness, in art and in science there are any number of approaches to a given revelation. Ten poets may conceive ten separate poems, each sharing no words, yet through each we behold essentially the same truth of human nature. Ten physicists may conceive ten separate cyclotron experiments, each looking like no other, yet through each we behold essentially the same truth of physical nature.

As to motivation, artists and scientists are addicted to inquiry. Artists itch to find out what their evolving works will reveal, as they gradually lift the curtain on their final creations. Their discoveries and pleasures come every little while in the journey of groping forth, setting and resolving suspense along the way, a surprise around every turn, getting truer and truer glimpses through the developing frame of their work. In every way this is like theoretical scientists who create pictures of how nature is.

As for empirical scientists who create experiments, which in turn create the pictures of how nature is, the main difference between them and artists concerns the timing of their finding out. With empirical scientists, the curtain remains down until all of a sudden every inch of it is up. It is the climactic discovery, the grand moment of truth, that they look forward to, itching to know.

Take the physicist Ernest Lawrence. Although he did not dislike his projects of conceiving the first cyclotron and its experiments—arrangements of magnets, power supplies, wiring, knobs, plugs, buttons and switches, and the directions for using it all—it was dull work next to the waiting prize that intrigued and drove him on, the secrets his cyclotron experiments would force nature to divulge.

As to freedom to create as one wants, where artists are individualists, scientists are participating individualists, with rules governing the participating part, not the individualist part. Research societies enforce norms for replicating experiments and drawing conclusions, ensuring the discoveries are sound and safe to build upon. Outside this orthodoxy, there is inexhaustible room for eccentricity to flourish in conceiving theories and experiments.

Finally, the majority of people hold science above art. They believe that products based on science, as medical drugs that promote a healthy body, have more benefit than artistic works, as Aaron Copland's *Appalachian Spring* and nature's Grand Canyon, that promote a healthy soul. Where is the majority's evidence?

Chapter Fourteen

The Work Of The Mathematician

Where artists project art, revealing human nature, and scientists project theories and experiments, revealing physical nature, mathematicians project proofs, revealing mathematical nature.

Consider that Pierre de Fermat proposed what is now called Fermat's Last Theorem. In effect it states that here is a lock to which there is no key, where the lock is an equation, and the possible keys are from an unbounded set of numbers. Precisely put, it is this: when n is any integer greater than two, no integers x, y, and z, none being zero, exist in all infinity such that the equation $x^n + y^n = z^n$ is satisfied.

During the three centuries following Fermat's time, millions of keys were tried and none fit, but millions are inconsiderable in an infinitude. The question remained, does this hold throughout the boundless unexamined rest?

Creativity enters mathematics in two places. The first is in creating a proposition that a certain mathematical idea is universally true, no one knowing for sure that it is. The second is in creating a proof, a series of deductive steps that resolves the question.

The proposition is necessary because the mathematician's project of creating a proof must start with a destination in mind.

Unlike science, where discoveries are sometimes made by stumbling onto important observations, as Galileo did in sighting four of Jupiter's moons, the mathematician who lacks a proposition has no orienting hypothesis to lay deductive steps toward. Striking out willy-nilly is unproductive; knowing where one is headed for is essential to making the logical linkups for getting there.

So with a proposition in mind, and guided by intuition, the mathematician selects a starting idea known to be true. Once it was a proposition itself, before someone proved it true, or it is an axiom, a defined truth. From the starting idea, the mathematician creatively assembles a train of true if-then ideas, the exit of one feeding into the entrance of the next, literally the ducts implied in the word deduction. The mathematician thinks: "Because this starting idea is true, then this second idea must be true," and "If this second idea is true, then this third idea is true" . . . , continuing on to the last link, perhaps "If this ninth idea is true, then this tenth idea, which bears on the proposition, is true." Accordingly, the truth of the starting idea runs like falling dominoes to the final deduction.

Two outcomes are possible. The final deduction may certify the proposition as definitely true, or as definitely false. Either way, the mathematician learns a fact of the mathematical landscape.

The mathematician subscribes to Emerson's "Everything good is on the highway." Only nominally are proofs means to certifying propositions; proofs are ends in themselves. Like the artist and the theoretical scientist, the mathematician's interest lies in the moment by moment thinking, thickening attention and telescoping time.

The mathematician's wastebasket is filled with crumpled and wadded sheets, frustrated steps which feed hidden progress. Examining an ironed-out published proof, we miss the crossed-out equations, the provisional trials of envisioning and designing, the complications that appear along the way, forcing the mathematician to create detours, to postulate and prove secondary propositions, legs of sub-journeys to sub-destinations within a leg of the larger journey. Nor do we see the mathematician planning to cast around for suggestions, giving seminars to colleagues on the work in progress, and scouting out articles in mathematical journals.

The truths that mathematicians fail to establish now, those who follow may. Time adds to the store of proven propositions, bringing more construction material, more stepping stones, more if-then deductive links to choose from, the better for getting there.

With the grace of time, Fermat's theorem, an Everest of a place, was eventually reached by a proof, a first ascent, a grand feat, through a lengthy, roundabout, rather ugly route, establishing its truth. Mathematicians will forever return to that mountain. Even if a time comes when every conceivable proposition that is true has been proved true, the mathematical landscape completely mapped, mathematicians will happily face an endless future of trying to get to already-visited destinations by simpler, shorter, more direct proofs. For its startling beauty, what mathematicians value above all is beeline logic.

Chapter Fifteen

The Work Of The Mechanic

Stresses scour the sheet metal of airplanes in flight, searching for microscopic heterogeneities: voids, inclusions of alloying elements, naturally occurring impurities, and corrosion around rivets. As the hours of loadings and releasings go by, the stresses quietly gnaw at the metal surrounding their prey, cutting out toeholds to disaster, tiny cracks uncomfortably close to the threshold of wholesale fatigue failure, every pilot's jack-in-the-box nightmare.

During the summer of 1933, as Charles and Anne Morrow Lindbergh were flying their seaplane across the North Atlantic, a small crack appeared in the engine cowling, and they put in for repairs at an outpost on the coast of Greenland. The mechanic they engaged, two people rolled into one—a diagnostician-engineer in restoring function, and an artist in restoring form—was closely concerned with solving problems he had yet to see the likes of. When he had finished, in place of the crack was a weld which could be trusted to last the life of the plane, and which nicely blended into the cowling's rounded lines. And in place of the Lindberghs' worries, they were free to continue their trip to Europe, on to Africa, and back to America.

Skimmed from his many deliberations are the following, without classifying or keeping in order where they occurred in the stages of his project:

Contain the crack by drilling holes and riveting metal strips underneath, or weld the aluminum, difficult to do dependably? And upon deciding to weld, remove the cowling or repair it in place? How large a safety factor to build in? How to make the work please the eye? What tools and materials to bring to the dock? At every spot in the welding, which size tip is best for the torch, in that a small one works well for pinpointing the flame but is poor for heating large areas? Where to put scratch marks before tacking the seam? At which points is the gap narrow enough to fuse with molten beads of aluminum, and where must it be bridged with melted welding rod? Where and for how long should heat be directed and applied to avoid wrinkling or warping the metal, which when cooled might strain the seam?

Mechanics engineer repairs. They are in company with surgeons sewing up wounds, psychologists healing minds, archeologists reconstructing ancient ruins, and counselors mending broken marriages. While many of their projects are routine, some are one of a kind, calling for original thinking beyond the procedures of shop manuals.

Although mainly driving this man was the need to improve human welfare, specifically to put goodness into the Lindberghs' lives, a considerable spiritual thrust boosted him as well. He was a mechanic's mechanic, working in a lonely place, against no rivals, unconcerned with stock options, awards, and titles. And no one goes to Greenland out of lust for public attention. He was there to serve excellently, to give his work the stamp of his soul, and by that the stamp of the caring collective human soul. Watching his discriminating hands at work, sweeping the blue-white flame in ovals, slanting the angle of attack, and sensing his merciless, looping, closing in on a job well done, the magical homing instinct having its magical hold on him, Anne Morrow Lindbergh recorded in her diary:

> It is marvelous to watch a man who knows exactly what
> he has to do, knows he can do it, has his tools and knows
> which to use, and sets about his work with speed, confi-

dence, and precision. Added to which this man has a thoroughness and capacity for work, a willingness to do his job perfectly, that is remarkable. He has worked all of two days, and some of the night, not bothering half the time about eating and resting, and he is not (modestly) satisfied with his work. He is impersonal about his work too—doesn't work for praise, but takes pride in its being well done.

No matter he spoke Danish, and the Lindberghs English; that is irrelevant to spiritual rapport. He communicated to them in the universal language of quality. He was in the same kind of flight as they were: selflessly devoted to doing one's work perfectly. How to explain people like this? Pierre Teilhard de Chardin would have put it in terms foreign to efficiency experts to whom cost-effectiveness is the thing. People like this mechanic, he would have said, are shot through with the fire of a cosmic passion. The efficiency experts would have said this explains nothing and is worth little. Teilhard de Chardin would have said it explains all and is worth everything.

Chapter Sixteen

The Work Of The Entrepreneur

What a magnifying glass does with the diffuse rays of the sun, entrepreneurs do with the ungathered talents of men and women. The entrepreneur is the vital force who creatively rounds up financing and facilities, chooses and shapes people into solidarity, and leads them to get a creative job done.

Entrepreneurial work is falsely stereotyped. The entrepreneur's vision is not always original, nor does it always put a premium on use rather than beauty. Nor does taking chances define the entrepreneur: risk figures into every kind of creative work. Nor must considerable lucrative stakes hang in the balance: the profit motive is frequently absent. Nor does anything near to national fame typically come to the successful entrepreneur: repute is often confined to a radius of several miles. Nor are investment bankers necessarily involved: pocket money covers the expenses in some cases.

This definition takes the surprise out of learning that certain entrepreneurial projects, completed in weeks, distinct from business, are exemplified by those of Elsa Maxwell. She was the instigating germ and fastidious organizer of dinner parties for people from the theater world. Envisioning and designing the ingredients that she intended would put them in high spirits, she scripted the list of guests and the seating arrangements of who would be next to whom, to best encourage congeniality; scripted the choice and setting of china, glassware, silverware, table linen, napkin rings, candle holders, and finger bowls; scripted the selection of the aperitif, the hors d'oeuvres, the wine, the main course, and the dessert; and into the role of host, scripted herself.

Planning to realize this, she assembled and guided a staff that arranged everything from polishing the water glasses and silverware, to obtaining prime meats and vegetables. With responses to contingencies carefully thought out, she was unlikely to be caught short in the event a waiter or a kitchen maid called in sick, or an invitation got delayed.

As entrepreneurs are, she was in a sense cousin to the scientist. Creating an experiment is interesting work to the scientist, but the greater interest is in running it. In the same way, it interested her to create the ingredients that set the stage for a party, but that was preliminary to what really mattered— when the guests assembled and her social enterprise was off and running.

Like creators of every stripe, entrepreneurs are out to manage their risks, to squeeze the adverse probabilities down toward zero, with the gamble that refuses to be squeezed further leaving a residual edge of excitement. Elsa Maxwell, readying her party experiments, troubled with minimizing, but could not eliminate, the chance that instead of getting a spontaneous evening of unpretentious diversion, a happy high point long after talked about, her guests might inexplicably behave like Easter Island monoliths.

Max Born was her counterpart in scientific research. He was the prime mover behind a long intellectual party, lasting approximately from 1921 to 1933 at the Physical Institute at the University of Göttingen. The ingredients he drew up and gathered were the leading atomic physicists of the day, and the party he set in motion generated what he was after: an exchange of ideas toward a more elemental understanding of matter, the sum of which was the beginning of quantum mechanics.

John Hunt was Elsa Maxwell's and Max Born's equivalent in mountaineering, fashioning the first party to climb Mount Everest. He united the world's principal climbers, studied and considered their personalities in assigning their roles, delegated responsibilities, mediated disputes and, when needed, intervened to staunch undercurrents of resentments. His vision and hand were in everything from hiring the porters, seeing to their orders, and putting the X's on the map that located the camps, to drawing up schedules for acclimatizing to altitude, and waging waiting games with the weather.

It may come as a surprise to think of Florence Nightingale as an entrepreneur, but she was. She was the torchbearer who during the Crimean War marshaled nurses and doctors to demonstrate that following sanitary procedures in sick wards curtailed disease. Partly on the opinionated grounds that she was a civilian and a woman, military bureaucrats tried to block her. Countering them, she capitalized detailed record-keeping procedures and graphical techniques of statistical display (the polar-area diagram, used today, is her invention) to bolster her argument and gain the overruling support of high governmental authorities. With her methods put into practice, deaths from disease, previously about 40 percent, settled at nearly zero.

Robert Fulton was an entrepreneur who aimed not to cut disease but travel time. By no means could a scavenger's hunt in the year 1800 have turned up a paddle wheel steamboat, yet easily could have located the material for it. Eight years later one was comfortably carrying passengers up and down the Hudson River, with the trip from New York City to Albany shortened from almost a week to 31 hours.

It is folly to believe this project fell into place without a central organizing magnet. Defying critics predicting that customers afraid of exploding boilers would stay away, Fulton formulated the steamboat and its service, and planned and supervised its making, toppling every barrier. He persuaded financiers and government officials to back its production, obtained a steam engine from

England, and oversaw boatwrights laying the hull, blacksmiths fixing the machinery into place, carpenters framing and finishing cabins, and agents scouting for passengers.

James Buchanan Eads was an entrepreneur without whom the present scene and inhabitants of St. Louis would be noticeably different. He conceived and saw to its completion in 1874 the Eads Bridge, spanning the Mississippi River to unleash an artery of commerce and the city's growth. His farsightedness, arm twisting, and obstinacy overcame both the entrenched ferryboat companies that transported people and supplies across the river, and the business interests in Chicago that wanted the gateway to the West to remain theirs.

Juan Trippe was one of those entrepreneurs who, after founding a company, go on to spend their lives nurturing its expansion. His vision and politic skills secured the airmail contract and lone airplane that spawned Pan American Airways, and fought off attempts of the established trading company, W. R. Grace Corporation, to put Pan Am out of business. In time he sold manufacturers on designing airplanes to his specifications, started excellent passenger service, and spread flights throughout Latin America and across the globe. Though his ability to create novel ideas out of nothing was average, his was a kind of genius that often finds its outlet in entrepreneurial work: he had what the book publisher Kurt Wolff has called a genius at grasping ideas of others, seeing profounder possibilities than they themselves do.

Occasionally entrepreneurs team up on large projects, making their decisions on constituent projects, mindful of the whole. Known as The Big Four, Mark Hopkins, Collis Huntington, Charles Cocker, and Leland Stanford were the entrepreneurs who got the western half of the U. S. transcontinental railroad conceived and built. They induced bankers to open their purse strings, and assembled legal staff to acquire roadway right-of-ways. They hired those who hired and managed the rest. Civil engineers, ironworkers, gang and section foremen, station men, yardmasters, brakemen, purchasing agents, expediters, accountants, signal engineers, telegraph and telephone operators, clerks, cooks, locomotive engineers and firemen, as well as doctors to care for them all, materialized. Culverts, crushed stone and gravel, rails and crossties and spikes by the millions, fencing material, signaling equipment, water towers, coal yards, stations, baggage carts, and rolling stock came into place—and the imagined railroad came to operate before the eyes.

For a last case, certainly entrepreneurial was the project to create the first nuclear submarine. Did it require assembling a hive of people having requisite talents, their efforts joined in a common aim? Yes, tens of thousands. Was the hive the result of a queen bee? Yes, Admiral Hyman Rickover was the enabling factor: the visionary, the nerve center, the project's lifeblood. Anyone but him was replaceable.

Rickover called his method *the orthodontic approach*. "The application of continuous, steady pressure over the years to achieve eventual change" is how his colleague and biographer, Theodore Rockwell, explains it. Rickover brought it to bear against deterrents of technological complexity and tactics of political obstruction that tried to deny him access to sufficient funds and the best engineers. By selling Congress on the idea, he was able to recruit top people, winning them over with promises of interesting and important work, and with their respect for him as the project's most toughly committed and aggressive worker, who put in the longest days. He set them to tackling unprecedented technical problems, compelling metallurgists to innovate new materials, and factories to produce them in quantities thought infeasible. And he instituted a model program of rigorous standards for selecting and training naval officers to operate the submarine. Eight years after the serious idea of it had first run in his head, the *Nautilus* put out to sea.

All the same, the majority of entrepreneurs are narrowly heard of, their projects of the pocket money kind, involving a handful of people. In a rural area, an entrepreneur takes the initiative to form an association to bring in touring chamber music groups. In a town, an entrepreneur determined to promote animal welfare solicits members and officers to begin a humane society. We would all be worse off without these unsung entrepreneurs than without the Andrew Carnegies, who by the sheer tonnage of their projects become household names.

Chapter Seventeen

The Work Of The Rock Climber

While the gloom of poor financial prospects weighed on the minds of Wall Streeters in early August 1932, four thousand and seven hundred miles away in the Dolomite Alps, Giusto Gervasutti and a climbing companion stood back from the base of a rock wall, buoyed by the bright promise of their recent vision. Up and across the wall they imagined a line spotted with sections that would occupy them to the full, prospecting for crannies, grooves, notches, lips, depressions, and rough surfaces; creating counterforces to gravity, allowing not an unguarded moment of deficit to sneak in.

Planning for their safety, they noted ledges for possibly bivouacking on, in case of storms. Back home, they consulted the weather forecast, decided on the day, went over their checklist of gear, clothes, and food; and drew up a timetable—start in the predawn before the sun warmed the ice above, releasing stones; be so far along by seven-thirty, at a certain place by nine.

Conceiving the overall project had its points, but what was to hold them long and fast was the ongoing work of recursively creating and trying out their moves, one minute a theorist, the next an empiricist. So on the designated morning, beginning shortly after roping up and lasting throughout the day, like Alice they were drawn into layers of their wonderland, subprojects embedded within the main project, and sub-subprojects within them, on down into the hierarchy, each level crammed with absorption compounded of curiosity and problem solving, doubts and elations.

This inclusion of projects inside projects is like mathematical fractals, having the property of self-similarity, for when any section of a fractal picture is magnified it has the makeup of the whole picture, and when any section of that is enlarged it is the same. No matter how many levels of magnification, there is no bottom to the pictures contained within pictures. And no matter that in climbing the embedded projects are consecutively more confined in space and time, each exacts total attention. The fractal effect packs living into living, and more living into that living, gathering spiritual nourishment in a morning and afternoon of climbing that could not come in months of ordinary living.

The fractal effect is thickest on pitches that slope away fearsomely. Even though safety ropes practically rule out getting hurt, the nervous system takes little comfort, at times sending a shiver up the spine, as if really within an inch of one's life. The thought that Old Newton might take over is essential. If somehow the ground below rose as climbers moved up, limiting falls to three feet, climbing would lose its attraction and remove them from its anvil.

"The laws of probability, so true in general, so fallacious in particular," remarked Edward Gibbon. Gervasutti envisioned and designed climbs that made the general probability of failing large, then gave his all to becoming the successful particular case. With the fractal effect in full swing, the spell of its motivating pleasures on high, the guiding hand ran most effectively, forming his capabilities in just the right way, enabling and encouraging him to go on to create climbs that rooted out and repaired his further weaknesses. Sometimes his calculated gambles went haywire, pitching him into unfamiliar creative territory, locating bottlenecks in himself, demanding he conceive saving subprojects, uncommon combinations of moves, no if-and-or-but excuses allowed. Practice climbing against made-up challenges was unsuited to do this, as he dimly perceived his critical shortcomings.

Thus more and more, Gervasutti became expert at distinguishing the part he played in his successes and failures from the part fortune and misfortune played, not allowing lucky results to lull him into taking credit, raising false confidence. More and more, he kept a cautious eye out for subtle shifts in normal mountain conditions to abnormal ones, where a usually safe decision, taken without a second thought, might trip the lever of calamity. More and more, he developed resistance against the temptations that gather voice as the summit is neared, to take unwise gambles just because the effort of getting so close has been spent and "it would be a shame to turn back now." More and more, he grew at reading the texture of rock and its opportunities; at widening the variety and combinations of his moves; at envisaging distantly ahead into the branching consequences of alternatives, and intuiting the worth of each; and at shaving allowances for safety without diminishing the safety.

Climbers as Gervasutti serve the world in a number of ways:

First, from the climber we sense quality point-blank, evoking the pervasive greatness of our species. The outer excellence of climbers' feats lays bare their inner excellence; automatically we grasp their extraordinarily self-reliant and courageous searches for solutions, free of extravagance, window-dressing, showmanship, pretense, and glossing over their mistakes. A kind of mathematician, climbers seek to create beeline proofs of genuine human being.

Second, climbers remind us that our ancient roots are in nature, God's creation. Climbing is alive on the material plane, where human flesh is at its ancestral home and belongs, with all fours touching earth—palms and thighs on timeworn smoothness and roughness and angularities of rock, sensing the warm and cool, the give and take of heat, all the while with companions of clouds and breeze, brook and wildflower meadow, sky and stars.

And on the transcendental plane, climbing is where human action is at its home and belongs, imitating and conforming with the beautifully recursive, creatively transforming processes of nature.

Third, climbers inspire us. On mountain walls, through the window of himself, Gervasutti saw into his species' ground nature. Subsequently by speaking and writing, he took his private window public, that all might see. Tens of thousands have been vitalized by his writing of the hours he was alone, halfway up the Matterhorn, Christmas Eve 1936, determined to reach the summit. Below in the village beckoned temptations of fireplaces, festivities, and animal comforts—high above in the cold, the icy route leading ostensibly to the top but really to Gervasutti's creating himself.

It is wrong to think a climb as this, to pay for itself in inspiration, has to directly stimulate millions to a profounder comprehension of themselves and their species, and to become more enterprising in their contributions. A climber's life, as Gervasutti's, indirectly ramifies like the trunk of a tree that gives spiritual nourishment to a hundred primary branches of climbers, teachers, detectives, journalists, artists, scientists, writers, inventors, engineers, doctors, pilots, and more. In turn, they each go on to better serve and inspire another hundred through their examples, and the branches spread to a hundred times a hundred, and on and on it goes, as the animating spirit makes its way far in generations and wide in vocations.

Fourth, climbers stand the meaning of escapism on its head. Serious climbers, freed from the wasteland of static and unimaginatively passed days, yesterday's events replayed, sparse with the kind of thinking that begins with the word "if," are among those most centered in the life that having a cerebrum fits us for.

Fifth, climbers teach us how to instill integrity. Unlike claim-jumpers who illegally seek title to gold ore without having to search for it, climbers own the precious process of searching, minute-by-minute gold. Naturally they shun unscrupulous means of reaching their goals, as taking a helicopter to within easy reach of the top. Naturally they refuse temptations to gild their work, making it seem better than it is. Any of this is certain to kill their spiritual thrust, stop their growth and journey, everything worthwhile to them. The lesson for educators and employers is clear. The more that the pleasures of the creative journey flourish in students and workers, the more they will act ethically—no rules, sermons, threats, or artificial rewards required.

Chapter Eighteen

The Work Of The Collector

There are two methods of creating, each with applications in many fields. Call the one the method of the artist. To this point in this book, it is the one discussed, with artists, mathematicians, and rock climbers among those who use it. It is marked by the almost continual generation of ideas and the judging of their worth, as with a painter standing before a canvas, recursively groping for thoughts and how to present them.

Call the other the method of the collector. It is used by those who create collections to illuminate an envisioned theme, as with collecting poems for an anthology. This is in contrast to collecting fossils, autographs, dolls, and the like, where the collection is an indiscriminate hodgepodge of items with no theme.

To illustrate the method's professional use, an art curator, wanting to stage an exhibition of paintings that illuminates an envisioned theme, faces blank walls. For the design, the curator selectively gathers paintings in the art community which their owners are willing to lend, and arranges the order of hanging them in a gallery.

To illustrate the method's amateur use, a button collector searches in antique shops and private collections, buying and making trades, to create a display in a button tray, mounting from 20 to 70 buttons in a geometric pattern, adhering to the rules of composition approved by the National Button Society. Perhaps individually the buttons are nothing special. Yet mounted together, the successful collection makes a unified whole of rare note.

My writing of this book relies on both methods. In creating the essay part, I am using the method of the artist. It is a whirl of generating ideas from scratch, provisionally trying them out, and discarding most. In creating the book's other part, I fish for remarks of creators, trying to create a compilation of quotations that makes a gestalt in ideas, and in the sincerity of the authors' words.

Being less intense, the method of the collector is less fatiguing than the method of the artist. It is wrong, however, to conclude it is inferior. An art curator may be able to assemble a set of paintings that illuminates a theme that no single painting could. Either method, well used, produces quality.

The creative skills required to do the method of the artist and the method of the collector are largely independent. Whether you can or cannot do one well predicts little about whether you can or cannot do the other well.

PART THREE

The Responsibilities
Of Creators

Chapter Nineteen

Guarding Against A Life
Given To Sensual Pleasures

Sensuality and creativity were at a soda fountain having chocolate sundaes when sensuality said, "You know, we're a bit different."

"I'd say that's putting it mildly," said creativity. "We're as different as sky rockets and driftwood. That's our kind of a bit different."

"But you have to admit," said sensuality, "different or not, we're equally valuable."

"You equal to me? I'll have you know I'm your better. Einstein was full of me. I made Einstein be Einstein."

"Hold on. I was in Einstein too. I was in the pipe smoke that went up his nose and soothed him while he thought. I was in the schnapps he sipped after work. I went sailing with him on vacations. Don't be stingy with the credit. I refreshed him so he could better use you."

"You were OK for him," said creativity, "but that's just because he had you under control. Many don't. Teenagers have been known to fill themselves with you by the time they first learn of me. Filled with you, they have no room for me."

The trouble with this exchange is that the claims, while true, are propped up by toothpicks. Belief wants pilings. Take the idea that sensualists and creators really do live in ways that are poles apart. Proof of this comes from two stories of a drop of water traveling intact in a river. Here is the first:

Born on the tip of a lodgepole pine needle, the drop falls to the clay bank and rolls into a tributary of the Yellowstone River, where it is sent downstream into discovery, in quick succession learning of bison and bald eagle, red squirrel and Alpine Laurel, beaver and Canada goose, and winding runs of rapids whose turns seem never to repeat.

To those just emerged from nothingness, everything is novel and rushes the senses, but the drop misses the fact and guesses high, concluding it is destined to be swept through a flux of delightful sensations, forever enlarging in kind and degree.

Yet not long after puberty and diving over the edge of Tower Falls into the rainbow mist below, the world begins looking less remarkable. The channel widens, the days merge. Ravens drifting overhead barely draw a gaze, and Yellow Paintbrush might as well be grey. With the possibilities of diversions mostly exhausted, fresh supplies exist only in the realm of impossible permutations: flying trout, waltzing crows, thunder before lightning, any unusual thing. But nothing appears but an awareness of why: that finite sets are finite; that early extrapolation inevitably lies; that boundlessness has a truer guise.

And so, slowing and losing its glisten, the drop passes the last ripple and comes to float like a twig in a current too weak to supply more than a lazy twirl, and entering the marshes of the Mississippi delta, it meanders back and forth among mazes of slender waterways, drifted less by currents than by the whims of rising gas bubbles, until washing out into the Gulf of Mexico and dissolution.

Now, the second story:

Rising from the Gulf of Nothing, the drop floats into being. The aimless drifting, the slow going, the fragile convictions, the false excursions up side channels—these belong to the delta of youth. By exploring and pledging itself to trials, even though unsure of where it wants to go and how, it tastes tentative purpose. And by pursuing such purpose, it gains competence; and competence in turn allows it to probe for firmer purpose; and out of this comes successively stronger conviction that it has found the way to live that its nature has intended it for.

At first, fewer than one in ten of its leaps takes it to the next higher shelf. It expects to be spilled back, to be bruised, to learn and prepare to try again. Sometimes it temporarily gives up and looks for less-steep side courses whose resistance better matches its capabilities, and when by ascending them it has strengthened itself, it returns to take on rapids as difficult as those that once forced its submission. And all the while, it aspires as much or more for the process of striving as for what it outwardly seeks, the next higher shelf.

As for why the upstreaming life of creating is better than the downstreaming life of sensuality, here are reasons:

From the standpoint of goodness, sensualists mistake what feels good for what is good. Voluptuous excitement from opiates, from drinking sprees, and from relieving pent-up sexual pressure lack goodness. Rather, goodness is what we put into others. They might not be aware of it at the time, or ever. It might not even feel good to them, or to the creators creating it, but the transaction does far-reaching good.

From the standpoint of the creative spirit, extreme sensualists—those who seek the nth degree of thrill, assaulting their senses weirdly and furiously, as being whiplashed, looped, and corkscrewed in barrels over waterfalls, getting cheek by jowl to full-blowing volcanoes, managing brushes with death, near calamities which momentarily cause loss of solid contact with the world—they mistake the emotions of being tumultuously disoriented or spectacularly towered over, for those of the spirit. Such events make us feel insignificant, whereas the creative spirit makes us feel cosmic.

From the standpoint of Homer's *Odyssey*, by whose authority is it that the downstreaming gang of carousers that courted

Odysseus' wife, that countered Descartes with "It's a kick; therefore I am," lived wrongly and Odysseus rightly? By those who for upward of 3,000 years have kept the *Odyssey* listened to and read. Never would they so respond if Homer had Odysseus shipped home on a luxury liner, pampered and coddled, obstacles whisked from his way, prizing his gonads above his cerebrum.

From the personal standpoint, the downstreaming life is wrong because it forsakes sensualists. Familiarity fouls their pleasure centers. Better kicks have been had, and what, with four or more decades to go, is there to do? With creativity, however, the more you use, the more you have to use, forestalling loss of interest.

From the standpoint of society, sensualists leave the world no better off. The human record barely awards them a place. Who has ever made a memorable statue of a sensualist? Try locating the names of sensualists in encyclopedias; a few bizarre curiosities are all, hedonists like King Faruk and the Marquis de Sade. At the same time, history and literature pay creative workers high tribute, making encyclopedias thick.

Finally from the Judeo-Christian standpoint of God, the downstreaming life is wrong. God created heaven and earth, a project. God created light, a project. God created the division of light, day and night, a project. God created the grasses and flowers, the trees and moss, the birds and fishes and every living thing, a project. And in His image, God created our potential to create goodness, a project. God, the foremost creator of goodness, comes down on the side of the creative worker.

Were God an out-and-out sensualist who had stumbled upon the universe already made, who carried on and failed to have Himself well in hand, as staging demolition derbies among galaxies, the Bible would not be. No one wants to read about a deity with warts.

Now as to the beneficial uses of sensuality, dashes of it, to be sure, spice creativity. But runaway sensuality has pervaded much of society, turning spice to poison. The lesser trouble is extreme sensuality, for it is rare. The greater is wholesale, ordinary sensuality: browsing through store merchandise; catering to one's looks; idling in amusement and bodily pleasure; spectating, directly and by secondhand accounts through news reports and gossip; and anything else that little relies on the cerebrum.

What few lesson books there are on limiting sensuality in one's life to its spice role is made up for by the greatness of one, the *Odyssey*. Odysseus is the upstreamer who relishes using his creative faculties, seeking excellence, goodness in the nth degree. With the Trojan War over, his project is to sail home to Ithaca and rejoin his wife, son, father, and neighbors. A number of times the gods cast appalling bullies into his path, for instance the Cyclops which seals him into its cave, sentencing him to a static, futureless existence like its own. Each time he fights to save his skin, in the case of the Cyclops exploiting its one-eyed blindness in foresight, escaping by his creative wits.

If the *Odyssey* was just about Odysseus's fighting to save his skin, libraries would shelve it next to Tarzan stories. Mainly it is about Odysseus's fighting to save his creative soul against temptresses out to sweep him off his feet and into their fool's paradise. He knows the difference between the satisfactions they hawk—satisfactions that merely stop complaint—and the satisfactions from work that aspires to quality—satisfactions that emanate from the creative soul. He knows that genuine life is of the cerebrum and our high nature, and that the tinny life results from sporting with our flesh and low nature.

And so he resists joining the drowsing herd of drugged Lotus Eaters who throw away their active imaginations to vegetate. He resists the bewitching strains of the Sirens, bent on drawing him into a pointless existence. He refuses Circe's seductive offer to spend eternity in frolicking, cuddling, and orgasmic excitement.

Some things have not changed since Homer's time. Now as then, the young despise boredom, time empty of pleasing events, the seconds lasting hours. Now as then, kicks are the cheapest solution. Years before the Muses can go to work on the young's high nature, sirens are enticing their low nature.

What has changed, and relatively recently, is that our age is far thicker with sirens. We call them marketeers, and they have made a science of their methods to infect us with the latest itches and to sell us the latest means of scratching. They are behind the self-indulgent carnival of people lusting hand-to-mouth in search of the next occupying or titillating moment, and it is not going too far to say that if Shakespeare was born today, his character, a sufficient shield against sixteenth century temptations, would quite possibly yield to the many ways of killing time. Merely the presence of shopping malls, television, and transportation to faraway places might be enough to distract him, dilute his concentration, dull his wits, blight his responsibility to develop his high nature to his limit, and rob us of his works.

Fighting fire with fire has a preventive role here. Educators have untapped power to be marketeers themselves, pitching the merits and attractions of the creative life to their classes, and showing it is superior to the sensual life. Let them steep the young in the history of creating, and in great examples of creating and creators. Let them help the young discover and build their special creative faculties, and advance toward the day their obsession and joy of creating turn on, and the itch of curiosity solves boredom naturally.

And let educators teach the young about the power of abnegation to combat sirens. Among the leading cases to discuss in the classroom is young Charles Lindbergh. As he tells in his autobiography, he knew that if sirens ever get the tip of their wedge in, the rest is easy for them. So when fame showered him with gifts, he went into solitude where reasons for self-restraint are always plainer and decisions easier. After landing his plane in the Utah desert to have the company of silence and stars, by morning he had resolved to give the gifts away, and never to sell his destiny to commercial interests. He would stay clear of material opulence. He would promote spiritual opulence. He would create great goodness for the world.

But can anyone who is already being swept mightily along on the downstream current do an about-face? Saint Augustine did. As a young man with little concern for ethics or the future, he gadded about looking for escapades, squandered his time on carnal lusts and playthings, and was a thief. One day, his identity crisis come to a head, he woke up feeling and thinking, I DISGUST MYSELF. Nothing short of being overtaken by the same feeling and thought about themselves can start the conversion of downstreamers to upstreamers.

Chapter Twenty

Raising Children

The parents a child is born to is either the opportunity or the misfortune of its life. Anne Morrow (Lindbergh) was lucky. She did not come as a spillover effect from two people selfishly after the fun of mating. Dwight and Elizabeth Morrow intended and dearly wanted her. Had department stores, not pregnancy, been the source of babies, she would have been ordered.

But her luck ran further. She was born to parents who lived religious precepts, and their civilizing example fostered in her the full range of sympathies. Her selfless life has been an active concern for the welfare of one and all, from people to moths.

Still, her luck ran further. Religion deals with but a part of living. It neither addresses nor mentions the giving of excellence through one's works. The Morrows knew—and this was Anne's furthest luck—that one can be warm and cheerfully acquiescent in daily affairs, inquire of neighbors, reach out dependably in times of crisis, never crush a gnat, stay above reproach, yet be sorely lacking. The fact is, people can come close to holy perfection by being something of a puppy dog.

There is a need for professional religion beyond ordinary religion. Think of the financial planner who wholeheartedly asks about a couple's child, but incompetently invests their life's savings. Or the congenial roofer who vexes customers with work that leaks and stains the plaster below. Or the gregariously entertaining teacher who permits students to graduate short of their best possibilities.

Ask who puts more goodness into the world. Is it ophthalmologist *A* who is sincerely concerned with curing your eye disease, comforting to talk with, who will say a prayer to put you in God's hands in the operating room, but who has complacently settled for average technical proficiency? Or is it *B*, poor at small talk, who declined to lend a hand cleaning up basements after last year's flood, but who is an ophthalmologist's ophthalmologist, taking on unthinkable cases and performing what seem miracles, not by prayer but by hard-acquired knowledge and talent? A little callously, the gruff one says, "Your eyesight is fixed, as good as new," with the unspoken implication, "now please get out of here." The other says, "I fumbled the job and your sight will be permanently impaired, but I love you all the same." To be content with making things so-so is to throw in the spirit's face an infidelity to our species.

Family size is no bound on raising righteous children. Any number can be taught agreeable manners, to be good Samaritans, and to keep to the letter of the law. But raising a child to discover the creative most of what it has, and to make the most of it, takes considerable time and money. Wealthier than a score of average families combined, the Morrows could have fed, clothed, and sheltered sixty children. They chose instead to concentrate their attention, preparing Anne with an upbringing that would let her someday contribute much to the world.

This meant giving her a steady regimen of excellent cultural outings—concerts, plays, museums, art galleries, and travel. It meant putting her in a climate of educating grandparents, aunts, uncles, and family acquaintances, who infected her with the habit of searching and skeptical inquiry, thinking up good questions and answering them in fine form. It meant, too, packing her off to a solitary spot on the coast of Maine during summers, for nature's perfections to rub off, shaping her standards of excellence, nurturing her latent spirit. So it was that Anne ripened into a young woman whose solution to boredom was not to go out and buy something new, but to think up something new.

The Morrow's final responsibilities were to send Anne to an excellent college and pay its appreciable tuition. One cannot gainfully be in a marathon of classes, subjects, penetrating thoughts, and enriching events while working to meet expenses.

What makes a college excellent? It is among the five or so percent that are nearest to an ideal college. Like George Orwell's exercise of imagining an ideal pub (which he named *The Moon Under Water*), it is instructive to imagine an ideal college with ideal features, that actual colleges and actual teachers and actual students may raise themselves toward.

Generally speaking, an ideal college covers the broad grounds of what is, what could possibly be, and what ought to be. It increases its students' empathy and reverence for all forms of life. It releases them from baselessly hidebound attitudes. It makes them public-spirited, selflessly vowing to do good not because it makes them feel good to do good, but because the principle of rightness demands it.

It is foreign to ideal teachers to assume that because students appear in class the first day that they are eager to learn. Rather, throughout the term the teachers captivatingly project their subjects. They work their students to rigorous intellectual and emotional standards. They plunge them into long terms of reading, writing, and debating. They lead them to turn the ideas and arguments of great books inside out and examine the seams, and to demolish stock responses that pretend to go to the heart of issues. They urge them to open up not clam up, placing their views before the public. An ideal college, moreover and particularly, does the following:

CULTIVATES A WIDE SPHERE OF KNOWLEDGE. The students equip themselves in every fundamental way to be universal artists, by acquiring interests and knowledge in a diversity of seemingly unrelated subjects that deal in ageless ideas and emotions, primarily from the perspective of goodness of beauty. By this, students fill the tank that supplies the spring of intuition. Obvious among the subjects are music, literature, mathematics, history, philosophy, writing, painting, dancing, and the natural world. Less obvious are subjects as computer programming, taught untraditionally to stress more its beauty of recursive logic than its commercial and technological applications.

Through this, each student builds a mongrel mind of mixed breeds, a start to being an original polymath. For laying practical skills on this foundation, there is graduate school and training on the job.

CULTIVATES A WIDE SPHERE OF THINKING SKILLS. The students acquire a many-side diversity in reasoning quantitatively and qualitatively, probabilistically and deterministically, inductively, deductively, analogically, heuristically and algorithmically, conditionally and unconditionally.

CULTIVATES DESCRIPTIVE SKILLS. "Nothing has really happened until it has been described," said Virginia Woolf. "Unless you catch ideas on the wing and nail them down [by describing them], you will soon cease to have any." An ideal college leads its students to nail down thoughts and feelings about behaviors, features, and relationships, by writing diaries, essays, and poetry, and by drawing with pencil and paper.

CULTIVATES THE CREATIVE SPIRIT. William Blake was creatively expressing the creative spirit when he wrote:

> To see a World in a Grain of Sand
> And a Heaven in a Wild Flower,
> Hold Infinity in the palm of your hand
> And Eternity in an hour.

The particular opens into the universal. Occasions of creating excellence or meeting it in the world bring forth the kingdom of great creators of all time and everywhere. A chorus is shaken loose. The kingdom resounds within us, uniting us with its members, a grand kinship above blood relation. With the energy of the timeless collective lending itself to the moment, quality flows into us, the creative spirit surges. We are increased to seek out and preserve excellence in nature, and to create our own excellent works.

To cultivate the creative spirit, it follows, cultivate the kingdom of great creators. Although time left to its haphazard devices may do this, an ideal college makes a point of it, shortening the period. An ideal college keeps examples of excellence before its students, enthusing them with an inspiriting cross-section of great creators. Four years of this instills a faceless composite of the noble best, separate paragons unified into a grand paragon, the sounding board of creative energy.

CULTIVATES THE DESIRE TO SOLVE IMPORTANT PROBLEMS. The teachers steer students away from intellectual stunt work: away from being more interested in style than in substance, away from using a lot of skill for a lot of nothing, away from aiming to be clever rather than profound, away from creating lively paths to nearly dead points.

The teachers steer students toward developing a sense of which projects promise major goodness and are to be pursued, and which minor goodness and are best dismissed. The students grow in the art of kindling the obscure glimmer of excellence, and at recursively working out its minute details into perfect radiance.

Where a problem is important it will be hard, and the thought may be to chuck it for easier work. An ideal college weans students from the temptation. Students are taught to take time to raise their knowledge and creative skills, putting hard solutions to important problems within reach.

CULTIVATES THE SKILLS OF DOING THOUGHT EXPERIMENTS. Those who believe that teaching by television or the Internet is the equal of teaching in the classroom have a point if the whole of education amounts to conveying impassive ideas. They have no point, however, if part of education is concerned with imprinting the heartfelt worth of ideas. For that, nothing substitutes for having students create thought experiments to be discussed with teachers and classmates.

Thinking and imagining skills join hands in thought experiments. We ask, "If this one part of the actual world were different, what would be the ramification?"

Science fiction stories are thought experiments, and students at an ideal college make science fiction of most every subject. Hypothetically, they add something of apparent worth to the world, deductively and probabilistically track the consequences, and hold them against their hearts, that they may better grasp whether or not the addition is worthwhile.

And students subtract a part of the world to imprint themselves with its value. The fact is, the more a thing is taken for granted, the less important it seems. Imaginatively denying the existence of the thing brings the heart to its senses. To demonstrate, rather then telling students about the privileges that the Magna Carta secured for people, which they will soon forget, have them imagine a world in which the Magna Carta never was. Have them write fictional essays in which they draw out how it would be to live without trial by jury and protection against arbitrary rule.

Likewise and to the point of this book, have them devise thought experiments to assess the importance of the creative spirit, by supposing that our species had always been spiritless. In tracing the path of a spiritless society, the need of the spirit for guiding and managing the creation of goodness, and in curbing evilness, is bound to emerge.

CULTIVATES THE SKILLS OF ANALYZING AND SYNTHESIZING. To analyze is to reduce, to decompose. Analysis melts complex notions down into their first principles, and resolves issues into their constituent parts. Analyzing the patient's symptoms, the doctor locates the cause. Analyzing a collapsed bridge, engineers determine why it failed.

To synthesize is to build up, to compose. Synthesis creates parts, or creatively gathers existing parts, and unites them into original wholes. Artificial hearts are synthesized. New bridges are synthesized.

Synthesis incorporates analysis. At each of synthesis' recursive steps, ideas are intuitively created and assembled, and the assembly is analyzed.

As ordinarily practiced in school, synthesis partly fits this definition but is an inferior approximation to the full thing. It amounts to the intellectual equivalent of assembling jigsaw puzzles. With jigsaw puzzles, a picture exists, has been cut into pieces, and the object is to reconstruct it. In terms of schoolwork, the teacher gives the students the pieces of a textbook problem, and the challenge is to assemble them according to the principles of the subject, arriving at the textbook solution. Or certain pieces are missing, and the students must realistically assume their shapes, and prepare a picture that comes out within a reasonable range, by the teacher's judgment and the norms of the subject.

Well and good as this is, such an approach would have us believe that George Gershwin one day found on his doorstep a shredded music manuscript, and went on to arrange and paste its notes back into their original order, conceiving *Rhapsody in Blue.* No, an ideal college helps students to practice full synthesis, as the Gershwins of all fields do. An infinity of pictures is conceivable, and the would-be creator hasn't a single piece. The aim is to recursively hunt for existing ideas or generate one's own, and to creatively associate the found or invented parts, working the design into a worthy whole. Four years and a million or two recursions of probing with intuitive thought, and of learning when to exercise the veto power of reason, and the student is on the road to millions and millions of recursions more, with a good chance of originating work that cheers the spirit. No solution to a textbook problem has ever cheered a spirit.

In several ways, the use of synthesis in art differs from its use in business:

Artists synthesize ends, works of art. Businesspeople synthesize means, products for winning an ulterior end, profits.

"We must spend our money in a way that gets results," businesspeople say. It is doubtful that any artist has ever used the term "get results." To artists as William Blake and Pablo Picasso, what corresponds to getting results is to work out their designs to the point of sitting perfectly well with their hearts.

A second difference is that artists synthesize in one step, businesspeople in two. Consider William Blake and his stanza above. He created the ideas for it and screened them, perfecting it. Had instead he followed the two-step approach, at the first step he would have synthesized a half dozen decent stanzas; and at the second, selected the best one. Such an approach, spreading effort and scattering attention, creates a work that is less good than it might be.

A third difference is that artists want complete creative freedom, not taking orders or suggestions from other people. Think of Pablo Picasso synthesizing his painting *Girl Before a Mirror*. His aim is personal. He has only to satisfy himself. At each decision point he consults only his heart, asking, Does the evolving work have prospects of attaining the excellence I demand of it?

With a thought experiment, let us make him be a commercial artist, cramping his freedom. For a client he prepares a number of sketches for a painting to be used in an advertising campaign. The client chooses the one having the best chance of promoting business, and in its style Picasso produces the finished painting.

A Picasso who does this over the years is guided from the outside, and his guiding of himself is confined within the channels of outside guidance. He is unable to fully discover and develop fully his latent artistic self. His works, missing what William Blake called the "minute discrimination" and "minute neatness of execution" upon which "all sublimity is founded," are incapable of touching people's souls. Next to the Picasso who actually was, this Picasso dies as an imperfectly completed person, his potentials unfulfilled. Worse still, society is denied his greatest works.

CULTIVATES THE SKILLS OF DECISION MAKING. Across campus from the departments of liberal arts are the departments of business and industrial engineering, which teach decision making. Students at an ideal college learn and practice it. Although the artistically disposed among them may never use it in their work, all must be critics of those who do. The phases of decision making that are most detrimentally prone to going astray are these:

1. Clearly and completely lay out the features of the desired outcome to be achieved before giving any thought to how to achieve it. How obvious this seems: first settle on where you want to go, then on how to go there. Yet how often it is done the wrong way round.

2. Be reasonably sure the desired outcome will be desired from the vantage point of thirty, forty, or more years ahead. How obvious this seems: be certain that where you want to go will be where you wanted to go once you have gotten there. Yet history teaches that people's values change. Think of society placing little worth on wilderness areas, destroying them, and after they are gone coming to feel they are precious.

3. In synthesizing alternative courses of action to achieve the desired outcome (including the do-nothing alternative), make sure the alternatives tolerably bridle the uncertainties that could produce a bad outcome.

4. For each alternative, identify the unwanted changes to the world that will accompany the achievement of the desired outcome, even if uncertainty is totally bridled. How obvious this seems: pay full attention to avoid so-called solutions that incubate cascades of aggravating problems, supposed improvements whose side consequences turn out to make things worse. Pandora's box.

5. Keep in mind that the proper decision may be to wait for more reliable, less sketchy information before deciding.

CULTIVATES AN UNDERSTANDING OF THE METHODS AND PROCESSES OF SCIENCE. Besides steeping students in scientific knowledge, an ideal college teaches them to analyze reports of research, judging whether or not the claims are as general and as soundly-drawn as their discoverers profess.

Science is a factory dispersed about the world in researchers' offices and laboratories. Its machineries are various methods, used to various tolerances, producing claims that such and such is so. To judge a new car, it is unnecessary to enter the factory and see how it was made. Not so with the knowledge science makes.

An ideal college teaches students to go inside the factory of science to the original journal articles, to examine the scientific methods that were used, to locate the "iffy" spots where errors may have escaped detection, and in the end to judge independently the claims, adopting another view if required.

CULTIVATES RESPONSIBILITY AS A VIRTUE. The inferior kind of responsibility is enforced with threats of "Act rightly or you will be punished." Run a red light, pay a fine. Steal property, hear the clank of iron.

Responsibility by threat works best when there is a high probability that wrongdoers will be caught. One of the circumstances that lowers the probability is having years between the act and its result. This is the situation in forestry, financial planning, teaching, and more. After a forester manages the planting of trees to grow them to an envisaged maturity, it takes longer for the forest to grow up than the forester has years of life. With slipshod work able to hide behind the smoke screen of time, what is to keep foresters honest?

The superior kind of responsibility comes from imprinting, as forestry schools imprint their students, the virtue of doing a job conscientiously. Again, whatever elements of learning that television or the Internet may effectively teach, imprinting virtues in not among them. Imprinting requires conscientious teachers and small classes, that duty-bound professional behavior may at close range seep out of the teachers and into their students' bones, like a mother goose imprints her goslings.

Of these preceding properties of an ideal college, Smith College had them in abnormal degree, except those concerning decision making and science, subjects that became full-blown and teachable after Anne attended college.

Now outside the classroom, students at an ideal college have only upstreaming classmates to be with and learn from. The further good consequence of this is that there are no downstreamers present who might divert students' attention to unimaginative, spiritually-barren activities, cheap and false to genuine human nature, leading to messing about in the company of people whose days go round and end up where they began.

And outside the classroom, an ideal college regularly has artistic performances to enlarge the reservoir of excellencies within the student. Here Anne is, her freshman year, reflecting in her diary on an instance of this:

> *Bach*, played by Harold Samuel.
> *Absolute perfection*–transporting, pure, clear, unearthly, untouched, and untouchable; escape into a world unbelievably perfect, apart; unattainable perfection caught and held there crystallized. Lucid, faultless, chaste.
> Such escape, after all the failures and imperfections of everyday things: of work for Mr. Patch, of papers for Miss Dunn, of poor expression in writing. We are always compromising, taking the imperfect.
> Here, here at last, perfection–absolute, cool, instantaneous–and its intangibility. Its beauty slipping liquidly away, while one listened in rapture and in tears.
> It doesn't matter that it can't last, that we don't find it more often. To know that there is such perfection, that there has been such perfection–it is worth living for. It *exists*. It *has been–it is*. One can contemplate it and feel a complete peace.
> The "wholeness," the completeness of such moments–I can stumble in imperfections for years to make up for it.

(Colleges today have largely gone from sponsoring artistic performances to sponsoring entertaining performances. By this they have gone from enlarging the reservoir of excellencies in students to placating their downstreaming urges. This is a sign that education places no paramount value on the creative spirit.)

By attending Smith College, Anne received several incidental benefits. One was confidence. She was constitutionally a mudder, but like most young mudders didn't know it. Had she attended a normal college, such as one of the typical state universities, she would have probably remained unsure of herself. That is because normal colleges have their students perform on a dry, manicured track clear of obstacles except the idealized homework problems. This bores mudders. Interesting possibilities flash upon them and steal their attention from the less interesting facts being written on the blackboard. Their grades may lapse, self-doubts may seize them. "You are obtuse," their college is telling them, when really their college is unfitted to educate them. The famous case is Albert Einstein.

Smith College prepared students for the everyday races in the real world, where settings ooze with unpredictables and unsure footings, where directions to head in are unannounced, and where to come in near the front requires strengths of character that normal colleges neither address nor grade, such as curiosity, intuition, creativity, patience, fortitude, and total dedication, all of which a student at a normal college can be weak in yet receive top grades.

Another benefit was that Anne's constantly involving herself in creating pushed outside worries from mind. A broken romance was unable to prey its fullest on her while she was poring over a creative school project, having a romance with her spirit.

Another benefit was that she was less likely to kill herself. A mother nurturing her child, Abraham Maslow noted in his journals, is enormously unwilling to commit suicide. He likewise believed that nurturing goodness into excellence is reason to live for. Just so, Anne's precious work in progress was her precious unborn child; for it someday to be, she must be.

This suggests a general lesson for those who mainly create for the joy and compulsion of the journey. If on top of this they cultivate a need to benefit the world with their creations, then if one day their joy and compulsion give out, they will want to carry on.

Another benefit was that Anne's work deterred her from using drugs, mental suicide. A student will sometimes say, "What about drugs improving creativity by stimulating your mind and giving you ideas?" Well, there isn't evidence they do more than sometimes flush ideas out in a short span that are bound to surface later. Besides, whatever their flushing effects on the main subconscious activities of projects—conceiving visions and strategies—they cause clogging effects in consciously dealing with the details of designing, of forming tactics, and of actually making.

Opium, by Coleridge's account, made him merry, and liquor elated F. Scott Fitzgerald. Still they rued the habits, believing it diminished the operation of their talents. Even granting they were wrong, unquestionably it killed them early, before their expressive powers had time to crest, robbing us and them of decades of excellence to come.

Another benefit was that Anne's education pried open opportunities which bigoted gatekeepers selectively try to shut. A supervisor will sometimes favor one employee over another who is as competent, letting incidental personal attributes into the equation—religion, sex, race, age, complexion, personality, looks, politics, where one hails from, how one holds the stem of a cocktail glass, the sound or origin of one's surname, and similarly silly measures. The preventive is superior competence; it shatters superficial pecking orders. Making oneself meritoriously indispensable to the world goes a long way to calling the intolerant to heel.

Each period of Anne's life prepared her to make much of the next. Her years to age eighteen brought her to a gentle boil; her four years in college, to the point of gushing patchily but promisingly; the years after, to the point of projecting a book that continues inspiring women to discover their inmost constitution.

What is there to conclude but that her parents are as much responsible for *Gift from the Sea* as she is? She was scarcely a born genius; this and her other books would scarcely have been if the Morrows had capitulated to the norms of child raising.

By her parents raising her as they did, they received her utmost love. Tally the hours of hugging and kissing they gave her and there will not be fifty. Count instead their hours of preparing the climate that shaped her toward a lifetime of creative work, and it will pass one hundred thousand. Hugs and kisses, Anne and they knew, are but a drop in the possible sea of parental love.

Chapter Twenty-one

Raising Oneself

The human lifetime is about 30,000 days. See your-
self as a society of 30,000 mes. The me of today builds itself, and
at midnight passes on to the me of tomorrow a more able mind
than it received from the me of yesterday.

On your last day, imagine, your 30,000 mes gather in
reunion. You want no backlash of older mes angrily accusing
younger mes of squandering time. The occasion should be
perfectly joyous—every me applauding its providers who came
before.

This cries for a social contract. By the usual notion of a social
contract, people contribute goodness to society with their work,
and receive in kind the same. The school crossing guard and the
electrician, the concert pianist and the forest ranger, the
landscape gardener, cabinet maker, and bookbinder give what
they do best, and welcome the best of others in return. Professors
teach airline pilots' daughters and sons; pilots transport professors.

The social contract for the society of mes differs, however, in
a way that William Wordsworth knew when into his poem, *My
Heart Leaps Up When I Behold*, he put the phrase, "The Child is
father of the Man." The giving among the mes is one-way, from
younger to older, like a whip in time that swells abilities toward
the tip. The young, living close to the whip's butt, own the

responsibility to invest their thousands of heirs with creative power. Will they, or will they ramble along in comfortable ignorance of their society's future?

When it comes to growth upon growth, investing in yourself runs rings around investing money. Each penny deposited in a bank account compounds at a rate it has no role in setting, and the principal and earned interest may be taken out but once. Whereas knowledge and skills you deposit in yourself give value to and receive value from the previous deposits. By myriad powers of ten, the repercussions multiply toward the tip of life, and are there for every me to draw upon.

Among the best artists and artisans, tenacious resolve to perfect one's work drives the investment in self. Think of William Charles Macready, an English actor of nearly two hundred years ago. Day-in, day-out, project after project, he prompted himself toward perfecting his acting, taking him above his best intentions, and high among the great actors of his century. Nothing but a large sample of entries from his diaries can show this, for resolve to be a perfectionist is invisible in anything less than a panoramic survey:

> [January 4, 1833] My acting to-night was coarse and crude–no identification of myself with the scene; and what increased my chagrin on the subject, some persons in the pit gave frequent vent to indulgent and misplaced admiration. The consciousness of unmerited applause makes it quite painful and even humiliating to me.
>
> [May 28, 1833] I acted Hamlet, although with much to censure, yet with a spirit, and feeling of words and situations, that I think I have never done before.
>
> [July 28, 1833] I have begun more seriously this month to apply to the study of my profession, impelled by the necessity which the present state of the drama creates. . . . To do my best is still my duty to myself and to my children, and I *will do it.*

[August 27, 1833] Acted particularly well William Tell, with collectedness, energy and truth; the audience felt it. I spoke in my own manly voice, and took time to discriminate. I was much pleased.

[August 29, 1833] At the rehearsal of *Lear* I found myself very deficient, undecided, uncollected; in short, unprepared for the attempt.

[October 22, 1833] Felt tired and dissatisfied with myself.

[November 20, 1833] Read Antony through the whole evening and discovering many things to improve and bring out the effect of the part. . . .

[December 9, 1833] I am ashamed, grieved and distressed to acknowledge the truth: I *acted* disgracefully, worse than I have done for years; I shall shrink from looking into a newspaper to-morrow, for I deserve all that can be said in censure of me.

[May 20, 1834] Before rising, thought over the madness of Lear, which now begins to obtain something resembling that possession of my mind which is necessary to success in whatever we desire to reach excellence.

[October 25,1834] Low and distressed; forgot the beginning of my first speech to Amintor; acted as I used to act three or four years ago, not like myself now. Could not do what I proposed at rehearsal.

[December 10, 1834] Went to the theatre, where I acted William Tell only tolerably; was a good deal distressed by the actors, imperfect and inattentive. . . .

[January 17, 1835] Acted King Lear unequally—wanted the sustaining stimulant of an enthusiastic audience—wanted in them the sensibility to feel quickly what I did. . . .

[March 6, 1835] Went to theatre and should have acted Oakley well, but that in the only scene in which the performers were not *very imperfect* with me, the prompter in every pause I made in a scene where the pauses are *effects* kept shouting "the word" to me till I was ready to go and knock him down.

[September 29, 1835] I returned to Macbeth. It is strange that I do not feel myself at all *satisfied* with myself: *I cannot reach in execution the standard of my own conception.* I cannot do it; and I am about to enter on the season which will decide my fortune, with the drawback of the consciousness of not being able to realize my own imaginations.

[October 16, 1835] Went to theatre and acted Hamlet, not as I did the last time–I felt then the inspiration of the part; to-night I felt as if I had a load upon my shoulders. The actors said I played well. The audience called for me and made me go forward. Wallace, Forster, and H. Smith, who came into my room, all thought I played well– but I did not. I was not satisfied with myself–there was effort, and very little free flow of passion.

[February 27, 1836] I acted Othello–I scarcely know in what way–not to please myself; the truth is, I have lost the tone, the pitch of voice, the directness of the part, and I strive in vain to recall it; perhaps and, as I believe, because I do not *strive enough.* . . .

[May 26, 1836] Rehearsed *Ion* with much care. Went to the theatre and acted the character as well as I have ever played any previous one, with more inspiration, more complete abandonment, more infusion of myself into another being, than I have been able to attain in my performances for some time. . . .

[October 10, 1836] Went to theatre. Acted Macbeth as badly as I acted well on Monday last. The gallery was noisy, but that is no excuse for me; I could not feel myself in the part. I was labouring to play Macbeth; on Monday last I *was* Macbeth. . . . Oh, God! Oh, God! *Shall I never learn to act with wisdom?*

[December 7, 1836] Mrs. Glover observed to me, hoping I should not be offended at the observation, that she had never seen such an improvement in my person as in myself lately. I told her I was extremely gratified to hear her say so, since every art needed study and was progressive in its course towards perfection.

[January 2, 1837] Acted Lord Hastings very, very ill indeed, in the worst possible taste and style. I really am ashamed to think of it; the audience applauded, but I deserve some reprobation. . . . Whatever is good enough to play is good enough to play well, and I could have acted this character very well if I had prepared myself as I should have done. Without study I can do nothing.

[June 19, 1837] I laboured through Richard, but it was labour, and most ineffectual. I was very bad, very bad.

[August 29, 1837] Acted Virginius miserably; it was painful to myself, and could have been satisfactory to no one.

[September 20, 1837] Acted Ion very languidly indeed; occupation through the day is scarcely compatible with a really successful performance. The nerves and spirits cannot keep their tone. How strange are the thoughts that pass through one's brain, when acting without being *possessed* by *the character.*

[April 7, 1838] Acted Foscari very well. Was very warmly received on my appearance; was called for at the end of the tragedy and received by the whole house standing up and waving handkerchiefs with great enthusiasm.

[February 18, 1839] Acted King Lear well. The Queen was present, and I pointed at her the beautiful lines, 'Poor naked wretches!' . . .

[April 16, 1839] Acted King Lear *very well*—as well, if not better than I had ever done.

[July 16, 1839] Rose and prepared to play in a very

depressed condition. My reception was so great, from a house crowded in every part, that I was shaken by it. I acted King Henry V better than I had yet done, and the house responded to the spirit in which I played.

[September 30, 1839] Acted Shylock, and tried to do my best; but how unavailing is all reasoning against painful facts—the performance was an utter failure.

[July 21, 1840] Began to act Jacques very fairly, but was thrown off my balance by a man in the gallery vociferating: "What do you go on for, spoiling Shakespeare," etc. I caught no more, for the audience was roused and he was turned out. But he was right in judgment, however barbarous and ungentlemanly his method of giving publicity to it.

[April 26, 1841] Acted Macbeth in my very best manner, positively improving several passages. . . . I have improved, Macbeth.

[February 23, 1842] Acted Gisippus, I must admit, not well, not finished; not like a great actor. . . . The effect of the play was success; but I am not satisfied.

[March 3, 1843] I entered this morning upon my *fiftieth* birthday. How very little of self-approval attends the review of my past life—how much of self-reproach!

[March 23, 1843] Acted Iago better, I think, than I ever have before done.

[June 14, 1843] I was resolved to act my best, and I think I never played Macbeth so well.

[October 23, 1843] Acted Macbeth equal, if not superior, as a whole, to any performance I have ever given of the character.

[January 19, 1844] Could not please myself in the performance of Hamlet. . . .

[March 1, 1844] Rehearsed King Lear, with a perfect consciousness of my utter inability to do justice to my own conception of the character.

[May 30, 1844] Acted Hamlet; the latter part, i. e., after the first act, in a really splendid style. I felt myself the man.

[November 21, 1845] Acted Hamlet as well, or better, than I ever did.

[January 12, 1846] Went to rehearsal, where I was much annoyed by the manifest indifference of those persons, who call themselves actors, in the scenes which I had several times rehearsed with them on Saturday. They made the *very same* mistakes, proving that they had never looked at their books, had made no memorandum, nor, in fact, ever thought upon the business for which they received the price of their daily bread.

[March 2, 1846] On reviewing the performance I can conscientiously pronounce it one of the very best I have given of Hamlet.

[May 11, 1846] Acted King Lear very languidly and not at all *possessed* with the character.

[June 18, 1847] Acted King Lear with much care and power, and was received by a most kind and sympathetic and enthusiastic audience.

[November 17, 1847] Acted Cardinal Wolsey, as I thought very well, to a very insensible audience. Am I deteriorating as I grow older?

[November 24, 1847] Acted Philip Van Artevelde ten times better than the last night.

[February 21, 1848] Acted Macbeth, *I think*, with peculiar strength, care, and effect. . . .

[December 2, 1848] Acted Hamlet with care and energy. . . .

[January 4, 1849] For the first time I saw in the glass to-day that I really am an old man. My mind does not feel old. . . .

[March 7, 1849] Acted Cardinal Richelieu; not to my satisfaction, being greatly disconcerted by—what?—

Ha! upon how small a thing the success of an actor's perfect identification depends—upon my beard being loose, and torturing me for four acts with the fear of its dropping off!!

[October 8, 1849] Acted Macbeth. . . . I never acted better, in many parts never so well, so feelingly and so true.

[January 18, 1850] Acted King Henry IV very well; and Lord Townly better, I think, than I have ever before done it.

[November 27, 1850] Acted Hamlet in my very, very best manner; it is the last time but one I shall ever appear in this wonderful character. . . . I acted with that feeling; I never acted better. I felt my allegiance to Shakespeare, the glorious, the divine. Was called and welcomed with enthusiasm.

[January 3, 1851] Acted Virginius, one of the most brilliant and powerful performances of the character I have ever given.

[January 16,1851] Acted Virginius, for the last time, as I have scarcely ever—no, never—acted it before; with discrimination, energy, and pathos, exceeding any former effort. The audience were greatly excited.

[January 22, 1851] Acted Iago with a vigour and discrimination that I have never surpassed, if ever equalled.

[February 26, 1851] Acted Macbeth as I never, never before acted it; with a reality, a vigour, a truth, a dignity that I never before threw into my delineation of this favourite character.

There are signs for telling if you are a perfectionist like Macready:

To begin with, could your prior mes stand in for your current mes and do as well? If so, your society of mes is complacently marking time. The two-way interplay between outer and inner excellence, the self-sustaining cycle of transforming present mes into superior mes, is sedentary. Conversely, have your current mes made your mes of six months ago obsolete, not up to doing a project you have just succeeded with? Then you are like Macready.

This test is most clearly decidable against a backdrop you seldom visit, a setting you pass through alone while dreaming of your aspirations. Suppose a Japanese student so dreams as she gazes from an airplane's window, on her way to enter Oxford University, her first time far abroad. Later, has she improved much? She will know most certainly when she is away from Oxford and on the plane back to Japan, pensively reconnected with the memory of herself during that flight to England.

Another sign for telling if you are a perfectionist like Macready is that your best friends are your younger mes. No one likes thieves who have made off with years of life's brief span and forsaken their descendants to spiritual poverty.

Another sign is that your accomplishments, despite throwing all your energies into them, are short of what you wish them to be. The disappointment lays self-doubt. Maybe you are poorly cut out for what you long to do? You could be Anne Morrow complaining to her diary:

> I want to write—I want to write—I want to write and I never never never will. I know it and I am so unhappy and it seems as though nothing else mattered. Whatever I'm doing, it's always there, an ultimate longing there saying, 'Write this—write that—write—' and I *can't*. Lack ability, time, strength, and duration of vision. I wish someone would tell me brutally, "You can *never* write *anything*. Take up home gardening!"

She was wrong about herself for three reasons:

One: she was making hidden progress. Her struggles were growing her and, soon or late, the effects would appear in her work. As such, the truly valuable work days are those we curse and wish never were, as we try mightily but futilely it seems, and drag homeward, questioning our purpose, muttering "What's the use?" These are the days of smoldering inner growth which, given time, is bound to blaze with a splendid result. The truly wasted days are the routine and unresisting ones, those of cheerful whistling and of going home sprightly, which leave us little changed.

Two: she was paying with disappointment the price for wanting to perform on a par with creators whose proficiencies took them until at least middle age to build. Next to the poems of the elder Rainer Maria Rilke, which set her standard, how could hers be more than tepid patter?

She shouldn't have worried. It is better to have advanced standards and modest proficiencies than modest standards and advanced proficiencies. Advanced standards often train and shape proficiencies of any level into greatness, as hers eventually did.

Three: it ill suited her to be cooped up by due dates. Her teachers made her themes due the next week, and this frustrated her perfectionist side. She was forgetting that the regimen of college permitted her to do her truncated best, not her very best. To do one's very best entails searching for ideas without timetables and deadlines, allowing favorable probabilities to speak when they are good and ready. No perfectionist, giant or junior, can reach doing his or her very best on a week's notice.

A final sign for telling if you are a perfectionist like Macready may come after youth has passed. Your résumé will feature excellence over quantity. Creating the best things possible in the best possible ways takes extraordinary patience, and a lifetime has room for a dozen or fewer great projects. Rare exceptions aside, those with résumés that go on and on have no spiritually significant works. Little haystacks with measly needles is their game.

Antoine de Saint-Exupéry's résumé signifies a perfectionist. He refused to hack out a score of books that pandered to what the public would buy but which fell short of spiritual significance. He devoted himself to creating three which give one of the truest conceivable perspectives on projects carried out by different hands, promising great goodness only if the members each do their devoted utmost for their common goal. The mutually responsible marriage of the workers gives rise to a collaborative soul, a soul in and of the social relations of the fellowship, threading its members.

Here is Saint-Exupéry in a letter defending his perfectionist nature, refusing to be pressured by his publisher into letting *Flight to Arras* go to press before he could give his message lasting expression:

> Don't tell me I'm wrong because my manuscript is "ready to go" and I won't be making any major changes. I won't make any great changes in the essential message—that's true—but I'll greatly change its impact. This is not a question of the material or the surface narrative. It's something that only begins to exist when one no longer sees why. And I know exactly what changes to make. They involve something that I can't define, which concerns the lasting quality of what I say. . . . Whenever I hear an echo, years later, from an article of mine . . . it is always, always, always an article that I rewrote thirty times. When I read a quotation of my own somewhere, it is always, always, always a phrase I rewrote twenty-five times. One sees no very noticeable difference between the first and last versions. It may even be that the final version seems less picturesque, but it is bound by an inner logic. It is a seed; the other was a plaything for a day. I have never, never, never been wrong about that.

The above explains the signs of a healthy society of mes, but what can be done to promote its health?

ON SPIRITLESS DAYS, ACQUIRE TECHNICAL PROFICIENCIES. Whoever heard of firefighters being put out of commission because their Muse deserted them? Yet those who create goodness of beauty rely on theirs. In psychological terms, saying the Muse is present means the subconscious mind is sending seemingly good intuitive ideas into the conscious mind. Saying the Muse is absent means little is bubbling up at the moment; for dealing with such times, the poet Josephine Preston Peabody had this advice:

> And how can an artist enlarge his technical resources too much? He should spend uncreative hours in patientest investigation (if only by half moments), in happy-go-lucky games with building-blocks—he should train his ears to consider the eloquence of daily sounds, the rhythms of trade and crafts; to simplify the complexities of things written and things said and things unsaid. He should have a thousand new rushes to spread before the Beloved when she comes, and never show her a chamber sparsely sprinkled with sand.

Taking this advice outside poetry—mathematicians, forsaken by their Muse in the midst of trying to prove a theorem, and writers who have run into writer's block, might do well to put their projects aside, trusting that their subconscious is working out the needed ideas and when ready will "send them up." Until it does, growing one's technical skills is best worth doing.

TAKE LEISURE. In painting, literature, music, sculpture, and all else where envisioning and designing are primary, where goodness of beauty is king, where absolute perfection is the goal, and where costs be damned, the ratio of leisure to work is three or four to one. Why?

Take the example of creative writing. First of all, designing, conceiving detail, is a practically nonstop sprint of recursive thinking, two or three times a minute generating, evaluating, and deciding on words, sentences, and their arrangement and organization. A few hours of this leaves one weary; leisure provides recuperation.

Second, leisure furnishes time for cogitating on novel problems that crop up in the course of creating, catching the subconscious mind off guard. In the midst of work, a writer may be stuck for a good way of phrasing an idea; later, relaxed and unforced, away from the work, the solution suggests itself.

And third, leisure furnishes time for the mind to leave the narrow, detailed path of work proper, to roam among broad ideas afield, which work proper is unlikely to visit, spawning revolutionary intuitions that may lead to undoing some of what has been done, and starting over.

Thus leisure is the longer, unhurried, relaxed, less visible and indispensable side of work. As Bernard Berenson put it:

> In my experience you can have ability without leisure, but ability only, and not creativeness. Real ideas come to me while relaxed, and brooding, meditative, passive. Then the unexpected happens. An illumination, a combination of words, a revelation for which I made no conscious preparation.

It is no surprise then that Nigel Nicolson, Virginia Woolf's biographer, noted that she "wrote only in the morning from 10 till 1, and usually she typed out in the afternoon what she had written by hand in the morning, but all day long, when she was walking through London streets or on the Sussex Downs, the book would be moving subconsciously in her mind. . . ."

It follows that universal artists shouldn't feel guilty about taking long recesses from work proper, relative to the norm for eight-to-five office workers. Nor should their employers disallow long recesses, as that will stifle beauty's creation. Computer programmers, for example, seeking to create beauty of efficiency, are best given generous limits within which they are free to manage their use of time.

Outside the arts—as in the work of bankers, merchants, sheriffs, and others where planning is primary, where goodness of use is king, and where absolute perfection of plans is a prohibitively expensive goal—the pace of recursive thinking is ten or more times slower, with shorter creative periods mingled with longer routine periods. Not overly taxing, the work goes through morning and into late afternoon or evening, and it is the ratio of work to leisure that is three or four to one.

BRANCH INTO NEW PHASES OR NEW KINDS OF WORK. The goal is to have a forever green old age. The goal is to avoid hardening of the creative arteries. The goal is to be never in the position of the mariner in Rainer Maria Rilke's lines, "I feel as though I had been sleeping for years or had been lying in the lowest hold of a ship that, loaded with heavy things, sailed through strange distances—Oh to climb up on deck once more and feel the winds and the birds, and to see how the great, great nights come with their gleaming stars. . . ."

It is not so much a loss of skill that may visit old age, but loss of interest. Added to this, maintaining youthful interest—never dropping below deck—is easier than reviving interest—easier than climbing up on deck once more. This is why the mathematician Paul Halmos, throughout his career, practiced anticipatory counteraction to head off declining interest. Periodically he gave his curiosity a new lease on life, going into fresh areas of mathematics. In his autobiography is the entry:

> In the late 1940's I began to act on one of my beliefs: to stay young, you have to change fields every five years. Looking back on it I can now see a couple of aspects of that glib commandment that weren't always obvious. One: I didn't first discover it and then act on it, but, instead, noting that I did in fact seem to change directions every so often, I made a virtue out of a fact and formulated it as a

piece of wisdom. Two: it works. A creative thinker is alive
only so long as he grows; you have to keep learning new
things to understand the old. You don't really have to
change fields—but you must stoke the furnace, branch
out, make a strenuous effort to keep from being locked in.

Beside branching into another subfield within one's field, the
branching may be into another field. Charles Lindbergh stayed
forever up on deck by being in turn a pilot, inventor, promoter of
civil aviation, and conservationist of nature. Heinrich Harrer trained
in geography, branched into slalom skiing, then to mountaineering,
then to helping free the Tibetan people, and from there to writing.

The trade you choose first, however, determines your freedom
to change fields. Jacob Bronowski's first was mathematics, and
from it he had no trouble turning his thoughts to biology. Had he
initially trained in biology, it would have been hard to go the
other way. Mathematics rides on strict deductive thinking; to do
it naturally and well, you must bring yourself up doing it.

BUILD A SUPPLY OF PRE-ENVISIONED PROJECTS. The poet William
Carlos Williams once explained to a correspondent how he
intended to keep his creative vitality into old age:

> . . . I have gradually made enough notes, here and there,
> to keep me busy clearing them up and developing them
> for a long time after I retire—if ever. I should dread an old
> age divorced from the thoughts and actions of my more
> vigorous years. Age should be a commentator, and what
> better than to comment upon one's own existence? Thus
> I have many projects in mind. And if I never catch up
> with them—wouldn't that be a misfortune. But I intend to
> try to do so.

Similarly, young Ansel Adams anticipated old Ansel Adams's
difficulties of traveling around the American West, of finding the
right places to photograph nature, and of waiting patiently for

the right moments of light. Young Ansel Adams did this work for the coming Ansel Adams, providing thousands of photographic negatives which old Ansel Adams, up until his last look on earth, took into his darkroom and teased out their spiritual substance.

Is his death regrettable? Not at all. We should think better of dying. God, placing the species above its individuals, has made us temporary dwellers. Death flushes out creators whose seven or eight decades have habitually fenced their thinking and feelings. Birth flushes in creators with unrestricted minds, free to take on and accomplish visions their predecessors wouldn't in ages have dreamed of. There is no end to it. Children can be quickly brought up to date in knowledge it took generations since antiquity to learn, then set off to create excellence beyond that of those whose places they took.

"O', if I could only live forever" is the wish that if granted would soon be regretted and unwished for. If after the first six billion people arrived on earth, a sign reading "filled up" had somehow been hung, with no more breeding allowed in return for a grant of immortality, the eternal accomplishments of those six billion fogeys, and so of the species, would have stagnated at a shabby, spiritless level, relative to that of today.

Those who most fear dying are those governed by pleasures of the flesh, and those who place themselves and their families above all else. To the contrary, those who hold the human species more precious than themselves, and above the particular people alive at the moment, know death's good side.

Still, it is possible to outlive one's flesh. Exemplifying this are certain African and Native North American cultures that distinguish between "the live-dead" and "the dead-dead." After people die, so long as their works remain a living presence in the community, the people are resistant to oblivion—not as they say, dead-dead, forgotten and depleted from contributing. Out of respectful gratitude, their places are set at ceremonial tables. These societies grasp the essence of the classic definition of immortality, "ourselves in others."

Chapter Twenty-two

Revering Every Form Of Life

More than ever before, causing pain or terror to people and animals, or enslaving them, or taking their lives impedes the creation and consumption of artistic excellence in society. News of heartless acts used to travel a short radius. Now, through television, newspapers, and the Internet, the worst of local cruelties enter global consciousness, saddening millions everywhere. Ending cruelty will clear the way for artists and universal artists to thrive as never before.

Several thought experiments illustrate how kindness, a form of beauty on the ethical plane, is conducive to having great beauty on the creative plane. The first shows that viewers sense no quality from an otherwise great painting if they learn it was produced by an evil creator:

Suppose we view Claude Monet's *Poppy Field, Argenteuil*. Its excellence opens the door on Monet's artistic excellence, inducing in us the sublime spiritual goodness that is quality. Just the same, upsets to the simplest human emotions put the higher emotions out of action. Suppose we get news that all is not right with Monet on the ethical plane. He is Jack the Ripper. Such a Monet is at the worst of cross-purposes. Creatively, he makes great goodness; in everyday dealings, great evil. Our spirit balks. *Poppy Field, Argenteuil*'s beauty remains as just a shell. The radiance of its beauty—its quality—refuses to be. Monet's dark deeds have sucked away its marrow.

A second thought experiment takes one step back to show that a villainous artist is incapable of producing great art:

Had Monet been Jack the Ripper, he could not have painted *Poppy Field, Argenteuil* in the first place. An angel before his easel, a barbarian away from it—going to any lengths with the paintbrush to create excellence for people, while with the razor determined to slash them—such defies every example in history.

Thus the case is made from two sides. From the producer's, a wicked Monet could hardly have created a great painting. Yet overlooking the impossibility and granting he could, from the consumer's side, if viewers knew of his vicious disposition, they would sense no quality from his work.

A third thought experiment shows that even allowing that the creator is morally sound, a background of meanness and misery in the world invites spiritual breakdown:

This time it is the real Monet, the gentle one, and we are looking at *Poppy Field, Argenteuil.* Does our spirit glow? Yes, as long as we are mostly happy with the human condition. Yet there is an extent of malevolence in society, a heat of pained sensibilities concerning those who receive ill, and outrage at those who deal it, that will discourage us about the world. Our heartache will smother the quality.

Taking the above to the last degree, imagine an absolutely vile world and we have imagined a creatively retarded, disenchanting place. Conversely, imagine a world in which all are acutely sensitive to the feelings of others, going out of their way to make life everywhere untroubled and tranquil, and we have imagined the creatively brightest of possible worlds.

HOW CRUELTY TO ANIMALS IMPEDES CREATIVITY IN SOCIETY. Those who drive animals torturously to the wall, hurting and robbing them of their tomorrows, cut compassionate people to the quick. With news of stony-hearted brutality to an animal spreading a sorrow about the globe, cruelty to animals by a few fills many with revulsion. How deeply and lastingly cruelty to animals can vex is conveyed in the words of John Galsworthy, speaking on the misery of caged animals:

> Travelling in California last spring, I had occasion to stay at an hotel where they always had a caged hawk for the edification of the guests. It was, they said, a new one practically every year, for the birds soon moped themselves to death. . . . When one reflects on the nature of [a hawk's] existence, the huge spaces that he covers, the way his eye is only fitted, as it were, for seeing at vast distances, the more one is forced to the conception of the utter misery he must suffer in a cage. It is as if some demon for no reason that we can fathom had seized one of us and shut us away from all the elements of our natural existence, pinned one of us down to perpetual suffering without rhyme or sense–this is what captivity must seem to a hawk. There is so much misery in the world, and that misery may at any moment fall on any one of us. To deliberately create misery seems to me the most dreadful thing that can happen to a man.

Thomas Hardy's sentiments were the same:

> It seems marvellous that the 20th century, with all its rhetoric on morality, should tolerate such useless inflictions as making animals do what is unnatural to them or drag out an unnatural life in a wired cell. I would also include the keeping of tame rabbits in hutches among the prohibited cruelties in this kind.

Besides caging animals, Hardy believed that slaughtering them goes against virtue and is nothing to boast about:

> . . . I hold it to be, in any case, immoral and unmanly to cultivate a pleasure in compassing the death of our weaker and simple fellow-creatures by cunning, instead of learn-

ing to regard their destruction, if a necessity, as an odious task, akin to that, say, of the common hangman.

Wronging animals by tormenting or stealing their lives may suit savages, but in a society that aspires to call itself civilized, it is a disgrace. So felt John Muir, and there is no question what he would say today of the countries of Japan and Norway. Their harpoons go into more than just a few whales, for more than just a few minutes. Their harpoons stab untold numbers of human hearts around the globe, and the hurt festers for years. In Muir's collected writings may be found scores of pities as this:

> A little schooner has a boat out in the edge of the pack killing walruses, while she is lying a little to east of the sun. A puff of smoke now and then, a dull report, and a huge animal rears and falls—another, and another, as they lie on the ice without showing any alarm, waiting to be killed, like cattle lying in a barnyard! Nearer, we hear the roar, lion-like, mixed with hoarse grunts, from hundreds like black bundles on the white ice. A small red flag is planted near the pile of slain. Then the three men puff off to their schooner, as it is now midnight, and time for the other watch to go to work.
>
> These magnificent animals are killed oftentimes for their tusks alone, like buffaloes for their tongues, ostriches for their feathers, or for mere sport and exercise. In nothing does man, with his grand notions of heaven and charity, show forth his innate, low-bred, wild animalism more clearly than in his treatment of his brother beasts. From the shepherd with his lambs to the red-handed hunter, it is the same; no recognition of rights—only murder in one form or another.

Of those who think themselves pious and at the same time victimize animals, Muir had these words:

> Making some bird or beast go lame the rest of its life is a
> sore thing on one's conscience, at least nothing to boast
> of, and it has no religion in it.

Advocates for animal welfare argue for laws giving animals rights, on the grounds that certain animals are similar to us in their capacity to feel pain (the marmot, the frog, . . .), or show something of our intelligence (the porpoise, the dog, . . .), or are morphologically our kin (the orangutan, the great ape, . . .), or have admirable human traits (the industrious beaver, the thrifty squirrel, . . .). The trouble is, there is no natural cutoff point fixing the extent to which an animal needs to be similar to people to be accorded rights. Like defining the moment that a mother's fertilized egg qualifies as a human, naysayers may rebut with, "That's just your opinion."

Advocates for animal welfare should be prefixing the word "rights" not with "animal" but with "people." Instead of arguing for animal rights, they should be arguing for laws that extend the right of humane people to have peace of mind. Person One's savagery to animals causes Persons Two through Ten-thousand heaviness of heart. That wounding the freedom or the flesh of animals wounds the feelings of those who want animals to go unmolested is a truth immune to rebuttal.

Governments protect us from physical and mental intrusions at the hands of others. No one may take a baseball bat to a person's skull. No one may rape a person. Advocates should make lawmakers realize that cruelty to animals rapes the sensibilities of a large and growing number of people who are unable to stomach instances of animals being made to experience hardships, maltreatment, sorrow, loss of life. People sympathizing with animal welfare should be protected against being helplessly aggrieved by knowing that somewhere in the world unsympathizing people are treating animals badly, and further aggrieved by the disillusionment with society over permitting the acts—aggrievement that rankles humane people to their core, and is not forgotten the next day or week but lingers in painful memory, even producing emotional turmoil lasting a lifetime, even turning people against humanity.

Enacting and enforcing laws prohibiting animal abuse will bring two social benefits. Millions of people will be cheered, good in itself, and by this society's capacity to create and to appreciate excellence will be less encumbered.

HOW KINDNESS TO ANIMALS PROMOTES KINDNESS TO PEOPLE. A more thorough compassion to animals will ripen into a more thorough compassion for people, furthering excellence more.

Albert Schweitzer's idea is that to have the most benevolent human-to-human ethic, we must have the strongest possible human-to-animal ethic. In calling for reverence for life, Schweitzer was after the prize of first importance: happiness in our ordinary affairs that accompanies peace, tolerance, and common decency for all people, the basis of being civilized. There is no indication that Schweitzer was thinking of the considerable second prize that accompanies reverence for life: that it removes a depressant on the creative spirit, a deterrent to carrying excellence to the highest heights. But there it is.

The cornerstone of reverence for life is carved of common sense. Bullying and killing humans comes easier after you have acclimated with bullying and killing animals. Beating your child or spouse seems a lesser crime when you think nothing of beating your dog.

The genius of reverence to life is that it seals off every practice that could in time slide toward harming people. It prevents selectivity and favoritism. It refrains from drawing an arbitrary line at lambs and allowing violence to creatures thought lower than lambs, which if once begun might spread to the day when lambs are fair game, and after lambs the next, until the inhumane insensitivity has people in its sights.

Reverence for life is a guideline. We are to treat every single one of God's creatures as equally sacred, from the tiniest, the ugliest, the peskiest, the most obscure, to the largest, the prettiest, and most prevalent, causing none the least misery. By following the guideline as faithfully as we can, we minimize the maltreatment and killing of creatures, not eliminate it. The guideline keeps us alert to the questions, "Must I really harm this creature? Isn't there another way?" The guideline asks us to justify why we can't go out of our way for the sake of a life. At times Albert Schweitzer slapped a mosquito that might carry disease, but only after determining he couldn't move indoors or use netting.

It is well to have Albert Schweitzer relate the logic and spiritually uplifting prospects of reverence for life:

> ... I then focused on the question of why ethics has such a weak influence on our society. Ultimately I concluded that ethics does not have full energy because it is nonelementary and incomplete. After all, it deals with the way people relate to one another instead of having us concern ourselves with our relationship to all living creatures. This complete ethics is far more elementary and far more profound than the usual ethics. It brings us to a spiritual relationship with the universe.

Schweitzer put his chief hope with the very young:

> Even children should reflect on themselves and their relationship to other beings and come to realize that reverence for life is the basic principle of goodness. Children should not just take over goodness as a tradition that they are taught, they should reflect and discover it within themselves as something intrinsic to them, that is theirs for a lifetime. Many teachers have told me that children are deeply impressed by the idea of the reverence of life because they possess it as experience and not just as something they are taught.

If mankind is not to be wiped out by wars with dreadful weapons, we have to develop an ethical civilization dominated by the idea of reverence for life. . . .

Reverence for life accomplishes what religions fail to. Religious precepts, by themselves, make for a shaky human-to-human ethic. Religions regularly prove themselves ineffective at preventing wars. In some religions, reverence for life is already written into their precepts, except that, like an old dusty law, it is merely "on the books," with violations winked at.

The lengths to which people go to practice reverence for life is a mark of its importance to them. The essayist, novelist, and poet John Cowper Powys habitually saved fish that became trapped in pools when the flow in the small river near his home dropped, sometimes walking "as far as a mile carrying a pail of them, till I found an adequate pool for their reception."

And about the clergyman and writer Charles Kingsley, his son Maurice Kingsley wrote:

> On the lawn dwelt a family of natter jacks (running toads), who lived on from year to year in the same hole in the green bank, which the scythe was never allowed to approach. He had two little friends in a pair of sand wasps, who lived in a crack of the window in his dressing-room, one of which he had saved from drowning in a handbasin, taking it tenderly out into the sunshine to dry; and every spring he would look out eagerly for them or their children, who came out of, or returned to the same crack. The little fly-catcher, who built its nest every year under his bedroom window, was a constant joy to him. He had also a favorite slow-worm in the churchyard which his parishioners were warned not to kill, from the mistaken idea prevalent in Eversley that slow-worms were poisonous. All these tastes he encouraged in his children, teaching them to love and handle gently without

disgust all living things, toads, frogs, beetles, as works
and wonders from the hand of a Living God.

Then there is the physicist Richard Feynman, who early in
his career was elected to the U. S. National Academy of Sciences. When he learned that the Academy supported
experimenting on animals, he resigned his membership.

One route to becoming reverent to life is through growing an
awesome esteem for animals as one of nature's excellencies. Such
was Charles Darwin's route. Brought up around many who enjoyed
shooting birds and hares, the young callous Darwin fitted right
in. It was his voyage on the *Beagle* that turned his values around.
The reformed Darwin later remarked, "It is absurd to talk of one
animal being higher than another. . . . People often talk of the
wonderful event of intellectual Man appearing–the appearance
of insects with other senses is more wonderful."

Janet Browne, a biographer of Darwin, notes that by the time
Darwin returned to England, "he had already virtually given up
shooting, viewing his former exploits as the activities of a
barbarian, or at least of an uncouth, unthinking oaf let loose
overseas. As his life of the mind expanded and took over, perhaps
this was inevitable. Nevertheless, he decided that killing animals
for pleasure was wrong. His hunting-shooting days were behind
him. The future would be devoted to altogether more civilised,
thoughtful, and intellectual preoccupations."

Likewise twice-born was Henry David Thoreau. The longer
he lived close to God through living close to nature, the more the
taking of animal life jangled out of tune with the universe's graces.
As he tells it:

I have found repeatedly, of late years, that I cannot fish
without falling a little in self-respect. I have tried it
again and again. I have skill at it, and, like many of my
fellows, a certain instinct for it, which revives from time
to time, but always when I have done I feel that it would

have been better if I had not fished. I think that I do not mistake. It is a faint intimation, yet so are the first streaks of morning.

If the change from killer to protector induces pangs of guilt over the remembered past, so much the better. It might be that long ago we thoughtlessly mistreated or killed an animal. Since then, we raised a conscience. Hindsight persists in hauling out our past insensitive acts, shaming us. We cannot issue errata like the printer, wiping out our wrongs. One good of the persecuting memories is they signify moral development. The sharper their sting, the better we have become. Another good is that the regret may prod us to atone with kind acts.

A second route to becoming more reverent to life, which may be taken along with the first, is to build a humanizing imagination. About this, Bernard Berenson had this to say:

> I love the words "human," "humanization," "humanized,"
> and "humanist" and "humanities." . . . [By "humanize"
> I mean] the faculty of putting oneself instantly and on
> every occasion under the skin, in the heart, in the muscles
> even of another, and in ideation to react as that other
> would. . . . And what is imagination but the same vivid
> and spontaneous putting oneself in another's place com-
> pletely? It is the lack of this imagination that leads to
> cruelties and atrocities, particularly where it is a matter
> of mass murders.

Berenson goes on to say that what we think of as the artistic imagination is the humanizing imagination:

> "Imagination" in the arts . . . is nothing but making one
> feel as the object impersonated is supposed to be feel-
> ing not only consciously but unconsciously, physiologi-
> cally, how he breathes, how he presses the ground when

> he stands, how he weighs when he sits, how his arms and
> hands and feet are relaxed. . . . All comes back to "Put
> yourself in his place," in all circumstances, and in all
> encounters and experiences.

André Gide was another who knew the importance of a humanizing imagination. Here he speaks of an instance of children failing in theirs, and the suffering their barbarity caused a dog, and from that caused two people distress:

> Em. was not able to sleep last night (nor I either, moreover), too angered and grieved by the imbecile cruelty of those children. I can explain it to myself only by their idleness . . . and their lack of imagination. Imagination alone, it seems to me, can bring out true pity.

Children are the key to a kinder world, and by that a more creative world, as well as a world less prone to war. Get to them before any unmerciful person has bent them away from kindness. Instill in them the habit of imaginatively climbing into the skins of every manner of life they meet. Have them be that jackrabbit, making its needs, joys and anxieties sympathetically theirs. Such will go a long way to drawing their sympathies beyond their noses.

Make their respect for all creatures so deep they will go out of their way to care for animals as their wards—so deep they will never grow into adults who dispose of their pets at animal shelters saying, "I can't keep her any longer," when they mean "I am unwilling to keep her." "I can't" is a condition of physical impossibility. "I am unwilling to" is a condition of failed ethics. The difference between them is responsibility.

Along with this, immerse children in the arts, especially painting and poetry, taught by merciful parents and teachers, thereby immersing them in goodness. How many fine painters and poets have ever been on a ten-most-wanted list?

Chapter Twenty-three

Knowing And Preserving Nature

Laying five topics together brings the subject into one view. WHY WE NEED NATURE. As most every school child comes to learn, nature is essential to our physical well-being. For one thing, nature sustains the balance of oxygen, carbon dioxide, and nitrogen in the atmosphere. For another, nature holds medically-useful molecular compounds, preventives and cures to be discovered in centuries ahead.

At the same time, little is heard of nature's second essential function. Nature, the part of earth that has never largely been affected by people, is necessary for our spiritual well-being. Nature keeps us close to God, nature makes us better creators, and nature gives us peace of mind.

As to keeping us close to God, a prominent idea in this book is that in beholding an excellent work, by reflection we behold its creator's excellence. Just so, the excellence of nature's works is the mirror through which we come face to face with the excellence of their Creator. The thought is age-old, having been around long before William Blake made it rightly felt with his poem, *The Tyger.*

Watching a tiger in the veldt of central India, sauntering in open view, brings the thought and feeling firsthand. Fearlessly unhurried, stately confident, its being leaps the bounds of the moment. A continental appreciation of the tiger species' timeless rightness wells up, evincing the Creator that recursively shaped not only tiger being but the whole of creature and plant being, sea, earth, and star being.

As to making us better creators, nature stirs us to conceive ideas we put into our works and into interpreting the works of others. Had our ancestors roamed an alabaster-smooth planet, Pythagoras wouldn't have been Pythagoras, nor Einstein been Einstein, nor Maxfield Parrish, James Russell Lowell, Joseph Haydn, E. E. Barnard, Wassily Kandinsky, Rachel Carson, and M. C. Escher been as creative as they were.

"In man's brain," writes Victor Weisskopf, "the impressions from the outside are not merely registered; they produce concepts and ideas . . . [which are] the imprint of the external world on the human brain." With nature having shaped the workings of our subconscious and conscious minds, nature stimulates these workings to create.

Haydn, for instance, was convinced that his habitually going out into the countryside and forests, drinking in the surrounding perfections, made his compositions, including *The Creation*, greater.

In Barnard's case, the fiery persistence of comets, nebulas, and stars stoked his fiery persistence to observe and catalog and comprehend their traits and laws.

In Kandinsky's case, he attributed his art to his "love of nature [consisting] principally of pure joy in and enthusiasm for the element of color," causing within himself "incomprehensible stirrings, the urge to paint a *picture*."

The chain of nature's uplifting and instructing influences runs indeterminably far. For example, marine life incited Rachel Carson to write *The Sea Around Us*, and one reader, M. C. Escher, has remarked to a correspondent that her "fascinating, precise and poetic" prose was to him "a stimulus for my spatial imagination about mother earth . . . [that] greatly inspires me to make a new print . . . in which I shall try for the hundredth time to give rein to my sense of suggesting three-dimensional space." In turn, Escher's prints have fired creators throughout the arts.

Inevitably the chains of influence branch from art into material application. Nature calls forth fresh beauties to painting, literature, mathematics, the basic sciences, and more, any of which may enthuse and call forth original ideas to inventors of practical products. Kandinsky explains:

> [Art's] advanced role in the creation of nonmaterial benefits, by comparison with other realms, derives naturally from that high degree of intuition that is essential to art. Art, producing as it does nonmaterial consequences, continuously increases the stock of nonmaterial values. But since from the nonmaterial is born the material, art, too, with time, freely and inevitably produces material values as well. What yesterday was a mad "idea" today becomes a fact, from which, tomorrow, will come material reality.

As to nature giving us peace of mind, John Cowper Powys explains in his autobiography that nature is a wick that draws away our "neurotic troubles," accepting and absorbing them "into its own magnetic life," so that "they lose their devilish power of tormenting." To live according to nature, Powys said, is "to possess the power to forget."

Powys often visited an ancient willow he called his Saviour-Tree. Touching it, his worries left him. He took this power of nature as "an outward and visible sign of an inward and spiritual grace."

Finally, it is best to experience nature in solitude. "The great flow from the subconscious to the conscious," said May Sarton, "is the good thing about solitude. There is no barrier between the subconscious and the conscious. . . ." Thus in solitude, our neurotic troubles escape from our subconscious, freeing our creative ideas to come easily into consciousness.

WHY WE NEED JOHN MUIR NATURALISTS. A naturalist is someone who, in sensing parts of nature with a mind trained in biology and ecology, and a heart trained in beauty, senses beyond the parts to a transcendental kingdom, the spirit of nature. A John Muir naturalist, beside being a naturalist, has John Muir's fight to see that wild nature is abundantly and perpetually preserved, sustenance for spiritual well-being, where nothing ever goes tiring or disappointing or betrays itself by a false note.

It is pointless to talk of protecting nature without specifying a purpose. One purpose will require one type and extent of protection; another, another. Of the two reasons mentioned for preserving nature for our physical well-being—clean air and water, and medical drugs—it means nothing if nature is scarred, or if there is no solitude, a billboard on every tree, loudspeakers by the streambanks, traces of human activity everywhere. But of the reasons for preserving nature for our spiritual well-being—connecting us closely to God, benefitting our creating, and cleansing us of our troubles—it means everything.

Although most environmentalists and conservationists are for preserving nature, that is their secondary concern. Environmentalists are primarily concerned with keeping the earth safe for our health, and conservationists with knowing how much of nature may be skimmed without endangering its ability to renew itself. If environmentalists succeed, the earth will not be a dumping ground for pollutants. If conservationists succeed, we won't run low on good topsoil, water, and plants and animals important to commerce. Yet their successes may come in ways that fail to keep the spirituality of nature alive. That duty falls to John Muir naturalists, those with John Muir's beliefs, as extracted from his collected writings and applied to today, which means the following:

1. John Muir naturalists believe that spiritual prosperity towers above mercantile prosperity. Reacting against the loss of nature, they ask that development be restrained, and the known and untold forms and interlocking relations of nature be sustained. Who in right mind wrecks a mountain for its coal? Where has it been proved that what cannot be advertised, wrapped, and

charged for is to be thought lowly of? And however controversial the issue of rights for animals and natural places may be, who dares deny that the first right of everyone is to be happy and content, and this is violated in those whose being is ripped by actions of those that cause animals to suffer; that confine species to smaller and smaller reservations, some consequently going extinct; and that gouge the hills, foul streams and oceans, and level forests to stumps?

2. John Muir naturalists believe that nature should be kept whole in its composition, the cast of species complete. Only at God's hands ought species come and go.

Nature's preciousness is spun of interrelated variety. Explaining this in another context, Charles Lamb wrote: "The going away of friends does not make the remainder more precious. It takes so much from them as there was a common link. A. B. and C. make a party. A. dies. B. not only loses A. but all A.'s part in C. C. loses A.'s part in B., and so the alphabet sickens by subtraction. . . ." Substitute "the going away of species" for "the going away of friends," and the truth remains. The sickening is more than ecological. It is spiritual.

Look at those passing sailors who clubbed the dodo out of existence for a short change of diet. The self-seeking impulses of these vandals destroyed more than the value of the dodo: they damaged a good deal of the value of the species linked with the dodo, including our species. A sensible tradeoff? For a while, a few have convenient meals; forevermore, billions and billions have nature's splendor taken a peg lower.

The John Muir naturalist knows that for the divine function of the Creation to work its spiritual wonders, earth must have God's authentic product in at least close to original size and scope. God's symphony is nature, species His instruments, and nature drained of even a few is like Beethoven's Ninth with the violins' strings cut. We do not improve a symphony or nature by taking away parts. With each dismemberment, we disproportionately cheapen the remainder.

Indispensable, therefore, are pure lakes and seas, and intact and spacious tracts of forests, prairies, deserts and tundra, not in token enclaves, perverted and curtailed imitations. Required is the full cast of God's creatures, every size, shape, behavior, and manner of plant and animal. God, in assigning us dominion over nature (according to Christian theology), has assigned us the perpetual duty of keeping it whole, that it may be perfectly echoic of Him.

Nor does the John Muir naturalist forget that God's symphony is being written, unfinished until our sun bulges into a red giant, stages of nature out-perfecting previous stages in kind and degree. Kill nature in its cradle, and we kill more than it is now. We kill what it is bound for.

3. John Muir naturalists place the human race above people. It is a club, we are its temporary members. One short-sighted lot of us, leaving fate to market forces and sales pressure, chances eroding nature's biological and spiritual integrity, past repair. If the word responsibility has any meaning, each generation must be on vigilant guard duty, fighting to keep the remaining wild places safe on its watch.

4. John Muir naturalists believe that the rampant increase in our numbers should be reined in. The issue is not of physical wasting but of spiritual wasting. It has been estimated, perhaps accurately, that the lands and seas could feed ten times the present population. Multiply the earth's area by the number of people a square mile can keep comfortably alive, and the figure is about eighty billion.

Developers, taking glee in this target, are without sorrow that eighty billion on earth will so raze nature that the spirit of God will be starved to oblivion. Fifty billion will do the same. Twenty billion, the same. As the upper limit, there should be no more of us than can be spiritually nourished. Incidental with this, there will be ample food to go around.

What of the possibility of a tradeoff between numbers of people and their per capita material consumption? Twenty billion existing frugally may have the impact on nature of six billion existing affluently. All the same, the possibility is irrelevant. Privacy is limiting. We need room to be in nature with none of our kind around.

Eat an ice cream sundae in company and it tastes the same, but intruding human sounds and sights are unnatural blemishes on wilderness, spoiling the beholder's spiritual taste. What is more, merely knowing that vast pristine spaces exist, as that the panda has widespread wild habitats and is thriving in its element on its innate terms, despite our never setting foot in China, is fundamental to keeping the spirit of God alive.

What is the rush to release a deluge of babies? In timeless eternity, souls bear no hardship in waiting to come onto earth. By having the flow of births moderate, everybody will eventually come here, and the here will not be a paved-over, nature-scarred, solitude-scarce, God-denying place.

5. John Muir naturalists place wild animals above paper laws, exempting animals from the boundaries of governments and the property rights of landowners. Wherever an animal walks or swims, it is a treasure belonging to people far and wide. If cranes come onto a farmer's field and eat grain, that is a cost of doing business, no less than if a mud slide came. The farmer or forebears bought the land with risks of this sort compensated in the price. The repercussions of a bullet striking a crane reach beyond the farmer's concerns to spiritually sensitive people, a harm outweighing any dollars the crane might subtract from the farmer's ledger.

In the same vein, what say should farmers, ranchers, and shopkeepers rightly have on the fate of wilderness areas next door to them? None more than those a continent away who care that wildernesses remain unspoiled. By no means does a treasure diminish by the distance from it.

6. John Muir naturalists believe that nature should be put off limits to recreation that mars the mirror of God or the solitude needed to reflect in the mirror. However much some clamor to drive machines up and down dunes and hills, and about lakes

and rivers–and businesses to sell the machines–what makes rec-
reational sense and commercial sense fails to make spiritual
sense.

The sound or sight of one machine crashing through sacro-
sanct wilderness, or marks left by one, closes the possibility of
being seized with the sacred enlargement of the present and the
place. Contradictory, isn't it, to bar machines from the Washington National Cathedral while inviting them into nature's
Cathedral? The joyriders are hardly after quiet and being alone;
crowds and noise amplify their excitement. Let them dodge their
boredom at stadiums, shopping malls, and race tracks.

7. The John Muir naturalist differs with possibly all commercial developers, and with plenty of economists, businesspeople,
politicians, administrators, and planners who line up in the
developer's camp. Where the developer thinks, "How stupid to
exclude bulldozers, cement mixers, oil wells, and open pit mines
from millions of square miles," the John Muir naturalist thinks,
"How blasphemous of humanity's godly needs to skin the land
for commerce, beyond a modest degree, and not keep the full
range of species and wildernesses, in rich abundance."

To developers, the spiritual loss is nothing. Nature is grist for
their money mill. They see wilderness as a nuisance squatting
on land they eye for expansion. Woodlands are for clearing and
building or farming on. Tigers are to shoot, whales to harpoon,
with the toucan's jungle home ideally put into coffee plantations.
And the starry sky takes distant second place to the outdoor
lighting that dims it from view.

The developer claims that the time when development stops
making amends for the nature it obliterates lies nowhere near–
that it is needless to worry while woods and under-story life are
sheared off for streets, houses, roads, and arable land, and as
air, water, and land receive waste chemicals of factories, power
stations, and mines, feedlots and farms, exhaust pipes and rup-
tured oil tankers.

The developer backs the claim with a number, the benefit-to-cost ratio. Economic analysts estimate the dollars that foreseeable industrial and residential developments may bring to the world. Against this, they estimate and quantify the impacts to health—so many wheezes, so many hacking coughs, so many lymphatic cancers resulting in lost wages and doctor bills. The net result, the benefit-to-cost ratio, shines a green light. Development, society is told, can be safely extended.

The John Muir naturalist sighs. The analysts widely understate the costs. They leave out that development denatures the earth, blighting the spirit before the body is endangered. The benefit-to-cost ratio actually tips the other way. The light really shines red.

John Muir naturalists, lest they be wrongly pictured, are not categorically against development. They welcome it, provided it and further development it may open the way for do not intrude on the health of the spirit. And where development already exists, they favor redevelopment, not destroying more of nature.

8. John Muir naturalists are for making known the true meanings of certain words and terms, used glibly by those for development, that subtly suggest that keeping nature whole is wrongheaded.

"Natural resources" is one of these. Meaning the raw stuff of nature, it carries the connotation that forests, bogs, swamps, animals, rivers, gravel, clay and the like are inferior to finished stuff that can be made with them. Redwood trees are labeled a natural resource, implying they are inadequate to the board feet of timber they can be sawed into and rung up on cash registers. Cougars and bears are labeled natural resources, implying they are better used by those who will pay for their experience of shooting them.

Similarly, everything that John Muir naturalists believe goes against a term economists invented, "rational man." This term lends an air of wisdom to whatever the greatest number do. The truth is, the so-called rational man is the majority materialistic person, intent of more and more possessions, diversions, and conveniences, and having them sooner than later, and as cheaply as possible. So-called rational man scarcely believes in leaving well enough alone. So-called rational man is the reason nature is less when we get up than when we went to bed. So-called rational man would label cumulus clouds a natural resource, could someone find a way to project advertisements on the sides and bottoms. So-called rational man is John Muir's foolish man.

9. John Muir naturalists protest that the economist's willingness-to-pay method is an improper gauge of the worth of nature. Using this method, economists find that the public spends more for tickets to football games than for preserving wilderness and species. And in canvassing people, asking how much they would consider contributing to a program to protect so many wild acres, most say they would give little or nothing.

Very well. Who puts van Gogh's *The Starry Night* up for auction before a roomful of people blind from birth, and concludes that the winning two-dollar bid represents its value? Who reasons that because wilderness and species whisper unassertively, enticing few to open their pocketbooks to save them from eradication, such things are inconsiderable? How much a person will pay is, John Muir knew, a measure of what feels good, not usually of what is good. Most everyone will pay to appease their hunger for immediate entertainment. Goodness, especially of the long run, doesn't sell on merit.

Materialists, shallowly versed in reflecting into nature, liking what they know, longtime followers of the primrose path, are asked how much they would pay regarding a spiritual future whose rightness for them and posterity they have yet to put themselves in position to know, and cannot until they school their hearts and minds in nature and the arts, and deepen into genuinely rational man.

10. For deciding the fate of natural areas, John Muir naturalists believe the one-person-one-vote principle suppresses total human happiness. Provided one has a working spirit, spiritual crimes are the most unbearable of all. To disintegrate nature more deeply wounds John Muir naturalists, more tears at their life basis,

more weights them with permanent sorrow, and more risks civil disobedience, than stopping developing bothers developers.

A thought experiment demonstrates. Assume it is announced that squirrels will be eliminated from earth unless some John Muir naturalists agree to go before a firing squad to guarantee eternal protection. Certainly there would be little trouble getting a thousand volunteers. Assume the opposite then, that development is to be banned unless just one developer goes before a firing squad. What developer would step forth, that unknown developers could continue their work?

11. John Muir naturalists want people to wake up to the danger of gradualism. Gradualism is how things get beyond shocking without shocking us. A string of small degrading steps, with pauses for acclimation, and by grains we land without protest in a condition that a full step to would repulse us.

Gradualism threatens every area of morality. People slightly descend from a moral principle, and that eases the way for another slight descent, and that to a third, and so on until they have descended entirely. Think of the man who cannot bear to think of killing his wife, but for some while yells at her. Once reconciled to that, he sometimes hits her lightly. Reconciled to that, he comes to knock her down regularly. Reconciled to that, he shoots her. Gradual reconciliation happens to the wife too. At the start, she would have left him if he had knocked her down once.

Outside the home, gradualism is behind our acquiescence to heinous crimes done to persons and animals. It is why we sit on our hands without outcry at the irreparable ravaging of species and wild places. How to strip the Amazon forest bare? Don't do it overnight while we are sleeping, or tomorrow there will be hell to pay. Do it as it is being done now. Pilfer it.

12. As a condition of holding office, John Muir naturalists want elected officials who make decisions having impacts on nature to be required to have had and passed a course in ecology, a course in aesthetic appreciation, and a course in the value of nature to mental health and creativity. Who would put

the operation of hospitals in the hands of unlearned, heartless surgeons?

In conclusion, John Muir naturalists present us with this choice. To join with them and go to any lengths to save God's one-time inventions of flora, fauna, air, water, and landscape, or to turn a blind eye as they are being irreversibly turned into museum material, letting those with marble hearts for anything they cannot cash in on monopolize the planet?

WHY CHILDREN SHOULD BE RAISED TO BE JOHN MUIR NATURALISTS. First of all, it leads them to see, in H. M. Tomlinson's words, "another sky than ours," letting them know what the creative spirit is. Although they are too young to sensitize their spirits by creating excellence or by appreciating it in human products, youth is no barrier to esteeming nature's excellencies. Thus with the glory of nature eliciting extrasensory enthusiasm for its Creator, tell them, "Someday when you create excellence, this is the quality, the spirituality, you will feel."

Another thing, educating children to be John Muir naturalists lifts their standards for casting their creative works toward, and for judging the works of others. That John Muir was the finest of writers is very possibly because nature's excellencies bred in him the highest conception of what excellence can be.

Furthermore, educating children to be John Muir naturalists arms them against impiety. The day will come that in the mirror of God they catch the reflection of the Divine. Even if they have professed themselves atheists, they must admit that nature is a creation. And admitting the absurdity of calling it a creator-less creation, they are forced to admit a Creator is behind it.

And believing in a Creator, they come to a comfort about their fate in eternity. Any or all parts of nature are avenues to this, as the plant world, the insect world, the mammal world, or the geological world. Edwin Hubble is an example of someone who did it with the cosmic world. Listen to what Edith Sitwell, in a letter to a private correspondent, said of him:

Did you, I wonder, know Dr Hubble, of the Expanding Universe–one of the greatest men I ever knew. One day, in California, he showed me slides of universes unseen by the naked eye, and millions of light-years away. I said to him, 'How terrifying!' 'Only when you are not used to them,' he replied. 'When you *are* used to them, they are comforting. For then you know that there is nothing to worry about–nothing at all!'

That was a few months before he died. And so I suppose now that he knows how truly he spoke. I was most deeply moved by that. I could never cease to be so.

Finally, educating children to be John Muir naturalists swells the ranks of future preservationists. They are sure to grow up resisting overrunning the world with people, to stand up to elected officials who are putty in the hands of developers, and to insist that nature remains fully here to know, not permitting the mirror of God to be further damaged or pared down.

How to raise children to be John Muir naturalists. Addressing the naturalist part of a John Muir naturalist, the path of raising children goes through subjects such as ecology and biology. Addressing the John Muir part, the path goes through subjects that deepen the impression of nature on the subconscious, advancing children's sensitivities to every form of natural beauty, offering them illumination into God.

Nature offers children all manner of figurative sunbursts through rifted clouds, but first children need to learn to see them. Hence, children should be taught to pay undivided attention to the shapes, hues, sounds, feels, smells, touches, moods, actions, needs, and interrelations of every live and not-live thing. By this, they will go some distance toward better making out the overarching radiance of the natural world that outsplendors the parts they sense at any moment.

Specifically, instill in children the habit of attentively sketching nature's features on paper, drawing everything from milkweed and aspen, to spider webs and worms, and from the constellations to the turning lines of schooling minnows and swallow flight. Thomas Huxley credited drawing with a value that cannot be "exaggerated, because it gives the means of training the young in attention and accuracy, the two things in which all mankind are more deficient than in any other mental quality whatever."

Instill in children the complemental habit of sketching directly on their imaginations. Encourage them to have always their imaginary bee at hand, placing it on leaves, sending it off on walks around the edges and up and down the veins, directly etching the forms and colors on their minds and hearts. They can never truly say they have made out leaves, birchbark, lichen, exposed limestone, and all else until they have watched their bee crawl about.

The sky, which the landscape artist John Constable called the "Organ of Sentiment," is of special consequence to the spirit, and a special subject to make out every day. Instill in them the habit of exchanging their bee for a boat, sailing it on imaginary trips hugging the cloud coasts, making the conscious impressions last a week, the unconscious perhaps indelibly.

Besides sight, instill in them the habit of paying undivided attention with their ears, selectively listening, as for the first cricket to chirp on the summer evenings, and nearby crickets to begin chiming in, and the chorus to mass, synchronize, modulate as one.

And instill the habit of paying undivided attention with words, describing nature in their journals. As a good model, have them study Rachel Carson's notes on the types and motions of clouds (in her book *Lost Woods*), where she works the technique of painting with words near to its limits of packing in accuracy and feeling.

And instill in them the habit of occupying themselves with the literary works of those poets and prose writers who go beyond seeing nature to inspecting it closely. To illustrate, of two young people, alike except that through the writings of Loren Eiseley the one has glimpsed into the inmost recesses of our ancestral relations with the natural world, that one has truer grasp of what Samuel Johnson defined as "that deepest part of us that cannot be opened to the eyes"–the soul, shaped by nature.

And instill in them the habit of going through the fractal mazes of scientific curiosities which excite wonder of nature. Among infinitely varied starting points is the migrating ruby-throated hummingbird that waits for just the right hour of tailwind before letting loose its wings and courage for its 30-hour journey across the Gulf of Mexico–the implausible desert downpour, collecting in rock basins, calling tadpoles to life–the globular clusters of stars, perhaps the one known as M2, a fuzzy jot in a small telescope, an eighth of an inch across at forty times magnification, where if a beam of light started on its right side and headed left, it would take more than 150 years to cross that eighth of an inch.

HOW TO SWAY THE PUBLIC TO SUPPORT THE PRESERVATION OF NATURE. Because most people take casual notice of nature, and are scarcely conversant about it, we should help them make nature out, deepening their senses, esteeming God's creation.

And we should help them to realize that "I am not unhappy," that "I have nothing to gripe about," that "I am gratified enough so as to stop complaint," a state achieved by appeasing bodily wants and staving off boredom with entertainments, is distant from "I am happy beyond what I thought happiness can be," a state achieved by sensing God's excellence through nature, and directing the power gained into creating excellence for others, and into creatively consuming the excellence of others, supplying the quality, the spirit, missing from "I am not unhappy."

And we should appeal to their reason, open their minds, make them feel for the sad vista of a future without nature, and question the wisdom of putting concrete in place of life.

Use argument to change their values? Surely that is naive. Don't likings of the adult heart exist independently of any logic for them? How often have appeals to reason stopped warring nations? What chronic drug user is not up to the neck in pleas to change? "Why give reasons for our preferences? How often have our preferences any reason?" asked H. M. Tomlinson in one of his essays.

Yet a preference is like a wagon parked on a hill in its long-accustomed spot, chocks under its wheels, and proper arguments can move it. Proper arguments appeal to listeners' self-interest: to their caring about themselves, about their children, and about their children's children to come. Proper arguments are given with variety that avoids wearing on the listener. Proper arguments are given with intensity that comes from the giver's basis. ("Intensity," Van Wyck Brooks noted, "always prevails. Whoever possesses intensity is bound to conquer other minds. . . .")

Because proper arguments are given however long it takes to change the listener's preference, those who give them must be patient. The arguments go to slow work dissolving the chocks. A fresh attitude takes years to ripen; in the meanwhile it appears no headway is being made. Yet in a decade or two, the wagon may sway, roll and stop on the spot the arguments favor, generally denying the arguments had anything to do with it.

In this way, seemingly hard-and-fast preferences that go against preserving nature can be reformed. Effective polemics, keeping in public notice that nature's plight is ours, appealing to the physical and spiritual roots of being, await only the creators who will invent them.

The hour is late, and each John Muir naturalist is at times bound to be dismayed by the thought, "I am but one. What chance do I have to convert the masses?" The answer is "high," if each takes to heart Václav Havel's observation about the gathering power of responsibility:

> Responsibility cannot be preached, but only borne, and . . . the only possible place to begin is with oneself. It may sound strange, but it is true: it is I who must begin.

One thing about it, however, is interesting: once I begin—that is, once I try—here and now, right where I am, not excusing myself by saying that things would be easier elsewhere, without grand speeches and ostentatious gestures, but all the more persistently—to live in harmony with the "voice of Being," as I understand it within myself—as soon as I begin that, I suddenly discover, to my surprise, that I am neither the only one, nor the first, nor the most important one to have set out upon that road. For the hope opened up in my heart by this turning toward Being has opened my eyes as well to all the hopeful things my vision, blinded by the brilliance of "worldly" temptations, could not or did not wish to see, because it would have undermined the traditional argument of all those who have given up already: that all is lost anyway. Whether all is really lost or not depends entirely on whether or not I am lost.

PART FOUR

Credos Of Creative Workers

T. H. WHITE

What is right or wrong (for a species)? Well, I can only suppose that it is Right for a species to progress in doing what ever it does. It would be quite wrong for a tortoise to attempt flight. It has no wings. In the end, you come down to the idea that a species must specialize in its own speciality. Follow that up, and you find that what is right for man depends upon his speciality, his wings, tail, beak, backbone, fins, antennae or whatever his most special speciality may be. And you will find that his most s. s. is his cerebrum. This (not the cerebellum) is as much overdeveloped in Man, as a species as, for instance, the nose of an elephant is overdeveloped from my nose.

W. N. P. BARBELLION

Youth is an intoxication without wine, some one says. Life is an intoxication. The only sober man is the melancholiac, who, disenchanted, looks at life, sees it as it really is, and cuts his throat. If this be so, I want to be very drunk. The great thing is to live, to clutch at our existence and race away with it in some great and enthralling pursuit.

ALAN SEEGER

I am not influenced by the foolish American ideas of "success" which regard only the superficial and accidental meanings of the word—advancement, recognition, power, etc. The essence of success is in rigorously obeying one's best impulses and following those paths which conscience absolutely approves, and than which imagination can conceive none more desirable.

JOAN MIRÓ

I am working as *much as I can*. People who have managed to do something have followed different paths, *but they have never deviated from hard work*. That has to be the most powerful objective of an artist's life.–When a person is really an artist this is an inexorable fact, the way night follows day.

– – –

It is remarkable–and very sadly so–to see how a man reacts the same whether he lives in a landscape where town and mountains are bitterly structured or when he observes a landscape in which everything is lyrical color and music. Everything moves him equally, he speaks in the same way, he is the same, and he paints the same; with the same feeling that he would paint Majorca, for example, he paints Toledo, changing only the "photographic" or realistic details. Apart from that he remains the same; he eats the same, walks the same, speaks the same.–The opposite sort of man sees a different problem in every tree and in every bit of sky: this is the man who suffers, the man who is always moving and can never sit still, the man who will never do what people call a "definitive" work. He is the man who always stumbles and gets to his feet again.–Not the other. He walks calmly; when he is tired he sits down and his works are of absolute perfection (!) both in drawing and color, faultless but empty. The other man is always saying *not yet, it is still not ready*, and when he is satisfied with his last canvas and starts another one, he destroys the earlier one. His work is always a new beginning, as though today he was just beginning to paint.

GEORGES BRAQUE

With me, the inception of a work always takes precedence over the results anticipated.

DOROTHY L. SAYERS

. . . The creator's love for his work is not a greedy possessiveness; he never desires to subdue his work to himself but always to subdue himself to his work. The more genuinely creative he is, the more he will want his work to develop in accordance with its own nature, and to stand independent of himself.

— — —

To feel sacrifice consciously as self-sacrifice argues a failure in love. When a job is undertaken from necessity, or from a grim sense of disagreeable duty, the worker is self-consciously aware of the toils and pains he undergoes, and will say: "I have made such and such sacrifices for this." But when the job is a labor of love, the sacrifices will present themselves to the worker—strange as it may seem—in the guise of enjoyment.

— — —

. . . That a work of creation struggles and insistently demands to be brought into being is a fact that no genuine artist would think of denying. Often, the demand may impose itself in defiance of the author's considered interests and at the most inconvenient moments. Publisher, bank-balance, and even the conscious intellect may argue that the writer should pursue some fruitful and established undertaking; but they will argue in vain against the passionate vitality of a work that insists on manifestation. The strength of the insistence will vary from something that looks like direct inspiration to something that resembles a mere whim of the wandering mind; but whenever the creature's desire for existence is dominant, everything else will have to give way to it; the writer will push all other calls aside and get down to his task in a spirit of mingled delight and exasperation.

— — —

. . . The writer is known to live by a set of values which are not purely economic: he beholds the end of the work. As a common-or-business man, he requires payment for his work and is often pretty stiff in his demands; but as an artist, he retains so much of the image of God that he is in love with his creation for its own sake.

Virginia Woolf

. . . to discover real things beneath the show.

— — —

. . . It's the writing, not the being read, that excites me.

— — —

It is worth mentioning, for future reference, that the creative power which bubbles so pleasantly in beginning a new book quiets down after a time, and one goes on more steadily. Doubts creep in. Then one becomes resigned. Determination not to give in, and the sense of an impending shape keep one at it more than anything.

— — —

And yet oddly enough I scarcely want children of my own now. This insatiable desire to write something before I die, this ravaging sense of the shortness and feverishness of life, make me cling, like a man on a rock, to my one anchor.

- - -

I write two pages of arrant nonsense, after straining; I write variations of every sentence; compromises; bad shots; possibilities; till my writing book is like a lunatic's dream. Then I trust to some inspiration on re-reading; and pencil them into some sense. Still I am not satisfied. I think there is something lacking. I sacrifice nothing to seemliness. I press to my centre. I don't care if it all is scratched out. And there is something there.

- - -

My grind has left me dazed and depressed. How on earth to bring off this chapter? God knows.

PIERRE TEILHARD DE CHARDIN

To grow and fulfil oneself to the utmost—that is the law immanent in being.

- - -

The greatest sacrifice we can make, the greatest victory we can win over ourselves, is to surmount inertia, the tendency to follow the line of least resistance.

- - -

. . . What fascinates me in life is being able to collaborate in a task, a reality, more durable than myself: it's in that spirit and with that in mind that I try to perfect myself and acquire a little more mastery over things. If death attacks me, it leaves untouched these causes, and ideas and realities, more solid and precious than myself. . . .

– – –

One of the things I have acquired this year is the conviction of the necessary effort, the effort without which *some part of being will never be achieved*. Only a fortnight ago, at Verdun, when I was seeing and experiencing the astonishing effort made by thousands of active units to mount an attack whose success was still in *the balance*, I had a profound impression of the *contingency* of any success in this world, and of its subordination to our own *tenacity*, to our own diligence. In fact, the sound principle is that of action that tackles everything resolutely and energetically, without wasting too much time in fruitless discussion. *'Don't chat, but try!'* That's always true.

NADIA BOULANGER

But the essential condition of everything you do, and not only in music, the touchstone, must be choice, love, passion. You do it because you consider that the marvelous adventure of being alive depends entirely on the atmosphere you yourself create, by your enthusiasm, your conviction, your understanding.

JEAN-PAUL SARTRE

It would be my own fault if I squandered my life.

– – –

One is totally responsible for one's life.

THORNTON WILDER

As to the young people who are going into writing—I beg them to have no impatience to be published. I tell them that the notion of acquiring some reputation in order to impress parents and friends is one of the enemies of good writing.

Do not aspire to earn your living by your pen–get some job to support you while you write at midnight, and take a job as little connected with writing as possible–teaching mathematics, I think, would be splendid. Having a gas station on the New Mexican desert would be wonderful.

ANDRÉ GIDE

I never am; I am becoming.

– – –

What could have been said by someone other than you, do not say it; what could have been done by someone other than you, do not do it; of yourself, be interested only in those aspects that do not exist except in you; patiently or impatiently create out of yourself the most unique and irreplaceable of beings.

– – –

I want to suggest . . . the influence of the book upon the one who is writing it, and during that very writing. As the book issues from us it changes us, modifying the course of our life. . . . Our acts exercise a retroaction upon us. "Our deeds act upon us as much as we act upon them," said George Eliot.

– – –

I believe that the major shortcoming of writers and artists today is impatience: if they knew how to wait, their subject would automatically compose itself slowly in their mind; by itself it would cast off the useless matter and everything that impedes it; it would grow like [the leading branches of] a tree. . . . It would grow *naturally*.

— — —

How often have I directed my attention, my study, to this or that fugue of Bach, for instance, precisely because in the beginning it discouraged me; through a need of doing myself violence and guided by that obscure feeling that what thwarts us and demands of us the greatest effort is also what can teach us most.

— — —

"True courage," said Napoleon, "is that of three a. m." He meant thereby, probably, that the courage he esteemed was that from which all intoxication, all vanity, all emulation were excluded. A courage without witnesses and without accomplices; courage when sober and on an empty stomach. . . . I cannot esteem the courage that is due, as so often happens, merely to a lack of imagination, just as fear is very often the result of an excessive imagination. . . . Before admiring the one who risks his life, I should like to be sure that he values it. So many young fellows, during the war, saw in the fact of risking their life a unique opportunity of winning some glory! Just imagine all of a sudden, among them, a person who feels himself to be the possessor of some secret message which, if he lives, will soon be a great boon to all the others; would not the truest courage, for him, be trying to preserve that secret?

— — —

The first condition of happiness is that man may take joy in his work. There is no real joy in rest, in leisure, unless joyful work precedes it.

— — —

... Man's happiness lies not in freedom but in the acceptance of a duty.

— — —

I am very much afraid that the shores of those islands, so charming in my childhood, have been as lamentably spoiled as the immediate surroundings of Cannes itself; as was also the coast of England of which Edmund Gosse speaks so eloquently in *Father and Son*; and as are all the most charming spots on this earth as soon as man begins to sprawl on them.

ISAAC ASIMOV

Staying power is an attitude. At the heart of it is a love of what you're doing. If I stopped writing today, my incoming royalties would let me live comfortably for the rest of my life. But last year, when I turned 65, I threw a huge non-Retirement Birthday Party for myself. It was the happiest birthday I ever had because I realized that no one could force me to retire.

If the world should suddenly come to an end, I hope it would find me at work. To me, stopping is like being defeated and I don't like being defeated. To quit is to kill the spirit that gives life its meaning and worth.

RICHARD HALLIBURTON

Dad, you hit the wrong target when you write that you wish I were at Princeton living "in the even tenor of my way." I *hate* that expression and as far as I am able I intend to avoid that condition. When impulse and spontaneity fail to make my "way" as *uneven* as possible then I shall sit up nights inventing means of making life as conglomerate and vivid as possible. Those who live in the even tenor of their way simply exist until death ends their monotonous tranquility. No, there's going to be no even tenor with me. The more uneven it is the happier I shall be. And when my time comes to die, I'll be able to die happy, for I will have done and seen and heard and experienced all the joy, pain, thrills—every emotion that any human ever had—and I'll be especially happy if I am spared a stupid, common death in bed. So, Dad, I'm afraid your wish will always come to naught, for my way is to be ever changing, but always swift, acute and leaping from peak to peak instead of following the rest of the herd, shackled in conventionalities, along the monotonous narrow path in the valley. The dead have reached perfection when it comes to even tenor!

R. A. Fisher

We must face the difficult and responsible task of getting good results actually accomplished. Good intentions and pious observances are no sufficient substitute, and are noxious if accepted as substitute. . . .

Jenny Read

more work = more problems
more problems = more solutions
more commitment = greater solutions

Vsevold Emilyevich Meyerhold

If the production pleases everyone, then consider it a total failure. If, on the other hand, everyone criticizes your work, then perhaps there's something worthwhile in it. Real success comes when people argue about your work, when half the audience is in raptures and the other half is ready to tear you apart.

CHARLES LINDBERGH

My civilized life did not encourage receptivity. There were too many details pressing for attention, too many problems, large and small, to occupy my mind. My time was a chattel of my obligations. My senses had less freedom than a slave's. But the juxtaposition that forms man also contains the capacity to change. In the future, I decided, I would devote more attention to the core without renouncing civilization. I would set a trend toward balancing the diverse elements of being, toward simplicity rather than more complications, toward appreciation rather than possessions, toward an objective I felt was before me but could not as yet define.

To select an objective and set a trend—how simple and routine that seems written in a sentence! And what momentous consequences can result in actual life! When I look back through my life, I realize that such selections and trends have had an extraordinary effect on its shaping. Usually I was conscious of their importance at the time.

– – –

The trend I decided to set that night on the Salt Lake desert involved more subtle problems than merely setting a trend to combat fear. I had no clear-cut objective. I was trying to combine two seemingly contrary objectives, to be part of the civilization of my time but not to be bound by its conventional superfluity. . . . I would cut down on all these activities. I would eliminate the superfluous, simplify my life, and let the trend develop. One thing seemed certain. The key to appreciation, to a balanced being, to joy and grace, lay in a basic simplicity beneath the elaborate garments of culture one chose or was forced to wear. I would reduce my obligations, give away some of my possessions, concentrate my business and social interests. I would take advantage of the civilization into which I had been born without losing the basic qualities of life from which all works of men must emanate.

The important thing was the core. But what was it: how much of it was physical, how much mental, how much spiritual? How could one reach one's core?

MARIA RAINER RILKE

Know, then, that art is this: the means through which singular, solitary individuals fulfill themselves.

— — —

Everything is gestation and then bringing forth.

— — —

Nobody can counsel and help you [about whether you should become a poet], nobody. There is only one single way. Go into yourself. Search for the reason that bids you write; find out whether it is spreading out its roots in the deepest places of your heart, acknowledge to yourself whether you would have to die if it were denied you to write. This above all—ask yourself in the stillest hour of your night; *must* I write? Delve into yourself for a deep answer. And if this should be affirmative, if you may meet this earnest question with a strong and simple *"I must,"* then build your life according to this necessity; your life even into its most indifferent and slightest hour must be a sign of this urge and a testimony to it.

— — —

The work of the artist has many dangers and often does not let one make out so clearly in detail whether one is going ahead or being driven back by the pressure of the too great forces with which one has become involved. Then it is a matter of waiting and holding out. . . .

— — —

Man has built his world; he has built factories and houses, he produces cars and clothes, he grows grain and fruit. But he has become estranged from the product of his own hands, he is not really master any more of the world he has built; on the contrary, this man-made world has become his master; before whom he bows down, whom he tries to placate or manipulate as best he can. . . . [Man] seems to be driven by self-interest, but in reality his total self with all its concrete potentialities has become an instrument for the purposes of the very machine his hands have built. He keeps up the illusion of being the center of the world, and yet he is pervaded by an intense sense of insignificance and powerlessness. . . .

— — —

Everyone must be able to find in his work the center of his life and from there be able to grow out in radiate form as far as he can.

KATHERINE MANSFIELD

Then I want to *work*. At what? I want so to live that I work with my hands and my feeling and my brain. I want a garden, a small house, grass, animals, books, pictures, music. And out of this, the expression of this, I want to be writing. . . . But warm, eager, living life—to be rooted in life—to learn, to desire to know, to feel, to think, to act. That is what I want. And nothing less. That is what I must try for.

−−−

I've always had a longing to *heal* people and *make them whole*, enrich them: that's what writing means to me—to enrich—to give.

Josephine Preston Peabody

I long to make use of everything I have and I long to have more of everything. And yet I shall feel such a sense of shame and fury if I only succeed in smattering. Heaven knows I have no desire to do many things a little: but I desire to do supremely well something definite, expressive, new, as anything sincerely and deeply wrought must be: and I wish to work richly, recognizing everything else as a help. . . .

−−−

To go out, sword at side and song in your mouth, knowing and believing that Beauty suffers imprisonment in every human spirit, that she waits and starves here, that she is almost dead there; that often enough she is so spent and tortured and dark you would not know her:—to go forth unafraid, with the Beauty in your own heart longing after her—and to rescue, rescue, rescue, greet, restore; to stand unmoved when she will not answer to her name, unmoved but never dismayed—and gathering all the time, light, potency, renewal. Beauty from Beauty—that is what I would beg to do—that is what I will do indeed—God willing.

Auguste Rodin

Art indicates to men their reason for being. It reveals to them the meaning of life; it illuminates their destiny and consequently orients them in life.

AN ANONYMOUS FRENCH SOLDIER

I think I see the work laid out for me, but I do not wish to indulge in any predictions based on this presentment, for every artist carries in him conceptions which never see light. Mozart, when he thought he was about to make a new flight, died, and Beethoven had planned a tenth symphony without knowing his end was so near. It is the artist's duty to bud regardless of the frost which may be close at hand. It is possible that God will permit some of my efforts to fructuate in the future. Though there is a marked homogeneity about my work, still my sketches and attempts at art have a youthful touch about them; there is a stammering in their execution which jars with the real loftiness of the intention. I feel that the art which is in me will not blow until I reach maturity. May God permit me to wait so long. This is my prayer.

FRANÇOIS JACOB

My obsession: a life that shrivels up, slowly rots, goes soft as a pulp. This worry about decline grabs me by the throat as I awake. In the brief interval between dream and waking, it flaunts before my eyes the frenzied dance of everything I would have liked to do, and did not do, and never will. As I turn over and over in my bed, the fear of the too-late, of the irreversible, propels me to the mirror to shave and get ready for the day. And that is the moment of truth. The moment for the old questions. What am I today? Am I capable of renewal? What are the chances I might still produce something I do not expect of myself? For my life unfolds mainly in the yet-to-come, and is based on waiting. Mine is a life of preparation. I enjoy the present only insofar as it is a promise of the future. I am looking for the Promised Land and listening to the music of my tomorrows. My food is anticipation. My drug is hope. As a child, unable to bear the absence of a goal, I made out of trifles what I called "little lights" to illuminate the coming day or week. In writing this memoir, I am neither to wallow in the mire of self-satisfaction nor to settle old scores, but rather to set myself a new purpose, and thus a new existence. It is to take my past and produce the future. I am bored by what has been done, and excited only by what is to do. Were I to frame a prayer, I would ask to be granted not so much the "strength" as the "desire" to do.

Paul Halmos

It is important to me to have something big and external, not inside myself, that I can devote my life to. Gauss and Goya and Shakespeare and Paganini are excellent, their excellence gives me pleasure, and I admire and envy them. They were also dedicated human beings. Excellence is for the few but dedication is something everybody can have—should have—and without it life is not worth living.

Louise Bogan

Sparrow said to me: You are resting on your laurels. You are finished. You are mummified. Take off your earrings and do some work. You didn't go about being a visible specimen of a fine high stern woman, well dressed and keeping her chin up, when you produced your early poetry. Look at the people about you, whom you often fear. They will be dead and forgotten and unmarked. But you and I are immortal. The only immortality is in the printed word. Get going.

Leo Tolstoy

One can live magnificently in this world, if one knows how to work and how to love, to work for the person one loves and to love one's work.

ANNE SEXTON

To work is to live. To create is to live. To perform (for me) is essentially false. Only as I write do I realize myself.

MERIWETHER LEWIS

This day I completed my thirty first year, and conceived that I had in all human probability now existed about half the period which I am to remain in this Sublunary world. I reflected that I had as yet done but little, very little, indeed, to further the hapiness of the human race or to advance the information of the succeeding generation. I viewed with regret the many hours I have spent in indolence, and now soarly feel the want of that information which those hours would have given me had they been judiciously expended. but since they are past and cannot be recalled, I dash from me the gloomy thought, and resolved in future, to redouble my exertions and at least indeavour to promote those two primary objects of human existence, by giving them the aid of that portion of talents which nature and fortune have bestoed on me; or in future, to live for *mankind*, as I have heretofore lived *for myself*.

SALVADOR EDWARD LURIA

The ability to live in the present has, I believe, served to counterbalance the self-doubt, the sense of personal inadequacy that my youthful experiences and my emotional upsets inevitably generated. I have learned that success depends in great part on concentrating whatever resources one has on the task at hand, without letting the feeling of inadequacy become an excuse for retreat. Concentration on realistic tasks was for me the expression of a commitment to effective activity. The resulting successes did generate a core of self-confidence that overcame the potentially stifling influences of childhood and later the effects of depression, a core of sturdiness that has stood me in good stead for seven decades.

Abraham Maslow

If you take into yourself something important from the world, then *you* become important. You have made yourself important thereby—as important as that which you have integrated & assimilated to self. At once it *matters* if you die, or are sick & can't work, etc. You must take care of yourself, respect yourself, get plenty of rest, not smoke or drink too much. You can no longer commit suicide—that would be too selfish. It would be a loss for the world. You are *needed*, useful. Easiest way to feel needed. Mothers with babies don't commit suicide as easily as nonmothers, I feel sure, because they are needed, because they're too busy to indulge themselves.

Easy medicine for self-esteem: become a part of something important. Be able to say: "We of the United Nations . . ." or "We physicians . . ." or "We psychologists have proven that . . ." (thereby participating in the glory, the pleasure, the pride, of *all* psychologists anyplace).

Marie Lenéru

My sole brake will be an extreme attention to my development *equally in all directions.*

There are saints, philosophers, men of letters, scientists, worldlings, artists. I do not choose in life, I have need of all its resources. I shall experience everything and I am even willing— I want even—to have had, or to have still further disagreeable experiences, provided I am not held too long in any one of them.

If the moment comes to break the balance, I shall know what I am doing.

GIUSTO GERVASUTTI

We stopped on a large rock terrace, about twenty yards from the dome of ice that forms the summit, and stretched ourselves out in the sun. It was hot, and we badly wanted to sleep. We felt no shiver of joy, no ecstasy in victory. We had reached our objective, and already it lay behind us. A dream had become reality—and I felt something close to bitterness. How much finer it would be, I couldn't help thinking, to long for something all one's life, to fight for it without respite, and never to achieve it!

But this was only another episode. Down in the valley again I should at once look round for some other goal, and if it didn't exist, I would create it! I do not know why people associate a man's happiness with the satisfaction of all his desires—a kind of eternal beatitude, which could just as well be a state of complete apathy. The completely happy man would have nothing left to say, nothing left to do. For myself I prefer an unattainable happiness, always near, always elusive: the prize which vanishes every time one grasps it, to give way to another, still harder, still more distant. The moments when the heart really overflows with happiness come when the sense of life is heightened by tension and struggle—the actual moments of conquest, or more often of defeat, and not the dead moments when victory has been achieved.

WILLIAM FAULKNER

By artist I mean of course everyone who has tried to create something which was not here before him, with no other tools and material than the uncommercial ones of the human spirit; who has tried to carve, no matter how crudely, on the wall of that final oblivion, in the tongue of the human spirit, "Kilroy was here."

That is primarily, and I think in its essence, all that we ever really tried to do. And I believe we will all agree that we failed.

That what we made never quite matched and never will match the shape, the dream of perfection which we inherited and which drove us and will continue to drive us, even after each failure, until anguish frees us and the hand falls still at last.

Maybe it's just as well that we are doomed to fail, since, as long as we do fail and the hand continues to hold blood, we will try again; where, if we ever did attain the dream, match the shape, scale that ultimate peak of perfection, nothing would remain but to jump off the other side of it into suicide.

JEAN COCTEAU

Work. I accept death. But I refuse to live and be dead. After my death, all this work must live in my place. I must create a robust health for it. Solid organs.

INGMAR BERGMAN

If I could not work, my whole life would be meaningless.

HYMAN G. RICKOVER

To seek out and accept responsibility; to persevere; to be committed to excellence; to be creative and courageous; to be unrelenting in the pursuit of intellectual development; to maintain high standards of ethics and morality; and to bring these basic principles of existence to bear through active participation in life—these are some of my ideas on the goals which must be met to achieve meaning and purpose in life.

ROBERT FULTON

As the component parts of all new machines may be said to be old . . . the mechanic should sit down among levers, screws, wedges, wheels, etc. like a poet among the letters of the alphabet, considering them as the exhibition of his thoughts; in which a new arrangement transmits a new idea to the world.

Rita Levi-Montalcini

I have become persuaded that, in scientific research, neither the degree of one's intelligence nor the ability to carry out one's tasks with thoroughness and precision are factors essential to personal success and fulfillment. More important for the attaining of both ends are total dedication and a tendency to underestimate difficulties, which cause one to tackle problems that other, more critical and acute persons instead opt to avoid.

Edwin Hubble

Labour which is labour and nothing else becomes an aversion. . . . Work, to be pleasant, must be toward some great end; an end so great that dreams of it, anticipation of it overcomes all aversion to labour. So until one has an end which he identifies with his whole life, work is hardly satisfactory.

George Orwell

From a very early age, perhaps the age of five or six, I knew that when I grew up I should be a writer. Between the ages of about seventeen and twenty-four I tried to abandon this idea, but I did so with the consciousness that I was outraging my true nature and that sooner or later I should have to settle down and write books.

E. B. White

I'm glad to report that even now, at this late date, a blank sheet of paper holds the greatest excitement there is for me—more promising than a silver cloud, prettier than a little red wagon.

It holds all the hope there is, all fears. I can remember, really quite distinctly, looking a sheet of paper square in the eyes when I was seven or eight years old and thinking "This is where I belong, this is it." Having dirtied up probably a quarter of a million of them and sent them down drains and through presses, I am exhausted but not done, faithful in my fashion, and fearful only that I will die before one comes out right. . . .

— — —

When I wrote "Death of a Pig" I was simply rendering an account of what actually happened on my place—to my pig, who died, and to me, who tended him in his last hours. . . . The death of this animal moved me, heightened my awareness. To confront death, in any guise, is to identify with the victim and face what is unsettling and sobering. As I said in the piece, "I knew that what could be true of my pig could be true also of the rest of my tidy world."

Kurt Wolff

I take pleasures in using my powers and seeing them grow with the tasks to be done, seeing them doubled by struggle and obstacles. I enjoy the give and take, the opportunity to make a difference, and although I may be mistaken, I believe that the small amount of good I am able to accomplish makes up for my errors.

Anne Frank

I can't imagine having to live like Mother, Mrs. Van Daan and all the women who go about their work and are then forgotten. I need to have something besides a husband and children to devote myself to! I don't want to have lived in vain like most people. I want to be useful or bring enjoyment to all people, even those I've never met. I want to go on living even after my death!

GILBERT K. CHESTERTON

The real trouble with this world of ours is not that it is an unreasonable world, nor even that it is a reasonable one. The commonest kind of trouble is that it is nearly reasonable, but not quite. Life is not an illogicality; yet it is a trap for logicians. It looks just a little more mathematical and regular than it is; its exactitude is obvious, but its inexactitude is hidden; its wildness lies in wait.

JOHN KEATS

. . . It is a false notion that more is gained by receiving than giving—no the receiver and the giver are equal in their benefits. . . .

— — —

I find that I can have no enjoyment in the World but continual drinking of Knowledge—I find there is no worthy pursuit but the idea of doing some good for the world—some do it with their society—some with their wit—some with their benevolence—some with a sort of power of conferring pleasure and good humour on all they meet and in a thousand ways all equally dutiful to the command of Great Nature—there is but one way for me—the road lies th[r]ough application study and thought.

SAMUEL TAYLOR COLERIDGE

. . . What I am depends on what I have been. . . .

– – –

Should children be permitted to read romances, and relations of giants and magicians and genii? I know all that has been said against it; but I have formed my faith in the affirmative. I know no other way of giving the mind a love of the Great and the Whole. Those who have been led to the same truths step by step, through the constant testimony of their senses, seem to me to want a sense which I possess. They contemplate nothing but *parts*, and all *parts* are necessarily little.

– – –

The *heart* should have *fed* upon the *truth*, as insects on a leaf, till it be tinged with the colour, and show its food in every the minutest fibre.

– – –

Think, in order that you may be able to *observe*! *Observe*, in order that you may have materials to think upon! And thirdly, keep awake ever the habit of instantly *embodying* and *realising* the results of the two; but always *think*!

– – –

I can *at times* feel strongly the beauties you describe, in themselves and for themselves; but more frequently *all things* appear *little*, all the knowledge that can be acquired child's play; the universe itself! what but an immense heap of *little* things? I can contemplate nothing but *parts*, and parts are all *little*! My mind feels as if it ached to behold and know something *great*, something *one* and *indivisible*. And it is only in the faith of that that rocks or waterfalls, mountains or caverns, give me the sense of sublimity or majesty!

JAMES RUSSELL LOWELL

You say that life seems to be a struggle after nothing in particular. But you are wrong. It is a struggle after the peaceful home of the soul in a natural and loving state of life. Men are mostly unconscious of the object of their struggle, but it is always connected in some way with this. If they gain wealth and power or glory it is all to *make up for this* want, which they *feel*, but scarce know what it is. But nothing will ever supply the place of this, any more than their softest carpets will give their old age the spring and ease which arose from the pliant muscles of youth. . . .

— — —

You must have first your chaos of jostling elements and forces, the fermentation of the yet uncrystallized idea; then the brooding of the creative imagination; and then the birth of your star or comet or, unhappily too often, of your meteor, which falls to earth a shapeless jelly.

— — —

. . . The older I grow the more I am convinced that [there] are no satisfactions so deep and so permanent as our sympathies with outward nature. . . . The flowering of the buttercups is always a great and I may truly say religious event in my year.

MARY BAKER EDDY

What I am remains to be proved by the good I do.

G. H. HARDY

The case for my life, then, or for that of any one else who has been a mathematician in the same sense in which I have been one, is this: that I have added something to knowledge, and helped others to add more; and that these somethings have a value which differs in degree only, and not in kind, from that of the creations of the great mathematicians, or of any of the other artists, great or small, who have left some kind of memorial behind them.

Raymond Chandler

Retiring is a kind of dying. The best way to revive is certainly what you have in mind. Work like hell at something just a little creative. No man grows old as long as he can create. You may die in the midst of it—so may I, who am older than you are—but you don't die of lethargy.

Charles F. Kettering

You have got to be a servant to somebody or something.

— — —

Failures, *repeated* failures, are finger posts on the road to achievement. One *fails forward* toward success.

— — —

The trouble is that we don't get interested in the commonplace things—and it is the commonplace things that go to make up the universe.

— — —

We have a lot of people revolutionizing the world because they never had to present a working model.

− − −

Do something different. My God, do something different!

HENRY ADAMS

My path is a different one; and was never chosen in order to suit other people's tastes, but my own. Of course a man can't do this without appearing to think a great deal about himself, and perhaps doing so in fact. The very line he draws requires care to observe, and is invidious to everyone else. In America there is [no] such class, and the tendency is incessant to draw everyone into the main current. I have told you before that I mean to be unpopular, and do it because I must do it, or do as other people do and give up the path I chose for myself years ago. Your ideas and mine don't agree, but they never have agreed. You like the strife of the world. I detest it and despise it. You work for power. I work for my own satisfaction.

JAMES AGEE

I care mainly about just 2 things. Sometimes they seem identical or at least like binary stars, & sometimes they seem like a split which can completely destroy. They would be (1) getting as near truth and whole truth as is humanly possible, which means several sorts of 'Truth' maybe, but on the whole means spiritual life, integrity and growth; and (2) setting this (near-) truth out in the clearest and cleanest possible terms. And I feel about it in two ways which may or may not be identical; one is I believe genuine 'hunger' toward it, and the other, if it is another, is ambition, which I think would kill it.

Lewis Carroll

And so you have found out that secret—one of the deep secrets of Life—that all, that is really *worth* the doing, is what we do for *others*? Even as the old adage tells us, "What I spent, that I lost; what I gave, that I had." Casuists have tried to twist "doing good" into another form of "doing evil," and have said "you get pleasure yourself by giving this pleasure to another: so it is merely a refined kind of selfishness, as your own pleasure is a motive for what you do." I say "it is *not* selfishness, that my own pleasure should be *a* motive so long as it is not *the* motive that would outweigh the other, if the two came into collision. The "selfish man" is he who would still do the thing, even if it harmed others, so long as it gave *him* pleasure: the "unselfish man" is he who would still do the thing, even if it gave him no pleasure, so long as it pleased *others*. But, when both motives pull together, the "unselfish man" is *still* the unselfish man, even though his own pleasure *is* one of his motives!

Charles Horton Cooley

We should not care for the cathedral if we did not sense the quarry behind it.

Anne Morrow Lindbergh

It seems to me—a simple enough thought—but just realized that if you really and sincerely and passionately want to do something (and wholeheartedly, with the whole of your sincerest self) it is by doing *that* that you will be most useful, will be giving the most, will be of most individual value. I am sure Colonel Lindbergh never fussed or gave a thought to where he would be most useful or where he could give the most. He just went ahead and did what he wanted terribly to do—what the whole of him wanted sincerely and in a selfless kind of passion to do.

— — —

For the natural selectivity of the island I will have to substitute a conscious selectivity based on another sense of values—a sense of values I have become more aware of here. Island-precepts, I might call them if I could define them, signposts toward another way of living. Simplicity of living, as much as possible, to retain a true awareness of life. Balance of physical, intellectual, and spiritual life. Work without pressure. Space for significance and beauty. Time for solitude and sharing. Closeness to nature to strengthen understanding and faith in the intermittency of life: life of the spirit, creative life, and the life of human relationships.

FLORENCE NIGHTINGALE

. . . If you think that my living the Robinson Crusoe life I do is the effect of Stoicism, there never was a greater mistake. It is entirely the effect of calculation. I cannot live to work unless I give up all that makes life pleasant. People say, 'Oh see the doctors have said these 8 years she could not live 6 months— therefore it is all a mistake'. They *never* say: she has lived 8 years when the doctors said she could not live 6 months by adopting this kind of life, of sacrificing everything else in order to work. . . . But I have ceased to try to make anybody understand this. I do hope I am getting wiser in this respect—not *explaining* . . . I NEVER said it was 'best for me'. All I said was, it was best for the work— or rather it is the only way in which the work could be done.

WILLIAM CHARLES MACREADY

As I reflect, look back on my past life, the thought of being rich, the ambition to be so, never once entered into my mind. I was most anxious to be independent. . . . Thus I am what the world would call a poor man. I trust, in reality, a contented and grateful one.

JEAN RHYS

. . . I know that to write as well as I can is my truth and why I was born.

LOUIS PASTEUR

When after long endeavor, certainty is reached, the reward is one of the keenest joys of which the human soul is capable.

OLIVER WENDELL HOLMES

. . . The true end of life is the exercise of one's faculties. . . .

LEO STEIN

It is commonplace that one must recognize one's faults in order to correct them, but one must be prepared to recognize one's false positions in order to evolve beyond them.

ALEXIS DE TOCQUEVILLE

It seems to me that my true worth is above all in works of the mind; that I am worth more in thought than in action; and that, if there remains anything of me in this world, it will be much more the trace of what I have written than the recollection of what I will have done.

ALDOUS HUXLEY

Society at large is obviously for ever doomed to a continual process of self-frustration; but for individuals there remain enormous potentialities, both physical and psychological–potentialities which, in the ordinary course of events, remain completely unrealized, but which, if one knows how and is prepared to take the trouble, one can realize. It looks as though the overwhelming majority of people were content to live at about twenty per cent of their potential capacities. The discovery of methods for realizing the full hundred per cent–this seems to be about the only sensible and constructive thing that one can do in this lunatic asylum we've gotten into.

MARY WOLLSTONECRAFT

Ah! my friend, you know not the ineffable delight, the exquisite pleasure, which arises from a unison of affection and desire, when the whole soul and senses are abandoned to a lively imagination, that renders every emotion delicate and rapturous. . . . These emotions, more or less strong, appear to me to be the distinctive characteristic of genius, the foundation of taste, and of that exquisite relish for the beauties of nature, of which the common herd of eaters and drinkers and *child-begeters* certainly have no idea. You will smile at an observation that has just occurred to me:–I consider those minds as the most strong and original, whose imagination acts as the stimulus to their senses.

KATHERINE ANNE PORTER

·I think it is the most curious lack of judgment to publish before you are ready. If there are echoes of other people in your work, you're not ready. If anybody has to help you rewrite your story, you're not ready.

JACQUES LIPCHITZ

I am still, like my father, putting one brick after another in the building of a house, attempting to make a final statement. I would like to be able to make this at the end of my life, or, as my father always said, "to come to the roof."

W. B. YEATS

My great wish being to do no work in which I should have to make a compromise with my artistic conscience.

JAMES MERRILL

Freedom to be oneself is all very well; the greater freedom is not to be oneself.

LOUISE BOURGEOIS

I am what I do.

MARIE HENRI BEYLE

Let us put the present to good use, for our minutes are numbered. The hour I've spent fretting has nonetheless brought me that much nearer death. Let us work, for work is the father of pleasure, but let us never fret. Let us reflect sanely before deciding on our course; once our decision is taken we ought never to change our minds. With a steadfast heart, anything can be attained. Give us talent; the day will come when I'll regret the time I've wasted. . . .

ANTON CHEKHOV

I rest all my hopes on the future. I am only twenty-six. Perhaps I shall succeed in doing something, though time flies fast.

— — —

Medicine is my lawful wedded wife, and literature my mistress. When one gets on my nerves, I spend the night with the other. This may be somewhat disorganized, but then again it's not as boring, and anyway, neither one loses anything by my duplicity. If I didn't have medicine, I'd never devote my spare time and thoughts to literature.

— — —

There is no doubt in my mind that my study of medicine has had a serious impact on my literary activities. It significantly broadened the scope of my observations and enriched me with knowledge whose value for me as a writer only a doctor can appreciate. It also served as a guiding influence; my intimacy with medicine probably helped me to avoid many mistakes.

— — —

Anyone who says the artist's field is all answers and no questions has never done any writing or had any dealings with imagery. The artist observes, selects, guesses and synthesizes. The very fact of these actions presupposes a question; if he hadn't asked himself a question at the start, he would have nothing to guess and nothing to select. To put it briefly, I will conclude with some psychiatry: if you deny that creativity involves questions and intent, you have to admit that the artist creates without premeditation or purpose, in a state of unthinking emotionality. And so if any author were to boast to me that he'd written a story from pure inspiration without first having thought over his intentions, I'd call him a madman.

— — —

If a man knows the theory of the circulatory system, he is rich. If he learns the history of religion and the song "I remember a Marvelous Moment" in addition, he is the richer, not the poorer, for it. We are consequently dealing entirely in pluses. It is for this reason that geniuses have never fought among themselves and Goethe the poet coexisted splendidly with Goethe the naturalist.

Amelia Earhart

Now and then women should do for themselves what men have already done—occasionally what men have not done—thereby establishing themselves as persons, and perhaps encouraging other women toward greater independence of thought and action.

Henry James

If I can only *concentrate* myself: this is the great lesson of life. I have hours of unspeakable reaction against my smallness of production; my wretched habits of work—or of un-work; my levity, my vagueness of mind, my perpetual failure to focus my attention, to absorb myself, to look things in the face, to invent, to produce, in a word. I shall be 40 years old in April next: it's a horrible fact! I believe however that I have learned how to work and that it is in moments of forced idleness, almost alone, that these melancholy reflections seize me. When I am really at work, I'm happy, I feel strong, I see many opportunities ahead. It is the only thing that makes life endurable. I must make some great efforts during the next few years, however, if I wish not to have been on the whole a failure. I shall have been a failure unless I do something *great*! . . .

ALBERT CAMUS

Unbridled sex leads to a philosophy of the non-significance of the world. Chastity on the other hand gives the world a meaning.

— — —

Any life directed toward money is a death. Renascence lies in disinterestedness.

— — —

Philanthropic Calvinists negate whatever is not reason because reason, to their way of thinking, can make them masters of all, even of nature. Of all except Beauty. Beauty eludes such a scheme. This is why it is so hard for an artist to be a revolutionary, even though he is a rebel as an artist. This is why it is impossible for him to be a killer.

— — —

The sea: I didn't lose myself in it; I found myself in it.

GAMALIEL BRADFORD

I was reading yesterday the *Letters* of Keats: the purest artist of our latter days. And they call me back to myself again; for lately I have been wandering. They teach me again that there is nothing in the world, for me at least, but art and beauty; that if I cannot live for that, I had better die. I wish that I could reveal the intense longing which I have to write something great; not for fame, not that the world may praise; but to know—not to dream, or fancy, or hope—but to know that the spirit of Beauty has laid her finger upon me and consecrated me to her service.

NAPOLEON I

We should not pass from the earth without leaving traces to carry our memory to posterity.

BEETHOVEN

From the heart—may it go to the heart.

SHERWOOD ANDERSON

If you handle your material in a cheap way, you'll grow cheap.

— — —

Impotence comes when men no longer shape things with their own hands.

— — —

Love of craft is to man what love of children is to women.

— — —

Give me a sunshiny day, a story to work on and I think life is fascinating.

JEAN JACQUES ROUSSEAU

Men do nothing excellent but by imitation of nature.

– – –

To live is not merely to breathe; it is to act; it is to make use of all our organs, functions, and faculties. This alone gives us the consciousness of existence.

H. G. WELLS

For me my master gift and passion is imaginative construction and especially in relation to the making for humanity of an ideal world-state. To that I seek to subordinate all my other gifts, powers and passion.

CHARLES DARWIN

Whenever I have found out that I have blundered, or that my work has been imperfect, and when I have been contemptuously criticized, and even when I have been overpraised, so that I have felt mortified, it has been my greatest comfort to say hundreds of times to myself that "I have worked as hard and as well as I could, and no man can do more than this."

– – –

It is absurd to talk of one animal being higher than another. . . . People often talk of the wonderful event of intellectual Man appearing–the appearance of insects with other senses is more wonderful. . . . Who with the face of the earth covered with the most beautiful savannahs & forests dare to say that intellectuality is only aim in this world.

CHRIS BONINGTON

When she married me, Wendy knew that I could never give up the mountains, they were too much a part of me. Nor could I start climbing at a lower standard, for, to me, the joy of climbing is to stretch my powers, my experience, my ability to the limit, and yet still have something in reserve. I don't enjoy danger for its own sake, certainly hate being afraid, as I inevitably am if things get our of control–if, say, I am out of condition on a climb that is too hard for me. But when on peak form, the exhilaration of climbing is at its greatest when I am in a potentially dangerous position yet feel in complete control.

GLENN GOULD

... I believe that the justification of art is the internal combustion it ignites in the hearts of men and not its shallow, externalized, public manifestations. The purpose of art is not the release of a momentary ejection of adrenaline but is, rather, the gradual, lifelong construction of a state of wonder and serenity.

J. R. R. TOLKIEN

We are finite creatures with absolute limitations upon the powers of our soul-body structure in either action or endurance. *Moral* failure can only be asserted, I think, when a man's efforts or endurance falls *short* of his limits, and the blame decreases as that limit is closer approached.

JOSEPH CONRAD

Everyone must walk in the light of his own heart's gospel. No man's light is good to any of his fellows. That's my creed from beginning to end. That's my view of life,–a view that rejects all formulas, dogmas and principles of other people's making. These are only a web of illusions. We are too varied. Another man's truth is only a dismal lie to me.

VITA SACKVILLE-WEST

Is it better to be extremely ambitious, or rather modest? Probably the latter is safer; but I *hate* safety, and would rather fail gloriously than dingily succeed.

D. H. LAWRENCE

'Be all things to all men.' That isn't my ideal, it seems like my fate. But really, one *can* only be towards each person that which corresponds to him, more or less.

- - -

When you come to think that we are such transitory little dots, it is no wonder we are sometimes lonely. Religion, work, love all link us on to an eternity—the one of singing, the other of influencing, the last of being.

JACK KEROUAC

As far as creative powers go, I have them and I know it. All I need now is faith in myself . . . [and] only from there can a faith truly dilate and expand to "mankind." I must change my life, *now*, I have reached 21 and I am in dead earnest about all things.

PHILIP LARKIN

Education should consist of helping a child to know its faculty—its ability, rather. Each man (generally) has one talent. Education should help him find it—should make the child say 'of course' as it recognises with delight what it has always potentially known.

Maria Callas

Singing for me is not an act of pride, but an effort to elevate towards those heavens where everything is harmony.

Ayn Rand

. . . I have only one religion: the sublime in human nature. There is nothing to approach the sanctity of the highest type of man possible and there is nothing that gives me the same reverent feeling, the feeling when one's spirit wants to kneel, bareheaded. Do not call it hero-worship, because it is more than that. It is a kind of strange and improbable white heat where admiration becomes religion, and religion becomes philosophy, and philosophy—the whole of one's life.

— — —

But the truth of the matter is that one finds worthwhile men and women among *people who work*. Follow me here very carefully, forgetting the cheap generalities which all our modern minds have been stuffed with. I do not mean LABOR. I do not mean people who have to earn their living. I do not mean proletarians. I do not mean tearooms. I mean what you and I understand by the term of "competent people." People who love to work, who are good at it, serious about it and concerned primarily with it. Bright, creative, productive, ambitious people. People who get money for their work, but who do not work primarily for the money—whether it's a weekly pay envelope or a thousand dollar bonus. People who are ambitious—not to climb socially, not to get wealth or titles—but ambitious to do more and more work of a better and better kind.

JACK LONDON

I look forward to a time when man shall progress upon something worthier and higher than his stomach, when there will be a finer incentive to impel men to action than the incentive of to-day, which is the incentive of the stomach. I retain my belief in the nobility and excellence of the human. I believe that spiritual sweetness and unselfishness will conquer the gross gluttony of to-day.

— — —

Every man, at the beginning of his career (whether laying bricks or writing books or anything else), has two choices. He may choose immediate happiness, or ultimate happiness. . . . He who chooses ultimate happiness, and has the ability, and works hard, will find that the reward for his effort is cumulative, that the interest on his energy invested is compounded. The artisan who is industrious, steady, reliant, is suddenly, one day, advanced to a foremanship with increased wages. Now is that advance due to what he did that day, or the day before? Ah, no, it is due to the long years of industry and steadiness. The same with the reputation of a business man or artist. The thing grows and compounds. He is not only "paid for having done something once upon a time," . . . but he has been paid for continuing to do something through quite a period of time.

— — —

A choice of ultimate happiness in preference to proximate happiness, when the element of chance is given due consideration, is, I believe, the wisest course for a man to follow under the sun. He that chooses proximate happiness is a brute: he that chooses immortal happiness is an ass; but he that chooses ultimate happiness knows his business.

Christopher Isherwood

I'm on my own. My life will be what I make of it.

Edward Abbey

I lie awake and think: Sitting in the Lobo Theater, Saturday afternoon, I was haunted by something like the conviction of sin. An original sin? The feeling of nothing, of nothingness. *Nihil ex nihilo.* A terrible dread. Why? The belief that I was, that I am, pissing my life away.

> *"Any way you turn*
> *Any way you look*
> *You have pissed away your life."*

I am now thirty-three, like Christ, and in the middle of the journey, like Dante. If there is any greatness in me, if I have a spirit and purpose here, then I must very soon drag it out of my guts. Tear truth from my entrails.

Winston S. Churchill

Come on now all you young men, all over the world. . . . These are the years! Don't be content with things as they are. . . . Enter upon your inheritance, accept your responsibilities. . . . Don't take No for an answer. Never submit to failure. Do not be fobbed off with mere personal success or acceptance. You will make all kinds of mistakes; but as long as you are generous and true, and also fierce, you cannot hurt the world or even seriously distress her. She was made to be wooed and won by youth. She has lived and thrived only by repeated subjugations.

CHARLIE CHAPLIN

If only someone had used salesmanship, had read a stimulating preface to each study that could have titillated my mind, infused me with fancy instead of facts, amused and intrigued me with the legerdemain of numbers, romanticised maps, given me a point of view about history and taught me the music of poetry, I might have become a scholar.

– – –

Over the years I have discovered that ideas come through an intense desire for them; continually desiring, the mind becomes a watch-tower on the look-out for incidents that may excite the imagination—music, a sunset, may give image to an idea.

I would say, pick a subject that will stimulate you, elaborate it and involve it, then, if you can't develop it further, discard it and pick another. Elimination from accumulation is the process of finding what you want.

How does one get ideas? By sheer perseverance to the point of madness. One must have a capacity to suffer anguish and sustain enthusiasm over a long period of time. Perhaps it's easier for some people than others, but I doubt it.

– – –

Even the beginner with talent must be taught technique, for no matter how great his gifts, he must have the skill to make them effective.

– – –

The whole scene lasted seventy seconds, but it took five days of retaking to get it right. This was not the girl's fault, but partly my own, for I had worked myself into a neurotic state of wanting perfection. *City Lights* took more than a year to make.

DAVID OGILVY

The mission of a great school should . . . be to inspire you with a taste for scholarship which will last you *all your life*.

BARBARA McCLINTOCK

I was just so interested in what I was doing I could hardly wait to get up in the morning and get at it. One of my friends, a geneticist, said I was a child, because only children can't wait to get up in the morning to get at what they want to do.

LANDON CABELL GARLAND

All true education is from within—the energizing of the mind itself. Your teachers cannot study for you. We may remove some obstacles from the way; we may save you from wandering into harmful bypaths, but you will have to do the hard and steady and systematic work . . . [although] all the learning in the world cannot substitute for a moral principle in shaping the conduct of life.

VOLTAIRE

Life is long enough for him who knows how to use it. Working and thinking extend its limits.

BERNARD SHAW

I never wanted to be a writer. I wanted to be a painter. I wanted to be a musician. But I couldnt draw. I couldnt compose. If anyone had taught me I could have been a mediocre artist or painter or actor or singer or pianist. But nobody taught me; and I was a born writer. You must use the talent you have, not the talent you have only a taste for. You cannot really taste the talent you are born with, just as you cannot taste water because it is always in your mouth. . . .

— — —

Happiness is not the object of life: life has no object: it is an end in itself; and courage consists in the readiness to sacrifice happiness for an intenser quality of life.

SIDNEY POITIER

There is a dimension not yet tampered with, at least by me, and that is to be able to work . . . in such a way that when the experience happens it has about it an encompassing effect on an audience. Encompassing, in that they become a part of the total, so that there is not a theatre and there is not a stage.

EDWARD O. WILSON

. . . Creativity in science, as in art, depends as much on self-image as on talent. To be highly successful the scientist must be confident enough to steer for the blue water, abandoning sight of land for a while. He values risk for its own sake. He keeps in mind that the footnotes of forgotten treatises are strewn with the names of the gifted but timid. If on the other hand he chooses like the vast majority of his colleagues to hug the coast, he must be fortunate enough to possess what I like to define as optimum intelligence for normal science: bright enough to see what needs to be done but not so bright as to suffer boredom doing it.

VÁCLAV HAVEL

. . . Human responsibility is precisely the agent by which one first defines oneself as a person vis-a-vis the universe, that is, as the miracle of Being that one is. On the one hand, it is only thus that one defines and so infuses meaning into one's dependency on the world; on the other hand, it is only thus that one definitively separates oneself from the world as a sovereign and independent being; it is only thus that one, as it were, stands on one's own two feet. I would say that responsibility for oneself is a knife we use to carve out our own inimitable features in the panorama of Being; it is the pen with which we write into the history of Being that story of the fresh creation of the world that each new human existence always is.

— — —

What does "responsibility" mean in this extreme sense, responsibility not only to the world, but also "for the world," as though I myself were to be judged for how the world turns out? . . . That curious feeling of "responsibility for the world" can probably only be felt by someone who is really (consciously or unconsciously) in touch, within himself, with "the absolute horizon of Being," who communicates or struggles with it in some way, who draws from it meaning, hope and faith, who has genuinely (through inner experience) grasped it. . . . In other words: by perceiving ourselves as part of the river, we accept our responsibility for the river as a whole. . . .

ALFRED TENNYSON

Come my friends,
'Tis not too late to seek a newer world.
Push off, and sitting well in order smite
The sounding furrows; for my purpose holds

To sail beyond the sunset . . . till I die . . .
To strive, to seek, to find, and not to yield.

DYLAN THOMAS

God is the country of the spirit, and each of us is given a little holding of ground in that country, it is our duty to explore that holding to gain certain impressions by such exploring, to stabilise as laws the most valuable of these impressions, and, as far as we can, to abide by them.

— — —

It's work that counts, madam, genius so often being a capacity for aching pains.

EUGENE IONESCO

The creation of a theatrical work is a walk in the forest, an exploration, a conquest, the conquest of unknown realities, unknown sometimes to the author himself when he begins his work.

— — —

One can't not be interested in technique. A writer can't not be interested in his means of expression, and in a sense the history of any art is the history of its means of expression. Only you should first of all be interested in what you have to say, then in the means that enable you to express it, and not first of all in technique. Actually, the quest for form and the quest for content should mean the same thing because everything is both form and content simultaneously. In art, you are trying to translate certain incommunicable things, incommunicable not because they cannot basically be communicated but because they have not yet been expressed. When you think about it, things are incommunicable in the beginning because they have not yet been communicated, and incommunicable in the end because the expressions that prop them up have been worn out. I personally am trying to express certain inner realities; images that suddenly loom up.

PRIMO LEVI

Sympathy is often a means of getting away with incompetence. Italy is full of attractive people who are very *simpatico* and don't know their trade.

– – –

Another virtue that the chemist's trade develops is patience, not to be in a hurry. Today chemistry is completely changed; it is rapid chemistry. Today the analysis of a mineral is no longer manual. It is done by machine and takes a few minutes, where before it took weeks. Naturally, it was inconvenient having to work a whole week to analyze the mineral, but this made it possible to develop other virtues, which in fact are those of perseverance, not getting discouraged, assiduous application. . . . It is clear that from a practical point of view a machine-made analysis is more convenient. But manual analysis, like all manual work, has a formative value; it is too similar to our origins as mammals to be neglected.

– – –

. . . A friend of mine used to say that in order to do things, "one mustn't have time." Time is an eminently compressible material.

WILFRED OWEN

Without offering anything definite, he interests himself in my future, mightily, and . . . tries to convert me to 'Business'. In particular he lauds the position of commercial traveller and apparently nothing would please him better than to see me fairly launched in that line. Now, I have a most praiseworthy desire to get at the root of all evil; but it seems to me that the digging would be too long and laborious. I have every confidence that if I wholly gave myself up to fortune building, and were content to work, and working, wait, I should 'arrive' within ten or twenty years. I consider, however, that that would be a literal losing of my soul; for that those things which my heart would put forth would then come out no more; and those things which my mind would take in, would then enter no more.

All I ask is to be held above the barren waters of want, and moving over the darkness of those waters to brood and to create. Woe is me, should I take to battling with the stream, and wet my wings of imagination!

M. CAREY THOMAS

An English man Joseph Beck was here to dinner the other day and he don't believe in the Education of Women. Neither does Cousin Frank King and my such a disgusson as they had. Mother of course was for. They said that they didn't see any good of a womans learning Latin or Greek it didn't make any more entertaining to their *husbands*. A woman had plenty of other things to do sewing, cooking taking care of children dressing and flirting. "What noble elevating things for a whole life time to be occupied with." In fact they talked as if the whole end and aim of a woman's life was to get *married* and when she attained that *greatest state of earthly bliss* it was her duty to amuse her husband and to learn nothing; never to exercise the powers of her mind so that he might have the *exquisite* pleasure of knowing more than his wife. . . . [They meant women] ought to be *mere dolls* for men to be amused with, to kiss, fondle, pet and love maybe, but as for associating with them on terms of equality they wouldn't think of such a thing. . . . I got perfectly enraged. How *unjust*—how narrow-minded—how *utterly uncomprehensible* to deny that women ought to be educated and worse than all to deny that they have equal powers of mind. If I ever live and grow up my *one* aim and consentrated purpose *shall* be and is to show that a woman *can learn can reason can compete* with men in the grand fields. . . . My greatest hope and ambition is to be an author, an essayist, an historian, to write hearty earnest true books that may do their part towards elevating the human race towards inducing some, at least, to let their money bags on which they are wasting such a wealth of hope and desire and intellect drop from their hands and aim at something higher than merely providing for our miserable earthly exhistance, to look higher than the miserable disappointments of every day life and . . . [live on] their duty to their fellow men. In the words of Longfellow

> "When departing leave behind me
> Footprints on the sands of time
> Footprints that perhaps another sailing
> on lifes dreary main
> A forlorn a shiprecked brother
> Seeing may take heart again."

It seems to me that is a purpose worth striving after. Oh may it not be *only* a purpose.

Jean Nicolas Rimbaud

I enjoy a certain consideration because of my humane behavior. I have never injured anybody. On the contrary, I do a little good whenever I can—it is my only pleasure.

W. Somerset Maugham

I am never so happy as when a new thought occurs to me and a new horizon gradually discovers itself before my eyes. A fresh idea dawns upon me and I feel myself uplifted from the workaday world to the blue empyrean of the spirit. Detached for a moment from all earthly cares I seem to walk on air.

F. Scott Fitzgerald

Now, insofar as your course is concerned, there is no question of your dropping mathematics and taking the easiest way to go into Vassar, and being one of the girls fitted for nothing except to reflect other people without having any particular character of your own. I want you to take mathematics up to the limit of what the school offers. I want you to take physics and I want you to take chemistry. I don't care about your English courses or your French courses at present. If you don't know two languages and the ways that men chose to express their thoughts in those languages by this time, then you don't sound like my daughter. You are an only child, but that doesn't give you any right to impose on that fact.

I want you to know certain basic scientific principles, and I feel that it is impossible to learn them unless you have gone as far into mathematics as coordinate geometry. *I don't want you to give up mathematics next year.* I learned about writing from doing something that I didn't have any taste for.

Luis W. Alvarez

At the University of Chicago a member of the gymnastics team told me that Chicago had the best coach and usually the best team in the Big Ten. I stopped by the gymnasium one afternoon in my freshman year and was hooked. I spent two hours every day for the next four years practicing gymnastics, winning a varsity letter in my senior year. When I watch gymnastic competitions today, I'm struck by the routines, most of which had not been invented when I was a gymnast. The single most important characteristic of my success in physics has been invention. Whenever anything has interested me, I have instinctively tried to invent a new or better way of doing it. Why didn't I invent any new gymnastic routines? I'm astonished that I could have spent ten hours a week for four years doing and watching gymnastics and never try to improve it. Intellectually I was a different person then from the person I later became.

The world of mathematics and theoretical physics is hierarchical. That was my first exposure to it. There's a limit beyond which one cannot progress. The differences between the limiting abilities of those on successively higher steps of the pyramid are enormous. I have not seen described anywhere the shock a talented man experiences when he finds, late in his academic life, that there are others enormously more talented than he. I have personally seen more tears shed by grown men and women over this discovery than I would have believed possible. Most of those men and women shift to fields where they can compete on more equal terms. The few who choose not to face reality have a difficult time.

Dad never claimed he might have won that Nobel Prize, but he did say more than once that he would have been a better researcher if he had occasionally let his mind wander over the full range of his work. He advised me to sit every few months in my reading chair for an entire evening, close my eyes, and try to think of new problems to solve. I took his advice very seriously and have been glad ever since that I did.

LINUS PAULING

My experience is that it is about as easy to do something myself as to get somebody else to do it, and if I do it myself I am satisfied with it, whereas if I get somebody else to do it I am not.

— — —

Some years ago I decided that I had been making use of my unconscious in a well-defined way. In attacking a difficult new problem I might work for several days at my desk, making appropriate calculations and trying to find a solution to the problem. I developed the habit of thinking about a problem as I lay in bed, waiting to go to sleep. I might think about the same problem for several nights in succession, while I was reading or making calculations about it during the day. Then I would stop working on the problem, and, after a while, stop thinking about it in the period before going to sleep. Some weeks or months, or even years might go by, and then, suddenly, an idea that represented a solution to the problem would burst into my consciousness.

SAMUEL JOHNSON

Nothing will ever be attempted if all possible objections must be first overcome.

EMILY DICKINSON

I have dared to do strange things—bold things, and have asked no advice from any.

Anne Bancroft

I think my job as an actress—the job of my talent or what I want to do with my talent—is to give to the people what I believe are certain realities of life, certain truths. Because I know one of the hardest things in life is to not only see a truth but to accept it. It's a very hard thing, reality—to see and accept and to realize it as a reality and a truth. I could get up and I could lecture and just lecture and lecture and lecture that this is a reality, that anything that puts the spirit in a dungeon is a sin, and that the greatest joy in the world is liberating that. And so I could get up and make a speech, but I don't think an audience would be quite so willing to accept it as they would be when it is embellished within an entertainment form, you see. If you put it in an entertaining form and then say what you want to say to the world—and you put it within the theatrical form—I think it gets to them easier, more easily. They don't feel that it's being thrust on them. They're not only getting a truth, but they're getting it done in this way, in this charming way or in this theatrical way or in this dynamic way—and it's easier, I think.

Alphonse Karr

You are not an author, as you are not an artist, unless from your own heart you add to the treasures of art something which would not have existed if you had not been born.

T. E. Lawrence

Writing has been my inmost self all my life, and I can never put my full strength into anything else. Yet the same force, I know, put into action upon material things would move them, make me famous and effective. The everlasting effort to write is like trying to fight a feather-bed.

\- \- \-

Some instinct tells me that the people who fuss about the money of the world are on the wrong tack.

GALEN

Employment is nature's physician, and is essential to human happiness.

JANE AUSTEN

I must keep to my own style and go on in my own way.

CYRIL CONNOLLY

A great writer creates a world of his own and his readers are proud to live in it. A lesser writer may entice them in for a moment, but soon he will watch them filing out.

FRANK LLOYD WRIGHT

The effect of any genius is seldom seen in its time. Nor can the full effects of genius ever be traced or seen. Human affairs are flowing. What we call life is plastic in everything; it is a becoming and is so in spite of all efforts to fix it with names, all endeavors to make it static to man's will. As a pebble cast into the ocean sets up reactions lost in distance and time, so does a man's genius go on infinitely, forever. For genius *is* an expression of principle. Therefore in no way does genius ever run counter to genius nor ever could.

— — —

Recounting facts does not constitute truth. Truth lies deeper. It is something we feel but can seldom touch with facts.

— — —

Escape is not freedom. The only freedom we have a right to ask is the freedom to seek—to be—to believe—and to love the beautiful as our souls conceive it, perceive it or as we can feel it.

— — —

Only Imagination using facts honestly as mere structural material can so imbue fact with Spirit as to make another life, the life of Man, take fresh inspiring Form. The work of art.

— — —

The Creative Conscience then lies in the artist, as in manhood, in himself. As the fashioner of FORM it demands the whole truth or suffers. It gives the whole truth—or suffers.

CHARLES SEIGNEUR DE SAINT-ÉVREMOND

It is a characteristic of great men never to precipitate anything and never to get impatient over anything. . . . It takes a certain period of time to bring great plans to maturity. Those who know how to wait are usually paid with interest for their patience; for, in many things, delaying achieves more than strength. . . .

ANTONÍN DVORÁK

To have a beautiful idea is nothing special. The idea comes from itself and if it is beautiful and great, man can take no credit for that. But to develop the idea well and make something great from it, that is the most difficult, that is—art!

— — —

To imitate the truth slavishly may be a good occupation, but to find the truth through one's imagination is better, much better.

BORIS PASTERNAK

I could never say, "The more poets—good ones and varied—the better!" because a multiplicity of people working in art constitutes unpromising, negative grounds for the emergence of someone, no matter who, someone extremely conscientious and humble, who will redeem their plurality with his singularity, redeem the broad exposure to their excesses with the laborious productivity of his suffering.

ALBERT EINSTEIN

Strenuous intellectual work and looking at God's Nature are the reconciling, fortifying, yet relentlessly strict angels that shall lead me through all of life's troubles.

— — —

The life of the individual has meaning only insofar as it aids in making the life of every living thing nobler and more beautiful.

– – –

[The scientist's] religious feeling takes the form of a rapturous amazement at the harmony of natural law, which reveals an intelligence of such superiority that, compared with it, all the systematic thinking and acting of human beings is an utterly insignificant reflection. This feeling is the guiding principle of his life and work, in so far as he succeeds in keeping himself from the shackles of selfish desire.

– – –

I have never looked upon ease and happiness as ends in themselves—such an ethical basis I call the ideal of a pigsty. . . . The ideals which have lighted my way, and time after time have given me new courage to face life cheerfully, have been Kindness, Beauty, and Truth.

– – –

That a man can take pleasure in marching in fours to the strains of a band is enough to make me despise him. He has only been given his big brain by mistake; unprotected spinal marrow was all he needed. . . . Heroism on command, senseless violence, and all the loathsome nonsense that goes by the name of patriotism—how passionately I hate them! . . . My opinion of the human race is high enough that I believe this bogey would have disappeared long ago, had the sound sense of the peoples not been systematically corrupted by commercial and political interests acting through the schools and the Press.

– – –

It is not enough to teach man a speciality. Through it he may become a kind of useful machine, but not a harmoniously developed personality. It is essential that the student acquire an understanding of and a lively feeling for values. He must acquire a vivid sense of the beautiful and of the morally good. Otherwise he—with his specialized knowledge—more closely resembles a well-trained dog than a harmoniously developed person. He must learn to understand the motives of human beings, their illusions, and their sufferings in order to acquire a proper relationship to individual fellow-men and to the community.

These precious things are conveyed to the younger generation through personal contact with those who teach, not—or at least not in the main—through textbooks. It is this that primarily constitutes and preserves culture. This is what I have in mind when I recommend the 'humanities' as important, not just dry specialized knowledge in the fields of history and philosophy.

– – –

Overemphasis on the competitive system and premature specialization on the ground of immediate usefulness kill the spirit on which all cultural life depends, specialized knowledge included.

– – –

The crippling of individuals I consider the worst evil of capitalism. Our whole educational system suffers from this evil. An exaggerated competitive attitude is inculcated into the student, who is trained to worship acquisitive success as a preparation for his future career.

\- \- \-

Imagination is more important than knowledge. Knowledge is limited, imagination encircles the world.

\- \- \-

If you want to live a happy life, tie it to a goal, not to people or things.

\- \- \-

We have to do the best we can. This is our sacred human responsibility.

ISAAC BASHEVIS SINGER

Every writer must write on his own topics, which are connected with his main passions, with the things he is pondering about, or brooding over. This is in part what gives a writer his charm and makes him genuine. It's only the amateur who will take any topic. He will go somewhere, he will hear a story—something, anything—and immediately it will become "his story." The real writer writes only stories which are connected with his personality, with his character, with his way of seeing the world.

JOHN BURROUGHS

A Mr. Clark has just called—an engineer on some northern railway, deeply interested in birds, and in psychology. His appreciation of my books knows no bounds. He says, as others often say, that I have little conception of what my books have done for people. I hardly know why I am so indifferent to such testimony. It goes in one ear and out the other. The reason probably is that I did not write my books to please the public. I wrote them to please myself. If I had made any sacrifices, or undergone any hardships or self-denial, to please others, I should be pleased if I found that I had succeeded. But there is no merit in my success; I could not help it; it was all for my own pleasure.

NICHOLAS BERDYAEV

In the case of man, that which he creates is more expressive of him than that which he begets. The image of the artist and the poet is imprinted more clearly on his works than on his children.

VIOLET TREFUSIS

The singing lyre that is vouchsafed to a thousand inarticulates—the artist god, yes! The artist who should be fed each day with new intuitions, new conditions, new loves and new hatreds to be kept singing for humanity! The artist—the supreme luxury that the gods toss to the world when it feels it must either speak or die!

And the woman perchance will smile when she reads this, and her friends will say what an ideal wife and mother she makes, which is true, but the artist will shrink in horror from the imputation of smugness that these words cannot fail to convey—

God knows it is aesthetically incorrect that the artist should be hampered by domesticity, Pegasus harnessed to a governess-cart, Marysas playing the harmonium. I shut my eyes, I seem to see, despite the Demeter-like attributes with which the woman is undoubtedly crowned, not the woman, but the artist striding the mountain tops, silent, inspired and alone.

WALLACE FOWLIE

Of all the arts, poetry is the one in which the power of man's spirit is best measured.

Federico García Lorca

I want to be a poet, from head to toe, living and dying by poetry. I'm beginning to *see clearly*. A high awareness of my future work is taking hold of me and an almost dramatic feeling of my responsibility constrains me . . . I don't know . . . it seems that *I'm giving birth* to new forms and an absolutely defined balance.

Edwin Arlington Robinson

How long do you think a man can live in hell? I think he can live there a good many years–a hundred, perhaps, if his bowels keep in decent order–but he isn't going to have a very good time. No man can have a very good time–of the right sort, at any rate–until he understands things; and how the devil is a man to understand things in an age like this, when the whole trend of popular thought is in the wrong direction–not only that, but proud of the way it is taking? The age is all right, material progress is all right, Herbert Spencer is all right, hell is all right. These things are temporal necessities, but they are damned uninteresting to one who can get a glimpse of the real light through the clouds of time. It is that glimpse that makes me wish to live and see it out.

S. M. Ulam

I also believe that changing fields of work during one's life is rejuvenating. If one stays too much with the same subfields or the same narrow class of problems a sort of self-poisoning prevents acquisition of new points of view and one may become stale.

John Steinbeck

This book is my sole responsibility and I must stick to it and nothing more. This book is my life now or must be. When it is done, then will be the time for another life. But, not until it is done.

ROBERT FROST

The greatest nonsense of our time has been the solution of the school problem by forsaking knowledge for thought. From learning to thinking—it sounds like progress. But it is illusory. Thought is good but knowledge is at least no worse and thought is no substitute for knowledge. Knowledge is certainly more material to the imagination than thought. The point is that neither knowledge nor thought is an end and neither is nearer an end than the other. The end they both serve, perhaps equally, is deeds in such accepted and nameable forms as the sonnet, the story, the vase, the portrait, the landscape, the hat, the scythe, the gun, the food, the breed, the house, the home, the factory, the election, the government. We must always be about definite deeds to be growing.

IVOR GURNEY

What the artist needs is not so much technique, as a greater appreciation of beauty so generally overlooked. Why should not the violet be considered as the chief work of God visible to us? And yet it is the bunch and the coloured vase that must make up most people's mental idea of that lovely thought of innocence. The Artist must learn to feel the beauty of all things, and the sense of instant communion with God that such perception will bring. "To feel Eternity in an hour". Blake knew that to attain to this height, not greater dexterity, but greater humility and beauty of thought were needed. And the composer must judge his work by this standard—that his work be born of sincere and deep emotion sufficiently controlled by the intellect to be coherent and clear. And if his thought be deep and worthy, who shall say it will not shape its proper expression?

VINCENT VAN GOGH

Of the drawings which I shall show you now, I think only this: I hope they will prove to you that my work does not remain stationary, but progresses in a reasonable direction. As to the money value of my work, I do not pretend to anything less than that it would greatly astonish me if in time my work did not become just as salable as that of others. Of course I cannot tell whether that will happen *now* or *later*, but I think the surest way, which *cannot* fail, is to work from nature faithfully and energetically. Sooner or later feeling and love for nature meet a response from people who are interested in art. It is the painter's duty to be entirely absorbed by nature and to use all his intelligence to express sentiment in his work so that it becomes intelligible to other people. In my opinion working for the market is not exactly the right way; on the contrary, it means fooling art lovers. The true painters have not done this; the sympathy they eventually received was the result of their sincerity.

JAMES JONES

But Ive taught myself a trick which is to do all my *thinking* when I am not *working*. Thus, in effect, I really employ two levels of creativity; the thinking level, and the working level. And I close the door on the one when I open the door on the other, and vice versa. I think up what I want to say when Im *not* working, and deliberately forget it when I *am* working. Thus I think up meaning, and organization and direction and often even individual episodes (which are the only things I make notes on), but when I sit down to work I close this part off and write only to make it real, and often in so doing find Ive changed course completely—while still hanging to the original skeleton. But it is a mistake to think I do not work *consciously*. I do. But when actually writing, I let intuition and instinct say for me what Ive already decided I want to say, but have deliberately and with malice aforethought made myself forget. The result is, I do not employ any conscious symbols or symbolisms in the work itself. In fact, a great deal of my hardest times come when for one reason or another I discover Ive forgotten to lock the door on the thinking and find it slipping in as symbol.

SINCLAIR LEWIS

Sirs:

I wish to acknowledge your choice of my novel *Arrowsmith* for the Pulitzer Prize. That prize I must refuse, and my refusal would be meaningless unless I explained the reasons.

All prizes, like all titles, are dangerous. The seekers for prizes tend to labor not for inherent excellence but for alien rewards; they tend to write this, or timorously to avoid writing that, in order to tickle the prejudices of a haphazard committee. . . . The Pulitzer Prize for Novels signifies, already, much more than a convenient thousand dollars to be accepted even by such writers as smile secretly at the actual wording of the terms. It is tending to become a sanctified tradition. There is a general belief that the administrators of the prize are a pontifical body with the discernment and the power to grant the prize as the ultimate proof of merit. . . . Only by regularly refusing the Pulitzer Prize can novelists keep such a power from being permanently set up over them. . . . Between the Pulitzer Prizes, the American Academy of Arts and Letters and its training-school the National Institute of Arts and Letters, amateur boards of censorship, and the inquisition of earnest literary ladies, every compulsion is put upon writers to become safe, polite, obedient, and sterile. In protest, I declined election to the National Institute of Arts and Letters some years ago, and now I must decline the Pulitzer Prize.

I invite other writers to consider the fact that by accepting the prizes and approval of these vague institutions, we are admitting their authority, publicly confirming them as the final judges of literary excellence, and I inquire whether any prize is worth that subservience.

Edna St. Vincent Millay

Ladies [of the League of American Penwomen]:

I have received from you recently several communications, inviting me to be your Guest of Honour at a function to take place in Washington some time this month. I replied, not only that I was unable to attend, but that I regretted this inability; I said that I was sensible to the honour you did me, and that I hoped you would invite me again.

Your recent gross and shocking insolence to one of the most distinguished writers of our time has changed all that.

It is not in the power of an organization which has insulted Elinor Wylie, to honour me.

And indeed I should feel it unbecoming on my part, to sit as Guest of Honour in a gathering of writers, where honour is tendered not so much for the excellence of one's literary accomplishment as for the circumspection of one's personal life.

Believe me, if the eminent object of your pusillanimous attack has not directed her movements in conformity with your timid philosophies, no more have I mine. I too am eligible for your disesteem. Strike me too from your lists, and permit me, I beg you, to share with Elinor Wylie a brilliant exile from your fusty province.

— — —

[Written to her mother] I was telling somebody yesterday that the reason I am a poet is entirely because you wanted me to be and intended I should be, even from the very first. You brought me up in the tradition of poetry, and everything I did you encouraged. I can not remember once in my life when you were not interested in what I was working on, or even suggested that I should put it aside for something else. Some parents of children that are "different" have so much to reproach themselves with. But not you, Great Spirit.

ARCHIBALD MACLEISH

Beauty is the means & the end. Beauty is what a man *sees*. Anything that he *sees* is beautiful which means merely that he sees it. For when our minds comprehend a thing, they love it, they *see* it; it is beautiful and they see it & it is beautiful. This is the function of art–to see first, then so to represent in terms of *other* beauty already known that the thing which the artist has seen is made to appear beautiful to other minds. (And art which does not translate but attempts to reproduce as nearly as may be the thing seen thus avoids that which is the true labor & all the justification of all art). Well, I saw all this. I saw what I must do. I must go about looking at things, laboring to see them. If I could understand them too then so much the better. But first I must see what they were–not to the chemist, or a biologist, or a sociologist, but to so much conscious life as was in me to see them with. Then I must think about them & I must find words for them. Then I must write poetry of these words.

MAX BORN

[Written to Albert Einstein] I read in the paper recently that you are supposed to have said: "If I were born a second time, I would become not a physicist but an artisan". These words were a great comfort to me, for similar thoughts are going around in my mind as well, in view of the evil which our once so beautiful science has brought upon the world.

JOHN CIARDI

I agree with what you have to say about fragmentation and disintegration. Our young poets are too often drawn to what I have to call "the trip culture." "Trip" is a term of the (now happily fading) drug generation. It means, at root, the hallucinatory experience (trip, voyage) brought on by drugs. It implies an eagerness for self-excitation (or drug excitation) of the mind. In poetry it seems to suggest (to the young) that all one needs to be a poet is the excitation of his own ignorance. Discipline and a true respect for the art, if follows, would stifle the overflow of one's excited feelings. The result is pap, but many young idiots, rejoicing in one another ("relating" to one another, as they call it) praise such clatter—because, as I suspect, they have never formed an attention capable of responding to the real thing. Whether it is the oratorical shouting of an Yevtushenko or the soul-spilling of a hallucinator, it is a self-exalting ignorance, and I can find in it nothing to hope for. I take my text from William Butler Yeats' poem, "Adam's Curse":

> A line may take us hours maybe,
> Yet if it does not seem a moment's thought,
> Our stitching and unstitching has been naught.
> Better get down upon your marrow bones
> And scrub a kitchen pavement, or break stones
> Like an old pauper in all sorts of weather,
> For to articulate sweet sounds together
> Is to work harder than all these, and yet
> Be thought an idler by the noisy set
> Of bankers, schoolmasters, and clergymen
> The martyrs call the world.

As I once said to a student: "I, too, want the impromptu, but I find that it's what begins to happen about the twentieth draft."

GABRIEL GARCÍA MÁRQUEZ

Not many years ago, I wrote a story of 15 pages and bought a package of 500 sheets of paper. When I finished the story, I had used up all 500 to write the 15.

PAUL KLEE

Art does not reproduce the visible; rather, it makes visible.

MICHELANGELO

The greatest artist does not have any concept which a single piece of marble does not itself contain within its excess, although only a hand that obeys the intellect can discover it.

GUSTAVE GEFFROY

Cézanne is one of the most liberal artists I have ever seen. He begins each sentence with 'For me, it's this way,' but he acknowledges that others can be equally honest and truthful with regard to nature, according to their convictions. He does not think that everyone must see in the same way.

PAUL CÉZANNE

Patience [is] . . . the mother of genius.

– – –

Keep good company, meaning: *Go to the Louvre.* But after seeing the great masters who rest there, one must hasten to leave and to revivify oneself through contact with nature, with the instincts and with the artistic sensations within us. . . . Studying well in Nature's presence, that's the best thing there is.

– – –

. . . If a strong feeling for nature—and mine is certainly intense—is the necessary basis for any artistic concept, and upon which rest the grandeur and beauty of future work, a knowledge of the means of expressing our emotion is no less essential, and can only be gained through long experience.

— — —

Michelangelo is a builder, and Raphael, great as he is, is an artist who was always restricted by the model. Whenever he tries to become reflective, he falls below the level of his great rival.

— — —

I am still working, and without worrying about criticism and critics, as a true artist should. The work must prove me right.

Edward Gibbon

Freedom is the first wish of our heart; freedom is the first blessing of our nature; and unless we bind ourselves with voluntary chains of interest or passion, we [will not] advance in freedom as we advance in years.

— — —

Every man who rises above the common level has received two educations: the first from his teachers; the second, more personal and important, from himself.

— — —

The love of study, a passion which derives fresh vigor from enjoyment, supplies each day, each hour, with a perpetual source of independent and rational pleasure. . . .

— — —

[An author's] social sympathy may be gratified by the idea that now, in the present hour, he is imparting some degree of amusement or knowledge to his friends in a distant land, that one day his mind will be familiar to the grandchildren of those who are yet unborn.

CLAUDE DEBUSSY

To complete a work is just like being present at the death of someone you love.

— — —

Search for a discipline within freedom! Don't let yourself be governed by formulae drawn from decadent philosophies: they are for the feeble-minded. Listen to no one's advice except that of the wind in the trees. That can recount the whole history of mankind. . . .

— — —

Art is the most beautiful deception of all! And although people try to incorporate the everyday events of life in it, we must hope that it will remain a deception lest it become a utilitarian thing, sad as a factory. . . . Let us not disillusion anyone by bringing too much reality into the dream. . . .

— — —

I believe the principal fault of the majority of writers and artists is having neither the will nor the courage to break with their successes, failing to seek new paths and give birth to new ideas. Most of them reproduce them twice, three, even four times.

They have neither the courage nor the temerity to leave what is certain for what is uncertain. There is, however, no greater pleasure than going into the depth of oneself, setting one's whole being in motion and seeking for new and hidden treasures. What a joy to find something new within oneself, something that surprises even ourselves, filling us with warmth.

— — —

Music is a mysterious mathematical process whose elements are a part of Infinity. It is allied to the movement of the waters, to the play of curves described by the changing breezes. Nothing is more musical than a sunset! For anyone who can be moved by what they see can learn the greatest lessons in development here. That is to say, they can read them in Nature's book—a book not well enough known among musicians, who tend to read nothing but their own books about what the Masters have said, respectfully stirring the dust on their works. All very well, but perhaps Art goes deeper than this.

— — —

Before the passing sky, in long hours of contemplation of its magnificent and ever-changing beauty, I am seized by an incomparable emotion. The whole expanse of nature is reflected in my own sincere but feeble soul. Around me the branches of the trees reach out toward the firmament, here are the sweet-scented flowers smiling in the meadow, here the soft earth is carpeted with sweet herbs. . . . Nature invites its ephemeral and trembling travelers to experience these wonderful and disturbing spectacles—that is what I call prayer.

CHRISTOPHER MILNE

The child's world is a single indivisible world in which all creatures, human and animal, live together as equals. Instinctively he feels this to be the truth—as indeed it is.

But in order to understand it, in order to learn how it works, we need to examine it bit by bit; and so we take it to pieces, separating it into its various layers—its species and subspecies, its races and classes. At school I learned how to distinguish a verb from a noun, a Cavalier from a Roundhead, a logarithm from an antilogarithm, and an atom from a molecule. When we have finished studying the world in this way and have learned all we can about it, perhaps we remember it as we once knew it. But can we ever put it together again?

This is the question that today faces not only the middle-aged adult but humanity as a whole. Can we, the human race, reassemble a world that, over the millennia, we have been taking apart? Can we put it together before it totally disintegrates?

There is not much time left. The child is waiting for us, beckoning to us. We must hurry.

— — —

How easy if my father had been a publisher instead of an author; for then I could have entered the family business and taken over from him when he retired. But an author has nothing tangible that he can hand on to his son. . . . These, really, were his two great talents: perfectionism and enthusiasm. He handed them on to me—and he could have given me nothing more precious.

There are two sorts of writer. There is the writer who is basically a reporter, and there is the creative writer. The one draws on his experiences, the other on his dreams.

Robert Henri

We are not here to do what has already been done.

A work of art is the trace of a magnificent struggle.

Art when really understood is the province of every human being.

It is simply a question of doing things, anything, well. It is not an outside, extra thing.

When the artist is alive in any person, whatever his kind of work may be, he become an inventive, searching, daring, self-expressing creature. He becomes interesting to other people. He disturbs, upsets, enlightens, and he opens ways for a better understanding. Where those who are not artists are trying to close the book, he opens it, shows there are still more pages possible.

The world would stagnate without him, and the world would be beautiful with him; for he is interesting to himself and he is interesting to others. He does not have to be a painter or sculptor to be an artist. He can work in any medium. He simply has to find the gain in the work itself, not outside it.

NANCY NEWHALL

Of all resources, the most crucial is Man's spirit.
  Not dulled, nor lulled, supine, secure, replete does Man create,
  But out of stern challenge . . .
From what immortal hungers, what sudden sight of the unknown,
surges that desire? What flint of fact, what kindling light of art or
far horizon, ignites that spark? What cry, what music, what strange
beauty, strikes that romance:
  On these hangs the future of the world.

VLADIMIR SHATAYEV

Discipline is the kind of concept that, if you doubt it partially,
you tear it down completely.

ROBERT OPPENHEIMER

I believe that through discipline, though not through
discipline alone, we can achieve serenity. . . . I believe that
through discipline we learn to preserve what is essential to our
happiness in more and more adverse circumstances, and to
abandon with simplicity what would else have seemed to us
indispensable; that we come a little to see the world without the
gross distortion of personal desire. . . . But because I believe
that the reward of discipline is greater than its immediate objective,
I would not have you think that discipline without objective is
possible: in its nature discipline involves the subjection of the
soul to some perhaps minor end; and that end must be real, if the
discipline is not to be factitious. Therefore I think that all things
which evoke discipline: study, and our duties to men and to the
commonwealth, war, and personal hardship, and even the need
for subsistence, ought to be greeted by us with profound gratitude;
for only through them can we attain to the least detachment; and
only so can we know peace.

KAREN HORNEY

To be free of sensuality means great power in a woman. Only in this way will she be independent of a man. Otherwise she will always long for him and in the exaggerated yearning of her senses she will be able to drown out all feeling of her own value. She becomes the bitch, who begs even if she is beaten—a strumpet. It is a different thing if through the muting of all other instincts, the one instinct has become a power in her, i. e., when she is only "female."

Otherwise eternal battling. And every victory of the senses a Pyrrhic victory, bought with loathing, ever deadly loathing afterwards.

And a man wants a woman calm and superior to these low instincts, of whose power he is only too well aware in himself. Everyone loves that which is higher.

— — —

The mind's only possession is thinking, is reason. Its goal is the truth. Hence happiness is the same as striving after the truth. For the truth is eternal, and the greater our striving, the greater our happiness. This is easy to understand, for happiness is absence of all influences from outside that threaten self-preservation.

An existence is defective, on the other hand, where outside influences predominate. Where intellect is hampered by passion, suffering remains. Thus the desire to please, voluptuousness, intemperance, greed, sensuality express surrender to the force of external things. There is suffering too if the mind strives for something transient, changeable, or where its noble striving attaches to perishable things.

I will look and go in 2 directions: *Strength of Will, Self-Discipline* and deep absorption in the natural sciences and philosophy, penetrating into the greatest poets and thinkers—above all, therefore, hard *work*.

Yes, and I long for one thing more: to learn how to listen to the delicate vibrations of my soul, to be incorruptibly *true to myself* and fair to others, to find in this way the right measure of my own worth.

ALFRED STIEGLITZ

When I make a photograph, I make love!

I am an idolator of perfect workmanship of any kind.

I have finally made *a print* from one of the negatives made 3 years ago.–It is a wonder. I guess I've made 50 prints during the 3 years always trying and trying over again–sometimes approaching–sometimes "fooling" myself into the belief that I had something satisfactory, always knowing there was still much leeway towards what I really wanted.

TONI BENTLEY

I learned, as one does in every rehearsal every day, that life goes on and rehearsal begins and ends no matter how despairing one may feel about such probabilities. I learned about the art of spending an hour with a peace derived from practice. How did I learn about this? By repetition and practice, like an animal. The only part my mind played was in formulating the learning into thought. I was an instrument going through the motions. Learning by way of repetition and routine is an avoidance and a waste of the human being's greatest gift of all—the gift of thought.

R. CARLOS NAKAI

We are born with severe limitations and shortcomings as human beings. Finding ways to overcome them . . . is our personal task.

EDDIE RICKENBACKER

Always be respectful to your superiors and elders as it is an acknowledgement of your capacity to appreciate the benefits acquired from experience.

This was evidenced by my answer to a query recently, "What advice can you give the younger generation, based on your greatest failure?" My answer was, "Failure to evaluate and understand the advice of my elders in my youth."

CHARLES SHEELER

Photography is nature seen from the eyes outward, painting from the eyes inward. Photography records inalterably the single image while painting records a plurality of images willfully directed by the artist.

CASPAR DAVID FRIEDRICH

The artist's feeling is his law. Genuine feeling can never be contrary to nature, it is always in harmony with her.

JEAN AUGUSTE DOMINIQUE INGRES

Have a religious feeling for your art. Do not suppose that anything good, or even fairly good, can be produced without nobility of soul. To become accustomed to beauty, fix your eyes on the sublime. . . . Go forward with your head raised towards the skies. . . .

OSCAR WILDE

Art, even the art of fullest scope and widest vision, can never really show us the external world. All that it shows us is our own soul, the one world of which we have any real cognizance. . . . It is Art, and Art only, that reveals us to ourselves.

GUY DE MAUPASSANT

Our eyes, our ears, our sense of smell, of taste, differing from one person to another, create as many truths as there are men upon earth. And our minds, taking instructions from these organs, so diversely impressed, understand, analyze, judge, as if each of us belonged to a different race. Each one of us, therefore, forms for himself an illusion of the world; and the writer (the painter, too) has no other mission than to reproduce faithfully this illusion, with all the contrivances of art that he has learned and has at his command.

CAMILLE COROT

Follow your convictions. It is better to be nothing than to be the echo of other painters.

Franz Marc

I am trying to heighten my feeling for the organic rhythm in all things, trying to establish a pantheistic contact with the tremor and flow of blood in nature, in animals, in the air. . . .

Max Beckmann

Art is creative for the sake of realization, not for amusement; for transfiguration, not for the sake of play. It is the quest of our self that drives us along the eternal and never-ending journey we must all make.

— — —

Learn by heart the forms to be found in nature, so that you can use them like the notes in a musical composition. That is what these forms are for. Nature is a marvellous chaos, and it is our job and our duty to bring order into that chaos and–to perfect it.

Henri Matisse

I have always tried to hide my own efforts and wished my works to have the lightness and joyousness of a springtime which never lets anyone suspect the labours it has cost. So I am afraid that the young, seeing in my work only the apparent facility and negligence in the drawing, will use this as an excuse for dispensing with certain efforts which I believe necessary.

Roger Fry

I am fully persuaded that the aim of all art and all life is ultimately the worship of God in its broadest sense.

— — —

Art is like religion; I'm not at all sure it isn't the same thing or rather an outcome of the same emotion—the emotion of the universal.

— — —

Art doesn't begin until you've got past the stage of ethics. Ethics is a balance of conflicting claims, Art is a free expression.

— — —

. . . [Art's] real use is a direct result of its detachment from any actual goal. It is there we must drink our fill of the absolute and not in matters concerning society. It is there one can break away from mechanization.

— — —

In general in painting [landscapes] I try to express emotions that the contemplation of forms produces in me and to extract fundamental relationships from the multiple, more or less chaotic and discordant shapes of Nature, relationships that are fundamental for my spirit and consequently for my fellows.

PIERRE AUGUSTE RENOIR

Craft is the pillar, the solidity of art. It is something one can only learn by putting one's hand to paint little by little. It is constant work that occupies you day and night for years and years, and that one never really knows, that escapes you just when you think you have grasped it.

— — —

Any work emanating from one's imagination is nothing compared to what has been created by nature. She alone can give us everything that makes art.

— — —

The greatest composer is the one who has best followed and understood the grand spectacles nature gives to those who love her. The greatest draftsman is the one who has scrutinized her down to the last detail.

— — —

Art is . . . immortal because it's the offspring, the product of nature filtered through different brains and colored by different eyes. It will never be monotonous, no more than a tree, a flower, and every natural form will ever be.

— — —

You'd better believe, young people, that your imagination is precious little if it's not helped along by everything that nature produces.

— — —

Machinism, the division of labor, has transformed the worker into a simple automaton and has killed the joy of working. In the factory, the worker, tied to a machine which asks nothing of his brain, sadly accomplishes a monotonous task of which he feels only the fatigue.

— — —

[A furniture worker said to me] Monsieur, for thirty years I've made the legs of chairs, another makes the backs, another assembles them, but I'm incapable of making a whole chair. There's the whole secret. A man who can no longer enjoy his work loses all trace of taste. He becomes like the machine which drives him. He slaves away without imagination and without brains. He earns his living but without joy, and that's what they call progress. Slavery has been abolished but the factory has been created. The slave doesn't exist any more, but there's the galley slave who sweats away in front of a machine which brutalizes and slowly kills him. I remember from my youth the lumbermen who sang while cutting their planks. Go and visit a mechanized sawmill and see if you hear laughter and singing.

LOREN EISELEY

Man is always marveling at what he has blown apart, never at what the universe has put together, and this is his limitation. . . . Man, the creation of the universe, after all created the bomb.

— — —

Idea of lecture: Man's loss of interest in visible nature just as he needs it.

LEONARDO DA VINCI

In youth acquire that which may requite you for the deprivations of old age; and if you are mindful that old age has wisdom for its food, you will so erect yourself in youth, that your old age will not lack sustenance.

\- \- \-

As a well-spent day brings happy sleep, so life well used brings happy death.

\- \- \-

Nature is full of infinite causes which were never set forth in experience.

\- \- \-

If you despise painting, which is the sole imitator of all the visible works of nature, it is certain that you will be despising a subtle invention which with philosophical and ingenious speculation takes as its theme all the various kinds of forms, airs and scenes, plants, animals, grasses and flowers, which are surrounded by light and shade. And this truly is a science and the true-born daughter of nature, since painting is the offspring of nature. But in order to speak more correctly we may call it the grandchild of nature; for all visible things derive their existence from nature, and from these same things is born painting. So therefore we may justly speak of it as the grandchild of nature and as related to God himself.

EDVARD MUNCH

Nature is the unique great realm upon which art feeds.

HANS HOFMANN

Nature: the source of all inspiration. Whether the *artist* works directly from nature, from memory, or from fantasy, nature is always the source of his creative impulses.

Eugène-Emmanuel Viollet-le-Duc

It cannot be repeated too often that only by following the order that nature herself observes in her creations can one, in the arts, conceive and produce according to the law of unity, which is the essential condition of all creation.

Odilon Redon

. . . The method that has been the most fruitful and the most necessary to my development is the copying of real things, carefully reproducing the objects of the exterior world in their most minute, individual and accidental details. After attempting to copy minutely a pebble, a sprout of a plant, a hand, a human profile or any other example of living or inorganic life, I experience the onset of a mental excitement; at that point I need to create, to give myself over to representations of the imaginary. Thus blended and infused, nature becomes my source, my yeast and my leaven. I believe that this is the origin of my true inventions.

Robinson Jeffers

. . . As to the importance of science for the artist and for the thinker. It seems to me that for the thinker . . . a scientific basis is an essential condition. We cannot take any philosophy seriously if it ignores or garbles the knowledge and view-points that determine the intellectual life of our time. . . .

For the contemporary artist science is important but not at all essential. He might have no more modern science than Catullus yet be as great an artist. But his range and significance would be limited accordingly.

– – –

Human happiness?–If a harmless drug were invented, under the influence of which all people could be intensely and harmoniously happy, only working enough to provide each other with sustenance and the drug,–would that be a good goal for men? That would be maximum happiness, minimum pain.

– – –

Man is a part of nature, but a nearly infinitesimal part; the human race will cease after a while and leave no trace, but the great splendors of nature will go on. Meanwhile most of our time and energy are necessarily spent on human affairs; that can't be prevented, though I think it should be minimized; but for philosophy, which is an endless research of truth, and for contemplation, which can be a sort of worship, I would suggest that the immense beauty of the earth and the outer universe, the divine "nature of things," is a more rewarding object. Certainly it is more ennobling. It is a source of strength; the other of distraction.

– – –

I believe that the universe is one being, all its parts are different expressions of the same energy, and they are all in communication with each other, influencing each other, therefore parts of one organic whole. . . . The parts change and pass, or die, people and races and rocks and stars, none of them seems to me important in itself, but only the whole. This whole is in all its parts so beautiful, and is felt by me to be so intensely in earnest, that I am compelled to love it, and to think of it as divine. It seems to me that this whole alone is worthy of the deeper sort of love; and that here is peace, freedom, I might say a kind of salvation, in turning one's affections outward toward this one God, rather than inward on one's self. . . .

– – –

I think that it is our privilege and felicity to love God for his beauty, without claiming or expecting love from him. We are not important to him, but he to us.

John Stuart Mill

It is not good for a man to be kept perforce at all times in the presence of his species. . . . Nor is there much satisfaction in contemplating the world with nothing left to the spontaneous activity of nature; with every rood of land brought into cultivation, which is capable of growing food for human beings; every flowery waste or natural pasture ploughed up, all quadrupeds, or birds which are not domesticated for man's use exterminated as his rivals for food, every hedgerow or superfluous tree rooted out, and scarcely a place left where a wild shrub or flower could grow without being eradicated as a weed.

Margaret Fuller

I entirely agree in what you say of *tuition* and *intuition*. The two must act and react upon one another to make a man, to form a mind. Drudgery is as necessary to call out the treasures of the mind, as harrowing and planting with those of the earth.

– – –

When I can exhaust myself in climbing, I feel delightfully; the eye is so sharpened, and the mind so full of thought. The outlines of all objects, the rocks, the distant sails, even the rippling of the ocean were so sharp that they seemed to press themselves into the brain. When I see a natural scene by such a light, it stays in my memory always, as a picture; on milder days it influences me more in the way of reverie.

— — —

Few have eyes for the pretty little features of a scene. In this, men are not so good as boys. Artists are always thus young. . . .

— — —

Surely I never had so clear an idea before of the capacity to bless of mere Earth, merely the beautiful Earth, when fresh from the original breath of the creative spirit. To have this impression one must see large tracts of wild country where the traces of man's inventions are too few and slight to break the harmony of the first design. . . . I feel much refreshed even by this brief intimacy with nature in an aspect of large and unbroken lineaments.

— — —

"From the brain of the purple mountain" flows forth cheer to my somewhat weary mind. I feel refreshed amid these bolder shapes of nature. Mere gentle and winning landscapes are not enough. How I wish my birth had been cast among the sources of the streams, where the voice of hidden torrents is heard by night, and the eagle soars, and the thunder resounds in prolonged peals, and wide blue shadows fall like brooding wings across the valleys! Amid such scenes, I expand and feel at home. All the fine days I spend among the mountain passes, along the mountain brooks, or beside the stately river. I enjoy just the tranquil happiness I need in communion with this fair grandeur.

Van Wyck Brooks

When the conscious mind is over-stimulated, the unconscious mind refuses to open its door.

– – –

The main thing in times like ours is not to lose the sense of the difference between the minor and the major.

– – –

It is a violation of some deep instinct in us to separate the aesthetic from the humane. . . . When Abraham Lincoln in his youth . . . saved a fawn's life by scaring it away from a rifle, he was acting in line with the discipline that requires writers to value life on pain of losing the power to recreate it.

– – –

How paradoxical is our age that praises both Hemingway's blood-lust and the quixotic humanity of Schweitzer and Gandhi,– Gandhi who removed silkworms from the leaves of a tree that were poisoning them and Schweitzer who rescues earthworms that are scorched by the sun.

Heywood Broun

. . . It is important that children learn the two-sidedness of history and from that grow to appreciate the double surface of all controversy. . . . If you train a child to think wholly on one side of any problem there's no telling when he may happen to hop off the particular plane on which you have placed him and become just as bigoted in dissent as he has been taught to be in conformity. To my way of thinking, Charles E. Hughes and Leon Trotzky come pretty close to being equally tight-minded. Neither of them seems capable of imagining the existence of any point of view but his own.

M. C. Escher

It may seem paradoxical to say that there are similarities between a poetical and a commercial mind, but it is a fact that both a poet and a businessman are constantly dealing with problems that are directly related to people and for which sensitivity is of prime importance. The business-like mind is sometimes described as being cold, sober, calculating, hard, but perhaps these are simply qualities that are necessary for dealing with people if one wants to achieve anything. One is always concerned with the mysterious, incalculable, dark, hidden aspects for which there is no easy formula, but which form essentially the same human element as that which inspires the poet.

God, I wish I could learn to draw a bit better! It takes so much effort and perseverance to do it well. Sometimes I am quite close to delirium with pure nerves. It is really only a question of battling on relentlessly with constant and, if possible, merciless self-criticism. I think that making prints the way I do it is almost only a matter of very much wanting to do it well. For the most part, things like talent are mere poppycock. Any schoolboy with a bit of aptitude might draw better than I; but what is usually lacking is the unwavering desire for expression, obstinacy gnashing its teeth and saying, "Even though I know I cannot do it, I still want to do it."

– – –

At times [on my new project], when I feel very enthusiastic, it seems as though no one in the world has ever made anything so beautiful and important. Shortly afterwards–a matter of hours–it suddenly looks useless and I am overcome by the utter pointlessness of all that pitiable fiddling. But having taken it on, I continue the next day as though my very life depended on it. I can even get truly terrified by the possibility of dying before this latest, so-called masterpiece is finished.

– – –

. . . Lazing about leads to unhappiness. I believe that the most important difference between man and other living creatures lies not so much in having or not having a "soul" or a "spirit", but in the astonishing fact that man must "work" as a condition of existence, while a bird does not need to.

MAY SARTON

I am at my desk from three to four hours every day. . . . It has to be the morning, before one's mind is all cluttered up, when the door to the subconscious is still open, when you first wake up. That's the creative time for me. Because you want, you see, that *primary intensity*. This is what my life is all about–creating a frame in which I can have that primary intensity for three hours a day.

– – –

Routine is the one way in which one learns not to waste time.

— — —

In poetry I know that I can't write in form unless the intensity is very great. In other words, I have to be inspired to use form. But when I am, then I can put a poem through sixty drafts to get that final crystalline thing that I want. I think of it when I'm teaching. The poem works like an aeroplane—it *flies* because of all the tension, the mechanical tensions within it. Every screw has to be screwed in exactly right, every single thing has to be balanced exactly right. And a poem is only as strong as its weakest word. It will not fly, doesn't soar in the mind unless it has form.

— — —

. . . I can go on revising when I'm really inspired. That's what I can't do what I'm not inspired. The critical self is just as alive and intense as the emotional self when you're truly inspired. So you can get things out of yourself that you really couldn't do except at white heat.

— — —

Every morning you have to conquer the demons who say, "This will *never* be any good. This will *never* be what I saw when I dreamed of it." But you just have to say, "Keep on, keep on," and finally it gets through.

— — —

It isn't the writing time, but the space around the writing time that matters. I only work three hours, but I'm thinking subconsciously all day long about what I'm doing.

– – –

Loneliness is the poverty of self and solitude is the richness of self. I don't think you can be happily living alone when you're very young, because you don't have enough inside you. I started really living alone when I was forty-five and bought an old farm in New Hampshire. From then on, I have been *happy* to be alone.

– – –

The crucial question seems to me to be this: what is the *source* of creativity in the woman who wants to be an artist? After all, admit it, a woman is meant to create children, not works of art. . . . A man with a talent does what is expected of him, makes his way, constructs, is an engineer, a composer, a builder of bridges. It's the natural order of things that he construct objects outside himself and his family. The woman who does so is aberrant. . . . Maybe it's this: the woman who needs to create works of art is born with a kind of psychic tension in her which drives her unmercifully to find a way to balance, to make herself whole. Every human being has this need: in the artist it is mandatory. Unable to fulfill it, he goes mad. But when the artist is a woman she fulfills it at the expense of herself as a woman.

EDMUND GOSSE

What is actually taught in early childhood is often that part of training which makes least impression on the character, and is of the least permanent importance. My labours failed to make me a zoölogist, and the multitude of my designs and my descriptions have left me helplessly ignorant of the anatomy of a sea-anemone. But I cannot look upon the mental discipline as useless. It taught me to concentrate my attention, to define the nature of distinctions, to see accurately, and to name what I saw. Moreover, it gave me the habit of going on with any piece of work

I had in hand, not flagging because the interest or picturesqueness of the theme had declined, but pushing forth towards a definite goal, well-foreseen and limited beforehand. For almost any intellectual employment in later life, it seems to me that this discipline was valuable.

WILLIAM CARLOS WILLIAMS

You, dear Bill, have a magnificent opportunity to enjoy life ahead of you. You have sensibility (even if it drives you nuts at times), which will be the source of keen pleasures later and the source of useful accomplishments too. You've got a brain, as you have been told *ad nauseam*. But these are the very things which are tormenting you, the very things which are your most valued possessions and which will be your joy tomorrow. . . . Wait it out. Don't worry too much. You've got time. You're all right. You're reacting to life in the only way an intelligent, sensitive young man in a college can. In another year you'll enter another sphere of existence, the practical one. The knowledge, abstract now, which seems unrelated to sense to you (at times) will get a different color.

Sooner or later we all of us knock our heads against the ceiling of the world. It's like breaking a record: the last fifth of a second, which marks the difference between a good runner and a world beater is the hardest part of the whole proceeding.

– – –

Everything we know is a local virtue–if we know it at all–the only difference between the force of a great work and a lesser one being lack of brain and fire in the second. . . . Art can be made of anything–provided it be seen, smelt, touched, apprehended and understood to be what it is–the flesh of a constantly repeated permanence.

CONRAD AIKEN

Is there any getting away from the fact that even the slightest step in literature, from the less to the more "poetic" is a step from the less to the more "arranged?" "Arranged" in the richest sense— embracing selection, order, emphasis. To "arrange" at all is, if you like, artificial: but it is an essential of all art. . . . I quite agree with you that the "less arranged" has its own cool sort of charm, adapts itself admirably to certain moods more colloquial and less intense; but I think its range is, in comparison with that of the "more arranged," infinitely small—Theoretically, one should seek in a work of art the utmost complexity, or arrangement, consistent with brevity—should one not?

SAMUEL BUTLER

We had better live in others as much as we can if only because we thus live more in the race, which God really does seem to care about a good deal, and less in the individual, to whom, so far as I can see, he is indifferent. After we are dead it matters not to the life we have led in ourselves what people may say of us, but it matters much to the life we lead in others and this should be our true life.

— — —

The question is what is the amateur an amateur of? What is he really in love with? Is he in love with other people, thinking he sees something which he would like to show them, which he feels sure they would enjoy if they could only see it as he does, which he is therefore trying as best he can to put before the few nice people whom he knows? If this is his position he can do no wrong, the spirit in which he works will ensure that his defects will be only as bad spelling or bad grammar in some pretty saying of a child. If, on the other hand, he is playing for social success and to get a reputation for being clever, then no matter how dexterous his work may be, it is but another mode of the speaking with the tongues of men and angels without charity; it is sounding brass or a tinkling cymbal, full of sound and fury signifying nothing.

– – –

All men can do great things, if they know what great things are.

– – –

Schools and colleges are not intended to foster genius and to bring it out. Genius is a nuisance, and it is the duty of schools and colleges to abate it by setting genius-traps in its way. They are as the artificial obstructions in a hurtle race—tests of skill and endurance, but in themselves useless.

– – –

The fight between [the theist and the atheist] is as to whether God shall be called God or shall have some other name.

PABLO PICASSO

The important thing is to create. Nothing else matters; creation is all.

– – –

A picture is not thought out and settled beforehand. While it is being done it changes as one's thoughts change. And when it is finished, it still goes on changing, according to the state of mind of whoever is looking at it.

– – –

When you begin a picture, you often make some pretty discoveries. You must be on guard against these. Destroy the thing, do it over several times. In each destroying of a beautiful discovery, the artist does not really suppress it, but rather transforms it, condenses it, makes it more substantial. What comes out in the end is the result of discarded finds. Otherwise, you become your own connoisseur. I sell myself nothing.

– – –

A picture used to be a sum of additions. In my case a picture is a sum of destructions. I do a picture—then I destroy it. In the end, though, nothing is lost; the red I took away from one place turns up somewhere else.

– – –

Have you ever seen a finished picture? A picture or anything else? Woe unto you the day it is said that you are finished! To finish a work? To finish a picture? What nonsense! To finish it means to be through with it, to kill, to rid it of its soul, to give it its final blow: the most unfortunate one for the painter as well as for the picture.

– – –

I too often tell myself: "It's not quite there yet. You can do better." I can rarely keep myself from redoing a thing—umpteen times the same thing. Sometimes it gets to be a real obsession. After all, why work otherwise, if not to better express the same thing? You must always seek perfection.

– – –

What one does is what counts and not what one had the intention of doing.

THOMAS CARLYLE

If I can do any work, it is a happiness to me; if I can do *no* work, all is an insignificance, an *un*happiness, and I had better be asleep than awake in such a world.

EZRA POUND

Great literature is simply language charged with meaning to the utmost possible degree.

– – –

Your perception of the "unit" is most gratifying. That of course is the artistic triumph.—To produce the whole which ceases to exist if *one* of its component parts be removed or permuted = or make the "whole" that has no "parts".

KATHERINE ANNE PORTER

I look forward to a world in which the artist has his place as a useful being, not for political purposes, but in his true function, which is that of a finder, a bringer, a giver of new forms of expression based on life, but seen with imagination and creativeness. First there must be bread for every one, but bread is not enough. Man eats his bread and looks about for something more, and the something more must be art (should be).

LOUIS ARMSTRONG

Joe Oliver has always been my inspiration and my idol. No trumpet player ever had the fire that Oliver had. Man, he really could *punch* a number. Some might have had a better tone, but I've never seen *nothing* have the fire, and no one created as much as Joe.

The way I see it, the greatest musical creations came from his horn—and I've heard a lot of them play. I think he was better than Bolden, better than Bunk Johnson. Buddy blew too hard—he actually did blow his brains out. Even Bunk didn't offer nothing but tone. He didn't have the get-up-and-go that Oliver did; he didn't create a phrase that stays with you. But Joe Oliver *created* things. . . .

— — —

When I joined the Joe Oliver Band in Chicago I was happy to find that Baby Dodds had stopped drinking excessively and settled down to music. He had always wanted to settle down but like so many good musicians, they would get that one too many drinks which would throw him off and cause some awful embarrassing moments. Good musicians have to guard against such things in music.

— — —

. . . As long as a person breathes, they still have a chance to exercise the talents they were born with. I speak of something which I know about and have been doing all of my life, and that's Music. And now that I am an elderly man I still feel the same about music and its creations. And at the age of "sixty-nine" I really don't feel that I am on my way out at all. Of course a person may do a little less—but the foundation will always be there. . . . There's no such thing as on the way out. As long as you are still doing something interesting and good. You are in business as long as you are breathing. "Yeah."

PEARL S. BUCK

I was not ambitious to be learned because of the honors it might confer, for I was taught that ambition itself was not the quality of a learned person. One must love learning for its own sake. One should not, or could not, consciously want to be learned for the sake of being a learned person or a scholar, for that curtailed the pleasure of acquiring learning. To acquire knowledge and hoard it, without allowing it to flower and bear fruit in admirable personal qualities, was to become an intellectual miser.

— — —

. . . Learning, in its process as well as in its accumulation, is the very heart of life. It is the secret to the enjoyment of life. And when we enjoy life we can accept hardship and deprivation with fortitude, because our treasure is secure. There is always more to know, more to understand, more to feel, more to express. There is always the means for growth. We renew ourselves through learning, we enlarge our habitations. Walls cannot confine us, sorrow does not destroy us. And learning is not mere escape—it is positive development, the entrance to wider horizons. We are enabled, through learning, to see ourselves in proportion to the whole of creation. We perceive that our world is not within the narrowness of one small human being.

— — —

. . . Our responsibility, as the company of the learned—to share what we have so that the benefits of human wisdom, with its infinite delights, may be enjoyed by all. When we have fulfilled our responsibility, I believe we shall find, incidentally, that we have achieved the blessed state about which we talk so much in every country today—and about which we do so little—the blessed state of permanent peace.

— — —

The secret of joy in work is contained in one word—excellence. To know how to do something well is to enjoy it.

Eleanor Roosevelt

People still ask me frequently how I planned my career and what over-all objective I had in mind. Actually I never planned a career, and what basic objective I had, for many years, was to grasp every opportunity to live and experience life as deeply, as fully, and as widely as I possibly could. It seemed to me stupid to have the gift of life and not use it to the utmost of one's ability. . . . I had really only three assets: I was keenly interested, I accepted every challenge and every opportunity to learn more, and I had great energy and self-discipline. . . . If you are interested, things come to you, they seem to gravitate your way without your lifting your hand.

— — —

It was not until I reached middle age that I had the courage to develop interests of my own, outside of my duties to my family. In the beginning, it seems to me now, I had no goal beyond the interests themselves, in learning about people and conditions and the world outside our own United States. Almost at once I began to discover that interest leads to interest, knowledge leads to more knowledge, the capacity for understanding grows with the effort to understand.

– – –

One curious thing is that I have always seen life personally; that is, my interest or sympathy or indignation is not aroused by an abstract cause but by the plight of a single person whom I have seen with my own eyes. It was the sight of a child dying of hunger that made the tragedy of hunger become of such overriding importance to me. Out of my response to an individual develops an awareness of a problem to the community, then to the country, and finally to the world. In each case my feeling of obligation to do something has stemmed from one individual and then widened and become applied to a broader area. . . . Actually I suppose the caring comes from being able to put yourself in the position of the other person. If you cannot imagine, "This might happen to me," you are able to say to yourself with indifference, "Who cares?"

Etty Hillesum

Now and then I join the gulls. In their movements through the great cloudy skies one suspects laws, eternal laws of another order than the law we humans make. This afternoon Jopie, who feels thoroughly sick and all in, stood together with his sister-in-arms Etty for at least a quarter of an hour looking up at one of these black and silver birds as it moved among the massive deep-blue rain clouds. We suddenly felt a lot less oppressed.

– – –

This morning one of my colleagues said, referring to all sorts of awful practices here: "Each moment of your life that your courage fails is a lost moment."

DIEGO RIVERA

Looking back on my work today, I think the best I have done grew out of things deeply felt, the worst from a pride in mere talent.

WILLIAM MICHAEL ROSSETTI

I read [Emerson] eagerly and with great admiration: and I think I can say that nothing ever exercised a more determining effect on my character than the essay "Self-Reliance." I was then very young–say barely 18–and in that state of feeling when I was liable to be biased either . . . towards self-reliance or towards deference to the authority of my betters.

FRANCIS CRICK

I learned that if you have something critical to say about a piece of scientific work, it is better to say it firmly but nicely and to preface it with praise of any good aspects of it. I only wish I had always stuck to this useful rule. Unfortunately I have sometimes been carried away by my impatience and expressed myself too briskly and in too devastating a manner.

– – –

It is interesting to note the curious mental attitude of scientists working on "hopeless" subjects. Contrary to what one might at first expect, they are all buoyed up by irrepressible optimism. I believe there is a simple explanation for this. Anyone without such optimism simply leaves the field and takes up some other line of work. Only the optimists remain. So one has the curious phenomenon that workers in subjects in which the prize is big but the prospects of success very small always appear very optimistic.

Thomas Turner

Oh, what a pleasure is business! How far preferable is an active busy life (when employed in some honest calling) to a supine and idle way of life, and happy are they whose fortune it is to be placed where commerce meets with encouragement and a person has the opportunity to push on trade with vigour. . . . It quite cheers the spirits and chases away the gloom that hangs on a melancholy brow.

E. M. Forster

I am a little doubtful perhaps about your application of 'psychology' to your difficulties, though your psychology is of course better than other people's. Science, when applied to personal relationships, is always *just wrong*–I refrain from adding in booming tones, 'and always will be', but it is certainly always just wrong at present. . . . Art is a better guide than Science.

– – –

One glance at the fields or the sky ought to prove the non-existence of spiritual evil.

Bernard Berenson

Everybody is an artist who enjoys his job and takes pride in making the best of it, putting his whole self into it–having what the Italians call *passione*. It matters not how humble or petty, shopkeeper or the higher occupations, from domestic servant to President of the U. S. A. or Prime Minister of England. It is the zest, the delight in his work, that something extra which he puts into it, that blesses him and those who benefit by him. Contrary to the person who enjoys his task so much that he puts payments, compensations, rewards, honours, last, the man or woman who does not enjoy his work wants to be exorbitantly paid for what he dislikes and even hates doing.

— — —

From an early age children should be taught to appreciate and value the beauty of things in themselves, and not only as painted or otherwise reproduced. . . . Sunset, sunrise, sky effects, all natural effects, the beauty of buildings, houses, street scenes, the charm of everyday objects in their places, the loveliness of human beings, not only of the young but of all ages, and of all animals of course, etc. That sort of education might lead people to value, appreciate, enjoy what costs them nothing, and at the same time turn them into potential super-painters. Then make them appreciate all the beauties, man-made, that cost them nothing or next to nothing, like the works of art in public museums.

Dmitri Shostakovich

Music illuminates a person through and through, and it is also his last hope and final refuge. And even half-mad Stalin, a beast and a butcher, instinctively sensed that about music. That's why he feared and hated it.

— — —

Fear of death may be the most intense emotion of all. I sometimes think that there is no deeper feeling. The irony lies in the fact that under the influence of that fear people create poetry, prose, and music; that is, try to strengthen their ties with the living and increase their influence on them.

— — —

When I hear about someone else's pain, I feel pain too. I feel pain for everything–for people and animals. For all living things.

— — —

I dedicated *Lady Macbeth* to my bride, my future wife, so naturally the opera is about love too, but not only love. It's also about how love could have been if the world weren't full of vile things. It's the vileness that ruins love.

John Galsworthy

I don't use "Beauty" in the mere narrow aesthetic sense. I include in it all that, of course; but I mean by it an increased conception of *the dignity of human life*. That dignity, I maintain, we shall never reach, until people increase in the sense of proportion, and come to revolt against disharmony, greed, and ugliness.

— — —

I think too much of town life has done us in; when we don't live (to some extent at all events) with Nature, we forget how to live at all.

Thomas Hardy

To distinguish truths which are temporary from truths which are eternal, the accidental from the essential, accuracies as to custom and ceremony from accuracies as to the perennial procedure of humanity, is of vital importance in our attempts to read for something more than amusement.

— — —

The human race being still practically barbarian it does not seem likely that men's delight in cruel sports can be lessened except by slow degrees. To attempt even this is, however, a worthy object which I commend.

Mary Somerville

I am now in my 92nd year (1872), still able to drive out for several hours; I am extremely deaf, and my memory of ordinary events, and especially of the names of people, is failing, but not for mathematical and scientific subjects. I am still able to read books on the higher algebra for four or five hours in the morning, and even to solve the problems. Sometimes I find them difficult, but my old obstinacy remains, for if I do not succeed to-day, I attack them anew on the morrow. I also enjoy reading about all the new discoveries and theories in the scientific world, and on all branches of science.

— — —

The short time I have to live naturally occupies my thoughts. . . . As I do comprehend, in some degree at least, the exquisite loveliness of the visible world, I confess I shall be sorry to leave it. I shall regret the sky, the sea, with all the changes of their beautiful colouring; the earth, with its verdure and flowers: but far more shall I grieve to leave animals who have followed our steps affectionately for years, without knowing for certainty their ultimate fate. . . . If animals have no future, the existence of many is most wretched; multitudes are starved, cruelly beaten, and loaded during life; many die under a barbarous vivisection. I cannot believe that any creature was created for uncompensated misery; it would be contrary to the attributes of God's mercy and justice.

— — —

We English cannot boast of humanity, however, as long as our sportsmen find pleasure in shooting down tame pigeons as they fly terrified out of a cage.

— — —

. . . I was much pleased to hear that Mr. Herbert, M. P., has brought in a bill to protect land birds, which has been passed in Parliament; but I am grieved to find that "The lark which at Heaven's gate sings" is thought unworthy of man's protection. Among the numerous plans for the education of the young, let us hope that mercy may be taught as a part of religion.

Thomas Paine

There is something in meanness which excites a species of resentment that never subsides, and something in cruelty which stirs up the heart to the highest agony of human hatred.

Charles Kingsley

[The perfect naturalist] must be gentle and courteous, brave and enterprising and withal patient and undaunted in investigation, knowing . . . that the kingdom of nature, like the kingdom of heaven, must be taken by violence, and that only to those who knock earnestly and long, does the Great Mother open the doors of her sanctuary, . . . always reverent, yet never superstitious, wondering at the commonest, yet not surprised by the most strange; free from the idols of size and sensuous loveliness, . . . holding every phenomenon worth the noting down; believing that every pebble holds a treasure, every bud a revelation; making it a point of conscience to pass over nothing through laziness or hastiness, . . . and looking at every object as if he were never to behold it more. . . .

John Greenleaf Whittier

Oh let us try to forget everything but our duty to God and our fellow beings.

— — —

I like to see Nature free and wild and untamed as when it came from the hand of its Creator.

— — —

I would encourage reading circles—healthful sports and exercises, and excursions amidst the serene beauty of Nature, so well calculated to exalt the mind towards that which St. Augustine speaks of as the "Eternal Beauty always new and always old."

— — —

How I wish I could show thee how lovely our river valley looks in the mellow light. The cold winds and rains have scattered the frosted foliage mostly, but the oaks still retain their many shaded brown leaves, and here and there a rock maple still flowers through the grey nakedness of the woods. It is still as a dream— one of those days which seem specially sent to assure us of the love of God.

William Morris

In the defacements of our big towns by all that commerce brings with it, who heeds it ? who tries to control their squalor and hideousness ? there is nothing but thoughtlessness and recklessness in the matter. . . .

Is money to be gathered ? cut down the pleasant trees among the houses, pull down ancient and venerable buildings for the money that a few square yards of London dirt will fetch; blacken rivers, hide the sun and poison the air with smoke and worse, and it's nobody's business to see to it or mend it: that is all that modern commerce, the counting-house forgetful of the workshop, will do for us herein . . . unless people care about carrying on their business without making the world hideous, how can they care about Art?

———

[I want] that these islands which make the land we love should no longer be treated as here a cinder heap, and there a game preserve, but as the fair green garden of Northern Europe, which no man on any pretence should be allowed to befoul and disfigure. I want all the works of man's hand to be beautiful, rising in fair and honourable gradation from the simplest household goods to the stately public building, adorned with the handiwork of the greatest masters of expression. . . .

———

Socialism is a theory of life, taking for its starting point the evolution of society; or, let us say, of man as a social being. Since man has certain material *necessities* as an animal, Society is founded on man's attempt to satisfy those necessities; and Socialism, or social consciousness, points out to him the way of doing so which will interfere least with the development of his specially human capacities, and the satisfaction of what, for lack of better words, I will call his spiritual and mental capacities.

GEORGE MACDONALD

As to [a person's natural] death itself that is not in any sense an evil, for it is not the thing it looks to the eye that looks on. I can well imagine the freed one exclaiming "Is this what they call death!"

— — —

You tell me about the sea and the sky and the shore so beautifully, so lovingly, so truthfully, that I love you more for it. . . . Tell me again about everything round about you; every expression the beautiful face of Nature puts on. Tell me, too, about the world within your own soul—that living world—without which the world without would be but a lifelessness. The beautiful things round about you are the expression of God's face, or, as in Faust, the garment whereby we see the deity. Is God's sun more beautiful than God himself? Has he not left it to us as a symbol of his own life-giving light?

— — —

Write to me about the sea & the sky, and all those never-ceasing beauties, ever changing yet still the same great truths. The *sense* of which makes a man feel great too. These truths ever the same yet ever presenting new aspects of beauty, different to the same mind at different times—yet ever in essence one and the same.

VERA BRITTAIN

Only when we are thoroughly acquainted with facts can we afford to disregard them; only after a thorough understanding of technique can we dare to reach beyond it. To attempt to achieve without knowledge is like beginning a journey along an unknown road on a dark night; knowledge is God.

– – –

The smart clothes I know I possess—the prettiness which people say is mine—what satisfaction can they give at the height compared with the slightest of intellectual achievements?

– – –

. . . If I am to have any distinction, I want it to be that of intellect & talent—so far, far more worth having than the pomp & circumstance that comes from being the possessor of wealth or the product of generations of intermarriage. Expensive lunatics, that are kept in motors & sables by an industrious nation's toil!

– – –

He said bitterly that I wanted to be famous & make a name for myself, but I should be none the better for it if I did etc. etc. I gently but firmly insisted again that I had no care for the material glory even of fame. . . .

I wonder if he could *ever* understand that my search, that my object, for which I enter upon taking exams. & university life, is the Beautiful & the True in every atom of created life . . . & that I learn & learn because I desire to have knowledge, believing that the more complete the knowledge, the nearer is one to Truth, my high ideal & final goal, as yet unseen but sometimes shining luminously through clouds. I wonder if he could understand how it is that I, leaning out & gazing at an earthly scene with a fierce yearning & aspiration which no friends or parents could either give or take away, feel something stir in my soul which is one with the glory, the diversity, of the world's Creator, and one with the best which is in all that is.

Late this afternoon there was one of the loveliest skies I have ever seen—warm & glowing in the west, with tiny rosy clouds floating above the horizon, while in the east was a heavy black cloud, & just below it a long streak of the purest silvery blue, against which the tall elm trees on the sky-line stood up dark. To raise one's eyes heavenward from the cold & gloomy lane was like gazing out of earth into Paradise.

Georgia O'Keeffe

Don't you think we need to conserve our energies—emotions and feelings for what we are going to make the big things in life instead of letting so much run away on the little things every day. Self-control is a wonderful thing.

I think we must even keep ourselves from feeling too much— often—if we are going to keep sane and see with a clear unprejudiced vision.

I am one of the intuitives—or subjectives—or whatever you call the type of person who comes to quick and positive decisions— and then sometimes—when it interests me—have to work for days or weeks or months to find out why I came to those decisions. . . .

A large proportion of the people who think they want to be Artists of one kind or another finally become commercial artists— and the work that they send out into the world is a prostitution of some really creative phase of Art.

– – –

I feel that a real living form is the natural result of the individuals effort to create the living thing out of the adventure of his spirit into the unknown . . . and from that experience comes the desire to make the unknown known—By unknown I mean the thing that means so much to the person that he wants to put it down—clarify—something he feels but does not clearly understand . . . Making the unknown known. . . .

– – –

One thing that gets me about . . . the Taos country—it is so beautiful—and so poisonous—the only way to live in it is to strictly mind your own business . . . and use your ears as little as possible—and keep the proportion of what one sees as it is in nature—much country—desert and mountain—and relatively keep the human being as about the size of a pin point—That was my feeling about my summer—most of the human side of it isn't worth thinking about—and as one chooses between the country and the human being the country becomes much more wonderful.

James Joyce

All things are inconstant except the faith of the soul, which changes all things and fills their inconstancy with light.

Siegfried Sassoon

One cannot be a good soldier and a good poet at the same time. Soldiering depends on a multitude of small details; one must not miss any of the details. Poetry depends on wayward moods and sudden emotions.

– – –

Heavens! what fortitude one needs, to become a decent writer. One runs madly through green thickets, enamoured of the bird-notes which last but a few moments; one stumbles, picks oneself up, and emerges into a barren waste; one ruminates miserably for a while, dragging desolate feet through the dust of dead dreams. And then, if one is lucky, one plunges into another fool's paradise of 'poetry'. And at the end, perhaps, one will meet death with half-a-dozen 'immortal' lines scribbled on half-a-sheet of note-paper. Lucky is he who does that!

RALPH HODGSON

There is one thing which seems to me worth doing. And that is for one man *to give birth to an idea* which two, or ten, or forty other men can develop. It may be an idea whose effect will have become dim and diluted in a few generations. But life seems to work that way, an idea being taken up by one decade after another until it has served its purpose and expressed what the world was waiting for.

EMILE ZOLA

. . . Put your dreams, those beautiful golden dreams, onto your canvases and try to pass onto them that ideal love you possess.

– – –

Think of art, of the highest art; do not consider form alone, because form alone is commercial painting; consider the idea, dream lovely dreams; the form will come with work. . . .

Edgar Degas

... The heart is an instrument which goes rusty if it isn't used. Is it possible to be a heartless artist?

— — —

A painting is above all a product of the artist's imagination, it must never be a copy. If, at a later stage, he wants to add two or three touches from nature, of course it doesn't spoil anything. But the air one sees in the paintings of the masters is not the air one breathes.

— — —

... There is nothing that can be done without the patient collaboration of time.

— — —

It seems to me that if one wants to be a serious artist today and create an original little niche for oneself, or at least ensure that one preserves the highest degree of innocence of character, one must constantly immerse oneself in solitude. There is too much tittle-tattle.

— — —

Drawing is not what one sees but what one makes others see.

— — —

I must impress upon myself that I know nothing at all, for it is the only way to progress.

GUSTAVE FLAUBERT

Of all lies, art is the least untrue. Try to love it with a love that is exclusive, ardent, devoted. It will not fail you. Only the Idea is eternal and necessary.

– – –

Fame! Fame! What is fame? It is nothing. A mere noise, the external accompaniment of the joy Art gives us.

– – –

Work, work, write—write all you can while the muse bears you along. She is the best battle-steed, the best coach to carry you through life in noble style. The burden of existence does not weigh on our shoulders when we are composing. It is true that the fatigue and the feeling of desertion that follow are all the more terrible. Let it be so, however.

– – –

I have no inborn gift. . . . Style is achieved only by dint of atrocious labor, fanatical and unremitting stubbornness.

– – –

Passion does not make verses; and the more personal you are, the weaker. . . . The less you feel a thing, *the more capable you are of expressing it as it is* (as it *always* is, in itself, in its universality, freed from all ephemeral contingencies). But one must be able to *make oneself feel it*. This faculty is, simply, genius: the ability to *see*, to have the model posing there before you.

– – –

The artist in his work must be like God in his creation—invisible and all-powerful: he must be everywhere felt, but never seen.

– – –

If everything around us, instead of permanently conspiring to drown us in a slough of mud, contributed rather to keep our spirits healthy, who can tell whether we might not be able to do for aesthetics what stoicism did for morals?

– – –

What seems to me the highest and most difficult achievement of Art is not to make us laugh or cry, nor to arouse our lust or rage, but to do what nature does—that is, to set us dreaming. The most beautiful works have this quality. They are serene in aspect, inscrutable. The means by which they act on us are various: they are as motionless as cliffs, stormy as the ocean, leafy, green and murmurous as forests, forlorn as the desert, blue as the sky.

– – –

You tell me that you are falling more and more in love with nature. My own passion for it is becoming uncontrollable. At times I look on animals and even trees with a tenderness that amounts to a feeling of affinity.

GEORGES BRAQUE

Limitation of means determines style, engenders new form, and gives impulse to creation. Limited means often constitute the charm and force of primitive painting. Extension, on the contrary, leads the arts to decadence.

— — —

The senses deform, the mind forms. Work to perfect the mind. There is no certitude but in what the mind conceives.

— — —

Nobility grows out of contained emotion. Emotion should not be rendered by an excited trembling; it can neither be added on nor be imitated. It is the seed, the work is the flower.

— — —

I like the rule that corrects the emotion.

L. S. LOWRY

The difference between an artist and everyone else is that everyone else is only happy when they stop working, an artist is only happy when he *is* working.

BERTRAND RUSSELL

Let us keep before our minds constantly the thought of serving the world, not some derivative principle, nor pride, nor desire to confute our opponents, but the positive desire to nourish life in the world rather than to minister to death. . . .

— — —

Work, when it goes well, is in itself a great delight; and after any considerable achievement I look back at it with the sort of placid satisfaction one has after climbing a mountain. What is absolutely vital to me is the self-respect I get from work—when (as often) I have done something for which I feel remorse, work restores me to a belief that it is better I should exist than not exist. And another thing I greatly value is the kind of communion with past and future discoverers. I often have imaginary conversations with Leibniz, in which I tell him how fruitful his ideas have proved, and how much more beautiful the result is than he could have foreseen; and in moments of self-confidence, I imagine students hereafter having similar thoughts about me.

— — —

My window looked out upon two Lombardy poplars, each about a hundred feet high, and I used to watch the shadow of the house creeping up them as the sun set. In the morning I woke very early and sometimes saw Venus rise. On one occasion I mistook the planet for a lantern in the wood. I saw the sunrise on most mornings, and on bright April days I would sometimes slip out of the house for a long walk before breakfast. I watched the sunset turn the earth red and the clouds golden; I listened to the wind, and exulted in the lightning. Throughout my childhood I had an increasing sense of loneliness, and of despair of ever meeting anyone which whom I could talk. Nature and books and (later) mathematics saved me from complete despondency.

SYLVIA PLATH

And there it is: when asked what role I will plan to fill, I say, "What do you mean, *role*? I plan not to step into a part on marrying—but to go on living as an intelligent mature human being, growing and learning as I always have. No shift, no radical change in life habits." *Never* will there be a circle, signifying me and my operations, confined solely to home, other womenfolk, and community service, enclosed in the larger worldly circle of my mate, who brings home from his periphery of contact with the world the tales only of vicarious experience to me. . . .

Writing is a religious act: it is an ordering, a reforming, a relearning and reloving of people and the world as they are and as they might be. A shaping which does not pass away like a day of typing or a day of teaching. The writing lasts: it goes about on its own in the world. People read it: react to it as a person, a philosophy, a religion, a flower: they like it, or do not. It helps them, or it does not. It feels to intensify living: you give more, probe, ask, look, learn, and shape this: you get more: monsters, answers, color and form, knowledge. You do it for itself first. If it brings in money, how nice. You do not do it first for money. Money isn't why you sit down at the typewriter.

I want to write because I have the urge to excel in one medium of translation and expression of life. I can't be satisfied with the colossal job of merely living.

MARK TWAIN

. . . I am writing with red-hot interest. Nothing grieves me now, nothing troubles me, nothing bothers me or gets my attention. I don't think of anything but the book, and I don't have an hour's unhappiness about anything. . . .

I am working but it is for the sake of the work—the "surcease of sorrow" that is found there. I work all the days, and trouble vanishes away when I use that magic.

Jules Renard

I was brought up by a library.

Beaumont Newhall

... The more I think of creative photography, the more I realize how true it is that what counts in art is what is inside of us. That is what separates the artist from the layman—the ability to recognize and the skill to transmit to others those observations and feelings.

Joseph Jefferson

The methods by which actors arrive at great effects vary according to their own natures; this renders the teaching of the art by any strictly defined lines a difficult matter.

— — —

In observing the works of great painters I find that they have no conventionalities except their own; hence they are masters, and each is at the head of his own school. They are original, and could not imitate even if they would.

— — —

... The work of an actor is fleeting: it not only dies with him, but, through his different moods, may vary from night to night. If the performance be indifferent it is no consolation for the audience to hear that the player acted well last night, or to be told that he will act better to-morrow night; it is *this* night that the public has to deal with, and the impression the actor has made, good or bad, remains as such upon the mind of that particular audience.

– – –

The author, painter, or musician, if he be dissatisfied with his work, may alter and perfect it before giving it publicity, but an actor cannot rub out; he ought, therefore, in justice to his audience, to be sure of what he is going to place before it. Should a picture in an art gallery be carelessly painted we can pass on to another, or if a book fails to please us we can put it down. An escape from this kind of dullness is easily made, but in a theater the auditor is imprisoned. . . . It is this helpless condition that renders careless acting so offensive.

WASSILY KANDINSKY

Painting is an art, and art in general is not a mere purposeless creating of things that dissipate themselves in a void, but a power that has a purpose and must serve the development and refinement of the human soul. . . .

– – –

I value only those artists who really are artists, that is, who consciously or unconsciously, in an entirely original form, embody the expression of their inner life; who work only for this end and cannot work otherwise.

– – –

Consciously or unconsciously [artists] are obeying Socrates' command–Know thyself. Consciously or unconsciously artists are studying and proving their material, setting in the balance the spiritual value of those elements, with which it is their several privilege to work.

— — —

The work of art consists of two elements; the inner and the outer.

The inner element, taken by itself, is the emotion in the soul of the artist. This emotion is capable of calling forth what is, essentially, a corresponding emotion in the soul of the observer.

As long as the soul is joined to the body, it can as a rule only receive vibrations via the medium of the feelings. Feelings are therefore a bridge from the nonmaterial to the material (in the case of the artist) and from the material to the nonmaterial (in the case of the observer).

Emotion–feelings–the work of art–feelings–emotion.

— — —

The inner need is built up of three mystical elements: (1) Every artist, as a creator, has something in him which calls for expression. . . . (2) Every artist, as child of his age, is impelled to express the spirit of his age. . . . (3) Every artist, as a servant of art, has to help the cause of art. . . .

— — —

The artist is not born to a life of pleasure. He must not live idle; he has a hard work to perform, and one which often proves a cross to be borne. He must realize that his every deed, feeling, and thought are raw but sure material from which his work is to arise, that he is free in art but not in life. . . . The artist is not only a king . . . because he has great power, but also because he has great duties.

Among the arts, painting has set foot on the path that leads from the practically purposeful to the spiritually purposeful.

The most modern musicians like Debussy create a spiritual impression, often taken from nature, but embodied in purely musical form.

EUGENE DELACROIX

With the majority of men, the intelligence is a field that lies fallow for almost all their lives. Seeing the multitude of stupid or at least mediocre people who seem to live only to vegetate, one has the right to be astonished that God should have given reason to his creatures, the faculty of imagining, of comparing, of combining, etc., to produce such small fruit. Laziness, ignorance, a passing situation, or chance throws them out of their course, and changes almost all men into passive instruments of circumstance.

We never know what we can get out of ourselves. Laziness is undoubtedly the greatest enemy to the development of our faculties. And so, *know thyself* would be the fundamental axiom of every society in which each of its members would perform his role exactly and would fulfill it to its limit.

I have told myself a hundred times that painting, that is to say the material thing called painting, was no more than the pretext, than the bridge between the mind of the painter and that of the spectator. Cold exactitude is not art: ingenious artifice, when it *pleases* or when it *expresses*, is art itself.

To feel that you have done what should be done raises you in your own eyes. After that, if you have no other reason for pleasure, you enjoy that chief of pleasures, which is self-content. The satisfaction of the man who has worked and made good use of his day is immense. When I am in that state, it is delightful for me, afterward, to enjoy my rest and even the mildest recreations. Indeed, I can find myself in the company of the most tiresome people, and feel no regret about it. The memory of the task that I have accomplished comes back to me and preserves me from boredom and sadness.

Nature is a dictionary; one draws words from it.

Delightful walk in the woods while my lodging is being arranged. A thousand various thoughts are suggested amidst this universal smile of nature. At every step in my walk, I disturb trysts—results of the spring season; the noise of my steps disturbs the poor birds who fly off, always in pairs. Oh! The birds, the dogs, the rabbits! Humble professors of good sense, all of them silent, all of them submissive to the eternal decrees—how far they all are above our vain and cold knowledge!

BERNARD DEVOTO

I should find it hard to state exactly what my ambition as a mature man is. It would run something like this: to do good work, to do work in which I may take some satisfaction and my friends some pleasure; at the utmost, as Frost once said of Robinson, to put something on the record that will not easily be dislodged.

- - -

The pursuit of truth–or the similitude that in an illusory world seems to be the truth–is the most splendid adventure open to us.

RUTH DRAPER

Last night a man who is staying here played divinely to us–Bach and Schumann–on and on–as I sat by the fire–all the noble and exalted beauty that they–Germans–have given to the world–and I shuddered to think of the contrast to the man [Hitler] they have set up as their God. The youth are all aflame with desire to fight, revenge and hate fill their hearts. Cruelty and brutality and lust for power are unleashed again. And I thought of my love–flying toward the stars–dying for his ideal–with his faith in life, in the universal, in aspiration–and the struggle and sacrifice that growth involves; one's thoughts get so tangled–one sees such triumph of materialism, such insoluble problems and blocks to spiritual enlightenment; then I think of him and I know he would still believe, still see beauty and be undismayed. I must go out and walk in the lovely Spring–blossoms, lambs and flowers everywhere–paradise save for the longing which makes it almost hell–

- - -

As long as we go on loving and working life is worth while.

- - -

Courage, enthusiasm, awareness–if only one can keep these to the end.

Lord Byron

The first thing a young writer must expect, and yet can least of all suffer, is *criticism*. I did not bear it–a few years, and many changes have since passed over my head, and my reflections on that subject are attended with regret. I find, on dispassionate comparison, my own revenge more than the provocation warranted. It is true, I was very young,–that might be an excuse to those I attacked–but to *me* it is none. The best reply to all objections is to write better, and if your enemies will not then do you justice, the world will. On the other hand, you should not be discouraged; to be opposed is not to be vanquished, though a timid mind is apt to mistake every scratch for a mortal wound. There is a saying of Dr. Johnson's, which it is as well to remember, that "no man was ever written down except by himself." I hope you will meet with as few obstacles as yourself can desire; but if you should, you will find that they are to be *stepped* over; to *kick* them down is the first resolve of a young and fiery spirit, a pleasant thing enough at the time, but not so afterwards. . . .

Wallace Stevens

To practice an art, to need it and to love it, is the quickest way of learning that all happiness lies in one's self. . . .

– – –

I want my powers to be put to their fullest use–to be exhausted when I am done with them. On the other hand I do not want to have to make a petty struggle for existence–physical or literary. I must try not to be a dilettante–half dream, half deed. I must be all dream or all deed.

— — —

What does not have a kinship, a sympathy, a relation, an inspiration and an indissolubility with our lives ought not, and under healthy conditions could not have a place in them.

— — —

To say that stars were made to guide navigators etc. seems like stretching a point; but the real use of their beauty (which is not their excuse) is that it is a service, a food. Beauty is strength.

LIANE DE POUGY

'What does he know, who has never been tested?' I read that fine line in yesterday's chapter of the *Imitation of Jesus Christ*. It is true that a satisfied, full-fed person who has been successful almost without a struggle is never sensitive or interesting. 'Who knows himself who has not suffered?' said the poet. Suffering is good, it purifies, sanctifies, enlarges, elevates.

— — —

This morning I went for a walk by myself in the grey, in the mist, in the warm wind which foretells a storm. I felt so good, alone in the universe, dreaming, cut loose. I no longer knew where I came from, I had no idea where I was going. Yesterday my chapter from the *Imitation* was about solitude and silence. I have just been granted an experience of it. I felt the sweetness of it. A great peace, a great calm and serenity flowed into me with the air I breathed.

THOMAS MERTON

My soul does not find itself unless it acts. Therefore it must act. Stagnation and inactivity bring spiritual death.

- - -

Who is willing to be satisfied with a job that expresses all his limitations?

- - -

Our being is not to be enriched merely by activity or experience as such. Everything depends on the *quality* of our acts and our experiences. A multitude of badly performed actions and of experiences only half-lived exhausts and depletes our being. By doing things badly we make ourselves less real. This growing unreality cannot help but make us unhappy and fill us with a sense of guilt. But the purity of our conscience has a natural proportion with the depth of our being and the quality of our acts: and when our activity is habitually disordered, our malformed conscience can think of nothing better to tell us than to multiply the *quantity* of our acts, without perfecting their quality. And so we go from bad to worse, exhaust ourselves, empty our whole life of all content, and fall into despair.

JAY WILLIAM HUDSON

Indeed, seek pleasure as if it were the only ideal in life and you never achieve it; it eludes you. The saddest and most jaded being on this earth is the professional pleasure-seeker. The life of pleasure, as in the case of Faust, comes upon its own tragic self-defeat.

— — —

A life of pleasure-seeking is anomalous and, in its degeneration into selfishness and aimlessness and finally boredom, it is on its logical way to one of two things, the destruction of the seeker, or the abandonment of the search.

ANTHONY TROLLOPE

For what remains to me of life I trust for my happiness still chiefly to my work–hoping that when the power of work be over with me, God may be pleased to take me from a world in which, according to my view, there can then be no joy. . . .

AGNES MILLER

Perhaps, it is true, there is no solution to this problem [of war] for the present but to let it wear on & fret itself away & for each of us to help as best he can in his or her own way looking steadfastly to the future & never doubting but that wrong will perish, right will triumph. But in the future we must all *strive & strive* to secure that there shall be no wars. I hate to hear wise and farsighted people declare that there will be another & just as terrible war before the century is out. I think they must be men of matter; but we must be men of spirit & we must prove to them & all the world that they are wrong.

OLAF STAPLEDON

But I guess that the more alive one is the more wide awake is one's sense of beauty, so that if one were a perfectly alive free soul unhampered by the tyranny of pleasure & pain one would recognise every message of every sense as a dazzling view of the world's soul.

JOHN GARDNER

I once asked a highly regarded music teacher what was the secret of his extraordinary success with students. He said, "First I teach them that it is better to do it well than to do it badly. Many have never been taught the pleasure and pride in setting standards and then living up to them."

— — —

Those who are most deeply devoted to a democratic society must be precisely the ones who insist upon excellence, who insist that free men are capable of the highest standards of performance, who insist that a free society can be a great society in the richest sense of that phrase. The idea for which this nation stands will not survive if the highest goal free men can set themselves is an amiable mediocrity.

VLADIMIR HOROWITZ

One suggestion I would offer is never to imitate. There is an old Chinese proverb which says, "Do not seek to follow in the master's footsteps; seek what he sought." Imitation is a caricature. Any imitation. Find out for yourself.

ALAN S. PARKES

. . . The more you want to believe a thing the harder you should look at it.

— — —

Two minds may strike from each other sparks which neither would have generated separately.

The greater the care, the fewer the young.

J. B. S. HALDANE

The churches are half empty today because their creeds are full of obsolete science, and their ethical codes are suited to a social organization far simpler than that of today. . . . If I thought that the aims of science and art were merely material I should belong to some church. But I believe that the scientist is trying to express absolute truth and the artist absolute beauty, so that I find in science and art, and in an attempt to lead a good life, all the religion that I want.

We have got rid of physical starvation. We still have intellectual, aesthetic, and spiritual starvation, which to my mind are greater evils than any mere economic inequality. Until our educational system is so altered as to give a fair deal to every boy and girl who desires a first-rate education and is capable of benefiting by it, my political views are likely to remain, as they are now, on the left.

— — —

We are all of us cut off from nature, and not only the town dwellers. It is perhaps important to remember something that we sometimes forget: that a field is as much a human product as a street. It is only on the seashore, on the moors, and in a few forests, that we see nature anything like what it was before man interfered with it. Yet if we are intellectually and emotionally cut off from nature, we suffer a loss which is hard to define. . . .

— — —

We ought . . . for our own good to have access to nature and knowledge of it. To my mind, it is monstrous that any child should grow up without some acquaintance with nature, and above all I would say without an opportunity for intimate knowledge of some individual plants and animals.

— — —

I am a part of nature, and, like other natural objects, from a lightning flash to a mountain range, I shall last out my time and then finish. This prospect does not worry me, because some of my work will not die when I do so.

Thomas Henry Huxley

I don't know and I don't care whether I shall ever be what is called a great man. I will leave my mark somewhere, and it shall be clear and distinct—T. H. H. his mark—and free from the abominable blur of cant, humbug, and self-seeking which surrounds everything in this present world—that is to say, supposing that I am not already unconsciously tainted myself, a result of which I have a morbid dread.

— — —

Science seems to me to teach in the highest and strongest manner the great truth which is embodied in the Christian conception of entire surrender to the will of God. Sit down before fact as a little child, be prepared to give up every preconceived notion, follow humbly wherever and to whatever abysses nature leads, or you shall learn nothing. I have only begun to learn content and peace of mind since I have resolved at all risks to do this.

— — —

... The cosmos remains always beautiful and profoundly interesting in every corner—and if I had as many lives as a cat I would leave no corner unexplored.

— — —

Even the best of modern civilisations appears to me to exhibit a condition of mankind which neither embodies any worthy ideal nor even possesses the merit of stability. I do not hesitate to express my opinion that, if there is no hope of a large improvement of the condition of the greater part of the human family; if it is true that the increase of knowledge, the winning of a greater dominion over Nature which is its consequence, and the wealth which follows on that dominion, are to make no difference in the extent and the intensity of Want, with its concomitant physical and moral degradation, among the masses of the people, I should hail the advent of some kindly comet, which would sweep the whole affair away, as a desirable consummation.

— — —

The politicians tell us, "You must educate the masses because they are going to be masters". The clergy join in the cry for education, for they affirm that the people are drifting away from church and chapel into the broadest infidelity. The manufacturers and the capitalists swell the chorus lustily. They declare that ignorance makes bad workmen; that England will soon be unable to turn out cotton goods, or steam engines, cheaper that other people; and the, Ichabod! Ichabod! the glory will be departed from us. And a few voices are lifted up in favour of the doctrine that the masses should be educated because they are men and women with unlimited capacities of being, doing, and suffering, and that it is as true now, as ever it was, that the people perish for lack of knowledge.

— — —

In an ideal University, as I conceive it, a man should be able to obtain instruction in all forms of knowledge, and discipline in the use of all methods by which knowledge is obtained. In such a University, the force of living example should fire the students with a noble ambition to emulate the learning of learned men, and to follow in the footsteps of the explorers of new fields of knowledge. And the very air he breathes should be charged with that enthusiasm for truth, that fanaticism of veracity, which is a greater possession than much learning; a nobler gift than the power of increasing knowledge; by so much greater and nobler than these, as the moral nature of man is greater than the intellectual; for veracity is the heart of morality.

———

There is a well-worn adage that those who set out upon a great enterprise would do well to count the cost. I am not sure that this is always true. I think that some of the very greatest enterprises in this world have been carried out successfully simply because the people who undertook them did not count the cost; and I am much of the opinion that, in this very case, the most instructive consideration for us is the cost of doing nothing.

———

Let every child be instructed in those general views of the phenomena of Nature . . . a general knowledge of the earth, and what is on it, in it, and about it. The child asks, "What is the moon, and why does it shine?" "What is this water, and where does it run?" "What is the wind?" "What makes the waves in the sea?" "Where does this animal live, and what is the use of that plant?" And if not snubbed and stunted by being told not to ask foolish questions, there is no limit to the intellectual craving of a young child; nor any bounds to the slow, but solid, accretion of knowledge and development of the thinking faculty in this way. To all such questions, answers which are necessarily incomplete, though true as far as they go, may be given by any teacher whose ideas represent real knowledge and not mere book-learning; and a panoramic view of Nature, accompanied by a strong infusion of the scientific habit of mind, may thus be placed within the reach of every child of nine or ten.

———

One of the most essential conditions, if not the chief cause, of the struggle for existence, is the tendency to multiply without limit, which man shares with all living things. It is notable that "increase and multiply" is a commandment traditionally much older than the ten; and that it is, perhaps, the only one which has been spontaneously and *ex animo* obeyed by the great majority of the human race. But, in civilised society, the inevitable result of such obedience is the reestablishment, in all its intensity, of that struggle for existence—the war of each against all—the mitigation or abolition of which was the chief end of social organisation.

John Rock

I would call our attention to the critical difference between *procreation*—bringing forth, begetting—and reproduction, that is making a copy, a likeness. Intellectually mature human beings do not reproduce, do not multiply themselves, when they merely beget.

— — —

Every couple owes it . . . to God . . . , to itself, to the community to procreate only those children whom it will be able to bring up and prepare adequately for life.

G. M. Carstairs

When, because of increasing over-population, the standards of living actually decline at the very times when people's aspirations have been raised, the stage is set for further outbreaks of collective irrationality and violence.

It is imperative that we recognise the gravity of this threat, because mankind today possesses weapons of such destructive power that the world cannot afford to risk outbreaks of mass violence; and yet the lesson of history points to just such a disaster, unless population control can be achieved before vast human communities degenerate into the semblance of concentration camp inmates, if not . . . pathologically aggressive apes.

JOSEPH HUTCHINSON

For make no mistake, the country [Britain] already carries a population as great as the environment can support without degeneration, and it will call for all the knowledge and skill it can command to prevent irreparable damage before we achieve a stable population, even if we set about sterilization without delay. Our greatest need is to master the threat of our own numbers.

HAROLD NICOLSON

My last day at the *Evening Standard*. I have learnt much in this place. I have learnt that shallowness is the supreme evil. I have learnt that rapidity, hustle and rush are the allies of superficiality.

– – –

It is approaching sunset and we get the best view of the [Grand] Canyon we have yet seen. The shadows are slate-blue and the rocks a dominant *sang-de-boeuf* trailing off to pink in places and in places to orange. We walk back thinking out comparisons. I say it is like a wood-fire–looking into the glow of logs. Viti says it is like nothing on earth. She adds that she feels 'increased'. I say that I do too.

RUPERT BROOKE

If you watch the great white cliff, from the foot of which the glacier flows–seven miles away, but it seems two–you will sometimes see a little puff of silvery smoke go up, thin, and vanish. A few seconds later comes the roar of terrific, distant thunder. The mountains tower and smile unregarding in the sun. It was an avalanche. And if you climb any of the ridges or peaks around, there are discovered other valleys and heights and ranges, wild and desert, stretching endlessly away. As day draws to an end the shadows on the snow turn bluer, the crying of innumerable waters hushes, and the immense, bare ramparts of westward-facing rock that guard the great valley win a rich, golden-brown radiance. Long after the sun has set they seem to give forth the splendor of the day, and the tranquillity of their centuries, in undiminished fullness. They have that other-worldly serenity which a perfect old age possesses. And as with a perfect old age, so here, the color and the light ebb so gradually out of things that you could swear nothing of the radiance and glory gone up to the very moment before the dark.

– – –

I'm going to put on my overcoat and sit in the snow and look at the Grand Canyon. It is very large and very untidy, like my soul. But unlike my soul, it has peace in it.

ROCKWELL KENT

Forever shall man seek the solitudes, and the most utter desolation of the wilderness to achieve through hardship the rebirth of his pride.

– – –

Being *alone* in one's youth is of the greatest importance in the development of one's latent personality and of all the faculties of reflection and imagination—and of practical self-reliance.

THOMAS GRAY

I own I have not, as yet, any where met with those grand and simple works of Art, that are to amaze one, and whose sight one is to be the better for: But those of Nature have astonished me beyond expression. In our little journey up to the Grande Chartreuse, I do not remember to have gone ten paces without an exclamation, that there was no restraining: Not a precipice, not a torrent, not a cliff, but is pregnant with religion and poetry. There are certain scenes that would awe an atheist into belief, without the help of other argument.

— — —

... At the bottom of a steep smooth lawn embosom'd in old woods, which climb half way up the mountain's side, & discover above them a broken line of crags, that crown the scene. Not a single red tile, no flaring Gentleman's house, or garden-walls, break in upon the repose of this unsuspected paradise, but all is peace, rusticity, & happy poverty in its neatest most becoming attire.

Philip James Bailey

Art is man's nature; nature is God's art.

Henry Miller

I have no respect for the artist, however great, who does not practice his art in living. Recently I observed with joy that I am able to act out my beliefs. One's behavior then becomes very simplified. All complications fall away. You have no fear of being either ridiculed *or* crucified. You have the deep joy of certitude. You know then, for the first time, so it seems to me, what the moral sphere really is. And, though you may disagree, I think the moral and the aesthetic are one. All is one. That's the utter, stark, simple beauty of it.

Konrad Lorenz

Aesthetic and ethical feeling appear to be closely related. . . .
The complete blindness to everything beautiful, so common in
these times, is a mental illness that must be taken seriously for
the simple reason that it goes hand in hand with insensitivity to
the ethically wrong.

— — —

Emotional loyalty to an institutionalized norm does not make
it a value, otherwise war, even modern technical war, would be
one.

— — —

Under the pressure of interhuman competition, all that is
good and useful, for humanity as a whole as well as for the
individual human being, has been completely set aside. The
overwhelming majority of people today value only that which
brings commercial gain and is calculated to outflank fellow
humans in the relentless race of competition. Every means serving
this end appears, falsely, as a value in itself.

— — —

[Among the processes] threatening to destroy not only our
civilization but mankind as a species . . . are:

1. Overpopulation of the earth, because of the superabundance
   of social contacts, forces everyone of us to shut himself off in
   an essentially "inhuman" way, and which, because of the
   crowding of many individuals into a small space, elicits ag-
   gression.

2. Devastation of our natural environment, with destruction not only of our surroundings but also of man's reverential awe for the beauty and greatness of a creation superior to him.

— — —

In America and England . . . it is not at all common [for fishermen] to slaughter a fish when it is caught. One fish after another is caught and tossed into the boat, where it dies a slow and cruel death by suffocation. Here is a case where a sense of pity, of conservation, of kindness to animals fails to exist because these people were not taught such sensibilities in their earliest childhood.

— — —

One doubts human ethics when one sees how animals are kept in close quarters for the purpose of financial gain. . . . [I mean] the production-line maintenance of animals, which is without a doubt one of the darkest and most shameful chapters in human culture. If you have ever stood before a stable where animals are being fattened and have heard hundreds of calves bleating, if you can understand the calf's cry for help, then you will have had enough of those people who derive profit from it.

— — —

. . . The acts of violence perpetrated by Greenpeace conservationists are often necessary in the face of the insurmountable difficulties we find in the world. Today, it is very difficult to uncover any remnants of truly unspoiled nature, and that which remains should be defended with all vehemence.

— — —

I don't believe that the Pope is infallible. . . . By his indirect demand that the poorest of the poor should bring an unlimited number of children into the world, the Pope has ruined the lives of many of my personal friends who were sympathetic toward Christianity.

JULIAN HUXLEY

The population explosion is making us ask . . . What are people for?

J. R. ACKERLEY

I have no animus against the human race, I simply want it painlessly but drastically reduced, for I don't believe it will ever reduce itself. I don't want nuclear war, it would destroy the animals and our treasures, which I wish to preserve. I want a beautiful plague, a human scourge, which would take off in a jiffy three-quarters at least of the entire population. . . . I can see no other solution to a doubled population . . . and the animals all gone.

— — —

I don't think anyone should attempt to gain possession of an animal heart unless they feel as sure as mortality can feel that they will never fail it. To get the confidence of any animal and then let it down seems to me almost the worst crime anyone can commit, human relationships matter less, people understand people, suffer though they may; animals understand nothing, only loss.

WILLIAM HAZLITT

. . . In our love of Nature there is all the force of individual attachment combined with the most airy abstraction. It is this circumstance which gives that refinement, expansion, and wild interest to feelings of this sort, when strongly excited, which every one must have experienced who is a true lover of Nature.

— — —

For him, then, who has well acquainted himself with Nature's works, she wears always one face, and speaks the same well-known language, striking on the heart, amidst unquiet thoughts and the tumult of the world, like the music of one's native tongue heard in some far-off country.

— — —

A fine poet thus describes the effect of the sight of nature on his mind:

> The sounding cataract
> Haunted me like a passion: the tall rock,
> The mountain, and the deep and gloomy wood,
> Their colours and their forms were then to me
> An appetite, a feeling, and a love,
> That had no need of a remoter charm
> By thought supplied, or any interest
> Unborrowed from the eye.

So the forms of nature, or the human form divine, stood before the great artists of old, nor required any other stimulus to lead the eye to survey, or the hand to embody them, than the pleasure derived from the inspiration of the subject, and 'propulsive force' of the mimic creation. The grandeur of their works was an argument with them, not to stop short, but to proceed. They could have no higher excitement or satisfaction than in the exercise of their art and endless generation of truth and beauty. Success prompts to exertion; and habit facilitates success. It is idle to suppose we can exhaust nature; and the more we employ our own faculties, the more we strengthen them and enrich our stores of observation and invention. The more we do, the more we *can* do. Not indeed if we *get our ideas out of our own heads*— that stock is soon exhausted, and we recur to tiresome, vapid imitations of ourselves. But this is the difference between real and mock talent, between genius and affectation. Nature is not limited, nor does it become effete, like our conceit and vanity. The closer we examine it, the more it refines upon us; it expands as we enlarge and shift our view; it 'grows with our growth, and strengthens with our strength'. The subjects are endless; and our capacity is invigorated as it is called out by occasion and necessity. He who does nothing, renders himself incapable of doing anything; but while we are executing any work, we are preparing and qualifying ourselves to undertake another. The principles are the same in all nature; and we understand them better, as we verify them by experience and practice. It is not as if there was a given number of subjects to work upon, or a set of *innate* or preconceived ideas in our minds which we encroached upon with every new design; the subjects, as I said before, are endless, and we acquire ideas by imparting them. Our expenditure of intellectual wealth makes us rich: we can only be liberal as we have previously accumulated the means. By lying idle, as by standing still, we are confined to the same trite, narrow round of topics: by continuing our efforts, as by moving forwards in a road, we extend our views, and discover continually new tracts of country. Genius, like humanity, rusts for want of use.

HENRIK IBSEN

The sea possesses a power over one's moods that has the effect of a will. The sea can hypnotize. Nature in general can do so.

BRUNO WALTER

Next to music, nature . . . has always been the strongest power in my life. And it surely did not penetrate into my soul merely through my vision, no matter how fervently I enjoyed the sight of beautiful mountains, valleys, lakes, sunny days, and moonlit nights. I was vouchsafed also a more immediate access: I felt akin and attached to the thicket and the ocean, to the rocky solitude and the thunderstorm, to the humming of insects, and to the noonday quiet. Saturated with nature, and feeling part of it, I was able early to enter into the sense of Faust's verses:

> *This glorious Nature thou didst for my kingdom give,*
> *And power to feel it, to enjoy it.*
> *'Twas not the stranger's short permitted privilege*
> *Of momentary wonder that Thou gavest;*
> *No, Thou hast given me into her deep breast*
> *As into a friend's secret heart to look;*
> *Thus teaching me to recognize and love my brothers*
> *In still grove, or air, or stream.*

— — —

Looking back upon my life, I find much cause for mourning, more for gratitude. I had gained strength from people dear to me, from those who were near to me in life, and from others who, influencing me by their work and example, nourished within me the comforting assurance of a community of the human spirit, beyond centuries and mundane boundaries. It was this invisible church that had sheltered me from the innumerable attacks with which the events of daily life shake man's power of resistance. Strength was given me by nature, to which I am as devoted today as I ever was. Strength was given me by the sheltering affection of my family, but also by interest in the sufferings of others and by aid I was at times able to render. It was given me by the little joys of life. But above all it flowed into me from music. There flows from music, irrespective of its ever-changing emotional expression, an unchanging message of comfort: its dissonances strive toward consonance—they must be resolved; every musical piece ends in a consonance. Thus music as an element has an optimistic quality, and I believe that therein lies the source of my innate optimism. Still more important, however, and of decisive influence upon my life is the exalted message conveyed to us from the works of the great masters, a message most sacredly expressed in the symphonic adagio. The Church knows why it calls upon the power of music at its most solemn functions. Music's wordless gospel proclaims in a universal language what the thirsting soul of man is seeking beyond this life. I have been vouchsafed the grace to be a servant of music. It has been a beacon on my way and has kept me in the direction toward which I have been striving, darkly, when I was a child, consciously later. There lie my hope and my confidence. . . .

C. S. LEWIS

The process of living seems to consist in coming to realize truths so ancient and simple that, if stated, they sound like barren platitudes. They cannot sound otherwise to those who have not had the relevant experience: that is why there is no real teaching of such truths possible and every generation starts from scratch. . . .

– – –

Many people—I am one myself—would never, but for what nature does to us, have had any content to put into the words we must use in confessing our faith. Nature never taught me that there exists a God of glory and of infinite majesty. I had to learn that in other ways. But nature gave the word "glory" a meaning for me. I still do not know where else I could have found one. I do not see how the "fear" of God could have ever meant to me anything but the lowest prudential efforts to be safe, if I had never seen certain ominous ravines and unapproachable crags. And if nature had never awakened certain longings in me, huge areas of what I can now mean by the "love" of God would never, so far as I can see, have existed.

ANAÏS NIN

How I love to walk among the trees stirred by a light February wind and in the fields where one can see the clear horizon. Ah, how I love that! How sweet it is to me! In those dreamy moments I feel as though I have left this sad earth, I feel as though I catch a glimpse, a tiny glimpse, of the air and fragrance of heaven, it seems as though I fly away toward the infinite. If my Maman's sweet voice didn't call me back, I would spend hours, long hours, contemplating nature . . . it's so beautiful! . . . it's the only thing that is pure and beautiful in this world.

– – –

To have a shining heart like the buttercup, to be as sublime as the plain pine tree that casts its shadow, as charitable as the stalk of wheat that nourishes us, as loving, caressing and consoling as . . . nature!

Everett Ruess

A love for everyone and everything has welled up, finding no outlet except in my art.

Music has been in my heart all the time, and poetry in my thoughts. Alone on the open desert, I have made up songs of wild, poignant rejoicing and transcendent melancholy. The world has seemed more beautiful to me than ever before. I have loved the red rocks, the twisted trees, the red sand blowing in the wind, the slow, sunny clouds crossing the sky, the shafts of moonlight on my bed at night. I have seemed to be at one with the world. I have rejoiced to set out, to be going somewhere, and I have felt a still sublimity, looking deep into the coals of my campfires, and seeing far beyond them. I have been happy in my work, and I have exulted in my play. I have really lived.

Ralph Waldo Emerson

The night is fine; the stars shed down their severe influences upon me, and I feel a joy in my solitude that the merriment of vulgar society can never communicate. There is a pleasure in the thought that the particular tone of my mind at this moment may be new in the universe; that the emotions of this hour may be peculiar and unexampled in the whole eternity of moral being. I lead a new life. I occupy new ground in the world of spirits, untenanted before. I commence a career of thought and action which is expanding before me into a distant and dazzling infinity. Strange thoughts start up like angels in my way and beckon me onward. I doubt not I tread on the highway that leads to the Divinity.

— — —

The maker of a sentence, like the other artist, launches out into the infinite and builds a road into Chaos and old Night, and is followed by those who hear him with something of wild, creative delight.

— — —

Do not waste yourself in rejection; do not bark against the bad, but chant the beauty of the good.

— — —

Like the New England soil, my talent is good only whilst I work it. If I cease to task myself, I have no thoughts.

— — —

Solitary converse with Nature is . . . perhaps the first [source of inspiration] and there are ejaculated sweet and dreadful words never uttered in libraries. Ah, the spring days, summer dawns, and October woods!

— — —

The good of going into the mountains is that life is reconsidered.

IRWIN EDMAN

For imaginative and sensitive minds, the passion called religious may find another object than the traditional image of God. Any intense allegiance or adventurous devotion is a faith. The artist in his creation, the worker in his work, the teacher in his teaching, if they are sincere and reflective of what they are doing, are performing acts of piety to the commands of an inner god. Permanent and stirring dreams constitute a heaven; a compelling and engrossing ideal is a god. To live governed by these invariables, to make no compromise where they are concerned is to lead something like what the theologians would call the spiritual life.

HENRY DAVID THOREAU

I learned this, at least, by my experiment: that if one advances confidently in the direction of his dreams, and endeavors to live the life which he has imagined, he will meet with a success unexpected in common hours. He will put some things behind, will pass an invisible boundary; new, universal, and more liberal laws will begin to establish themselves around and within him; or the old laws be expanded, and interpreted in his favor in a more liberal sense, and he will live with the license of a higher order of beings. In proportion as he simplifies his life, the laws of the universe will appear less complex, and solitude will not be solitude, nor poverty poverty, nor weakness weakness. If you have built castles in the air, your work need not be lost; that is where they should be. Now put the foundations under them.

— — —

Be not simply good; be good for something.

— — —

Superfluous wealth can buy superfluities only.

— — —

Thank God man cannot lay waste the heavens as he has the earth!

– – –

We need the tonic of wildness–to wade sometimes in marshes where the bittern and the meadow-hen lurk, and hear the booming of the snipe; to smell the whispering sedge where only some wilder and more solitary fowl builds her nest, and the mink crawls with its belly close to the ground.

– – –

At the same time that we are earnest to explore and learn all things, we require that all things be mysterious and unexplorable, that land and sea be infinitely wild, unsurveyed and unfathomed by us because unfathomable. We can never have enough of Nature.

– – –

All sensuality is one, though it takes many forms; all purity is one. It is the same whether a man eat, or drink, or cohabit, or sleep sensually. They are but one appetite, and we only need to see a person do any one of these things to know how great a sensualist he is.

– – –

We are all sculptors and painters, and our material is our own flesh and blood and bones. Any nobleness begins at once to refine a man's features, any meanness or sensuality to imbrute them.

– – –

He is blessed who is assured that the animal is dying out in him day by day, and the divine being established.

— — —

Goodness is the only investment that never fails.

— — —

No humane being, past the thoughtless age of boyhood, will wantonly murder any creature, which holds to its life by the same tenure that he does. The hare in its extremity cries like a child. I warn you, mothers, that my sympathies do not always make the usual phil-*anthropic* distinctions.

John Cowper Powys

The word "science" covers every kind of atrocity; and the issue is perfectly clear. My opposition to vivisection, particularly to the vivisection of dogs, is based upon an argument that is unanswerable. This wickedness contradicts and cancels the one single advantage that our race has got from what is called evolution, namely the development of *our sense of right and wrong.*

— — —

When, on that great flight of steps at Rome leading up from the Piazza del Spagna to the Pincian Hill, I suddenly got an ecstacy of mysterious exultation, in which I said to myself, "Let *me* pass and perish, as long as this magical stream of life, so noble in its heroic continuity, still goes on!" What I really did was to sink my own solitary personality in the innumerable personalities of all men and women who for generations had gone up and down those historic steps.

\- \- \-

The astronomical world is *not* all there is. We are in touch with other dimensions, other levels of life. And from among the powers that spring from these *other levels* there rises up one Power, all the more terrible because it refuses to practise cruelty, a Power that is neither Capitalist, nor Communist, nor Fascist, nor Democratic, nor Nazi, a Power *not of this world at all*, but capable of inspiring the individual soul with the wisdom of the serpent and the harmlessness of the dove.

And thus it comes to pass, even while we are still in life, that when our soul loses itself in the long continuity of kindred lives, it does not lose itself in any power less gentle, less magical, less universal than itself, or less the enemy of cruelty; for what it finds is what it brings, and what it sees is what it is; and though the First Cause may be both good and evil, a Power has risen out of it against which all the evil in it and all the unthinkable atrocities it brings to pass are fighting a losing battle.

Albert Schweitzer

What we need is to hope for a new spirit so that human responsibility toward all living creatures becomes something that is taken for granted! Here, as in all things, we have to rely on the spirit!

\- \- \-

The most important among [great people] are those who create ideas that spell spiritual progress for humanity.

\- \- \-

The idea of spiritual solidarity with the world through reverence for life is the goal of everything I write and do.

--- --- ---

. . . It was only the phrase "reverence for life," which surfaced mysteriously and unconsciously in my mind, that made me realize ethics would have a much deeper and greater energy by taking heed of all creation because it would put us in a spiritual relationship with the entire universe.

--- --- ---

A complete ethics . . . requires kindness and mercy toward all life, for any living creature can suffer. Kindness knows no limits. It is boundless. Only a profound and complete ethics is able to create an ethical civilization.

Thomas Mann

In the depth of my soul I believe—and consider this belief to be natural to any human soul—that this earth has a central significance in the universe. In the depth of my soul I entertain the presumption that the act of creation which called forth the inorganic world from nothingness and the procreation of life from the inorganic world, was aimed at humanity; a great experiment was initiated whose failure by human irresponsibility would mean the failure of the act of creation itself, its very refutation.

Rosalyn Tureck

They knew I was serious about my music. Succeeding at it was a normal, natural event. I felt no pressure because I knew my direction and the family simply let it lead me. Glamor, exploitation, special attention were out; work was in. Brilliant-Liven and her husband were extremely disciplinary and extremely serious-minded musicians; they never let me forget my purpose. The whole idea was that, as a musician, you just devote all your energies to your work. I had to be a serious student of music, or none at all.

— — —

As you can see from the collection of books I've amassed over the years, the subject matter covers philosophy, literature, art, science, etc. The collection includes almost any subject you can think of. They all deepen my perspective of life in some way. Next, my great love is nature, especially the sky. I walk in the countryside whenever I can because I can see the sky so much more clearly there. Much as I would like to have enjoyed sports, I never indulged in any except on occasional moments because of possible injury to the hands. The only exception to this is swimming, although I'm certainly not the world's greatest. Snorkeling, for me, is a fantastic activity because I see such variety of life under the sea. I have done snorkeling in the Mediterranean, in the south of France. It's another world, and it gives me a great sense of the immensity and the individuality of nature. When I first saw underwater life, I thought, "My God, what music a composer could have written had he seen this!"

Robert Louis Stevenson

A faint wind, more like a moving coolness than a stream of air, passed down the glade from time to time; so that even in my great chamber the air was being renewed all night long. . . . I have not often enjoyed a more serene possession of myself, nor felt more independent of material aids. The outer world, from which we cower into our houses, seemed after all a gentle habitable place; and night after night a man's bed, it seemed, was laid and waiting for him in the fields, where God keeps an open house. I thought I had rediscovered one of those truths which are revealed to savages and hid from political economists.

FRED HOYLE

. . . In the Lake District, there was a spotted flycatcher that came back from central Africa each year to make its nest no more than five yards from our front door. The ability to navigate four thousand miles to this degree of precision would seem to me impossible without employing concepts similar to those we use in mathematics. The accuracy of the flycatcher and the accuracy of our calculations in quantum electrodynamics seem to me to spring from the same source, a source behind and independent of words, a source that . . . [is] the godlike bit in all of us.

— — —

I rather expect that historians of the future will see our present age as one of low inventiveness all round, to be explained as a combination of too much affluence and the ubiquitousness of communications and media pressure.

— — —

. . . I have developed a strong distaste for scientists who experiment on animals.

— — —

I was never a great one for taking eggs from birds' nests, for the reason that I could see no interest in them once they were taken. . . . I found it far more interesting to watch what happened if you left the eggs where they were. On one occasion when I was scouting alone I found a kingfisher's nest. . . . I told one of the lads about it; whether he took the eggs or someone else did I never knew. When I found the nest empty, it seemed an absurd waste. Here had been something that would have made marvelously colored birds that were then not to be.

WILLIAM WORDSWORTH

There is a spiritual community binding together the living and the dead; the good, the brave, and the wise, of all ages. We would not be rejected from this community; and therefore do we hope. We look forward with erect mind, thinking and feeling: it is an obligation of duty: take away the sense of it, and the moral being would die within us.

[The Poet] considers man and nature as essentially adapted to each other, and the mind of man as naturally the mirror of the fairest and most interesting properties of nature. And thus the Poet, prompted by this feeling of pleasure, which accompanies him through the whole course of his studies, converses with general nature.

Let then the Youth go back, as occasion will permit, to Nature and to Solitude. . . . A world of fresh sensations will gradually open upon him as his mind puts off its infirmities, and as instead of being propelled restlessly towards others in admiration or too hasty love, he makes it his prime business to understand himself. New sensations, I affirm, will be opened out–pure, and sanctioned by that reason which is their original Author: and precious feelings of disinterested, that is self-disregarding, joy and love may be regenerated and restored:–and, in this sense, he may be said to measure back the track of life which he has trod.

[Much as natural] scenes have been injured by what has been taken from them . . . [it] is not the removals, but the harsh *additions* that have been made, which are the worst grievance—a standing and unavoidable annoyance.

John C. Van Dyke

Art is an illusion of nature produced by a personality.

– – –

Even the people who write prose, and are not popularly supposed to be bothered with fine frenzies, have their troubles in describing the [Grand] Canyon. They have not enough adjectives to go around or to reach up and over. Language fails them. The tourist who comes out to the Rim for the first time and exclaims "Good God!" comes as near description as the more elaborately wordy if by his exclamation he means not only his own surprise but the greatness and goodness of God.

– – –

The aesthetic sense—the power to enjoy through the eye, the ear, and the imagination—is just as important a factor in the scheme of human happiness as the corporeal sene of eating and drinking; but there has never been a time when the world would admit it. The "practical men," who seem forever on the throne, know very well that beauty is only meant for lovers and young persons—stuff to suckle fools withal. The main affair of life is to get the dollar, and if there is any money in cutting the throat of Beauty, why, by all means, cut her throat. That is what the "practical men" have been doing ever since the world began. It is not necessary to dig up ancient history; for have we not seen, here in California and Oregon, in our own time, the destruction of the fairest valleys the sun ever shone upon by placer and hydraulic mining? Have we not seen in Minnesota and Wisconsin the mightiest forests that ever raised head to the sky slashed to pieces by the axe and turned into a waste of tree-stumps and fallen timber? Have we not seen the Upper Mississippi, by the destruction of the forests, changed from a broad, majestic river into a shallow, muddy stream; and the beautiful prairies of Dakota turned under by the plough and then allowed to run to weeds? Men must have coal though they ruin the valleys and blacken the streams of Pennsylvania, they must have oil though they disfigure half of Ohio and Indiana, they must have copper if they wreck all the mountains of Montana and Arizona, and they must have gold though they blow Alaska into the Behring Sea. It is more than possible that the "practical men" have gained much practice and many dollars by flaying the fair face of these United States. They have stripped the land of its robes of beauty, and what have they given in its place? Weeds, wire fences, oil-derricks, board shanties and board towns–things that not even a "practical man" can do less than curse at.

– – –

. . . There is, perhaps, a satisfaction in thinking that some things in nature are beyond man's power. It is a pleasure to think of mountains, for instance, that no one can till them or fell them or destroy them, that commercially or economically they cannot be capitalized and sold on the market, that even artistically they are hardly to be captured and lugged into the drawing-room. Evidently, the best that man can do about them is to wonder over them and admire them.

– – –

Of what avail the struggle of races, the clashing of social systems, the ascending cry of the human! Serene above it all, the Great Mother never hears, never heeds. The law of the kingdom– look to the law. Raise no hand of protest to the throne. There is no appeal. If you would cry out, go to the forest; if you would moan, stand on the prairie; if you would implore, look up at the sky and the sunlight. Learn from these. The law is written on them. Through all the ages of the earth's endurance that law has not failed to teach obedience, patience, peace.

— — —

The deserts should never be reclaimed. They are the breathing-spaces of the west and should be preserved forever.

ABRAHAM PAIS

. . . It is evident that if humanity is to have a future, then the untrammeled capitalism we have known, and which is at the root of the environment's decline, can have none.

JOSEPH WOOD KRUTCH

[In defense of Thomas Gray's spending his lifetime for making a few excellent poems instead of many average ones] Can one accuse of ineffectiveness or of waste a man who writes even one immortal poem?

— — —

[An] "economy of abundance" is a meaningless phrase unless one asks, "Abundance of what?". A society could have an abundance of physical space and also an abundance of spiritual space. It could have an abundance of leisure, of contemplation, of intellectuality, and of spirituality. It might even have an abundance of manners. And it might have all these things without having any more of many other things; might indeed find it easier to keep the one abundance if it did not have thrust upon it more of the other.

Yet of this obvious fact few seem ever to think. Most take it for granted that the abundance which is desirable is the abundance which manifests itself most conspicuously in, say, juke boxes, television sets, organized playgrounds, and even, perhaps, of schools and of museums. They seem not even aware of the fact that much has grown scarcer while these things have been becoming more abundant, and that many things threaten to grow even scarcer still.

I am no ascetic and, so at least I believe, no fanatic of any other sort. I am not praising want and I have no romantic notion that distresses should not be relieved. But I do, in all seriousness, question the assumption that endless progress implies the needless multiplication of goods and gadgets, even that "real wages" and "production per man hour" are necessarily an approximate index of welfare. I am not saying that a reduction in the standard of material living automatically brings with it an increase in happiness or nobility, but I do doubt that the converse is true, and I do find it astonishing that this doubt seems so seldom shared.

Victor F. Weisskopf

But there was one older physicist who made a greater impression on me than any of the others and shaped my attitudes toward physics: He was P. Ehrenfest . . . [and he] taught me for the first time to distrust the complicated mathematics and formalisms that were then very popular in Göttingen. He loved to ask, and encouraged others to ask, "stupid" questions; he refused to admit that something is understood if one understands only the mathematical derivation. He showed me how to get at the real physics, how to distinguish between physics and formalism, how to get at the depth of things: "Physics is simple, but subtle," he used to say. The older I get, the more aware I am of his influence.

— — —

Human experience encompasses much more than any one given system of thought is able to express within its own framework of concepts. We must be receptive to the varied and apparently contradictory ways of the mind when we are faced with the realities of nature, our imagination, and human relations. There are many modes of thinking and feeling, and each of them contains a part of what we may consider the truth. Science and technology comprise some of the most powerful tools for deeper insight and for solving the problems we face. But science and technology provide only one path toward reality; others are equally needed for us to comprehend the full significance of our existence. Indeed, those other avenues are necessary for the prevention of thoughtless and inhuman abuses of the results of science. The survival of our civilization is severely threatened by nationalism, religious fundamentalism, and other intolerant, one-sided views. We will need to use many different approaches in order to overcome the grave problems that we face today. Only then do we stand a chance of achieving a better world.

— — —

Human existence depends upon compassion and curiosity. Curiosity without compassion is inhuman; compassion without curiosity is ineffectual.

— — —

The lack of awareness of sense and purpose has led culture to become increasingly shallow. When the most important needs have been provided for, the content of life may amount to no more than a desire for entertainment or pleasure. In the extreme, the lack of a sense of meaning of life may lead to such excesses as the use of drugs. The damage to our society by drugs, with all their terrible consequences, is more threatening today than the receding danger of nuclear war. . . . . What is missing in too many individuals is a feeling of deep commitment to a great cause beyond our own personal interest—a cause whose value is never questioned.

— — —

In man's brain the impressions from outside are not merely registered; they produce concepts and ideas. They are the imprint of the external world on the human brain. Therefore, it is not surprising that, after a long period of searching and erring, some of the concepts and ideas in human thinking should have come gradually closer to the fundamental laws of this world, that some of our thinking should reveal the true structure of atoms and the true movements of the stars. Nature, in the form of man, begins to recognize itself.

Adolf Weissmann

The de-romanticizing of the world, which we now face, was set in motion already before the war, but it was completed by it. . . . The machine, which conquers distances in shorter and ever shorter times, is self-evidently opposed to the romantic. The romantic thrives on distances, and even creates them artificially. With the discovery of the railroad, the romantic certainly was not killed, but the commerce and worldwide traffic that the railroad set in motion gave it its first and painful wound. A glorious isolation of the artist became a rarity. . . . By necessity, a leveling process will spread throughout the world. To the extent the machine shines in all corners of the world, then the romantic must die.

Mark Van Doren

Society continues to change, and there are those who say it is already the monster we have feared. Whatever in truth it is, the artist ought to be one of the first to understand it, to sympathize with its predicament, and to start making it better at the core. He might even become a philosopher or a politician in order to do this well; but short of that, he can think more deeply and feelingly than he has done about the courage it now takes to be the sort of individual whose dignity matters more than wars and revolutions, more than welfare and the sovereignties of states. Such dignity is given to no one. It has to be created in the mind, by slow and painful stages, amid the total darkness of other men's refusal to make the attempt at all. But once it is created, it proves everything. And once it is created in an artist whose ambition is otherwise unbounded—and whose skill—it becomes the final excellence of which the rest of us had dreamed. It could even change again the changing world.

John Ruskin

When love and skill work together expect a masterpiece.

– – –

The noblest scenes of the earth can be seen and known but by few; it is not intended that man should live always in the midst of them, he injures them by his presence. . . .

– – –

The whole force of education, until very lately, has been directed in every possible way to the destruction of the love of nature. The only knowledge which has been considered essential among us is that of words, and, next after it, of the abstract sciences; while every liking shown by children for simple natural history has been either violently checked . . . or else scrupulously limited to hours of play: so that it has really become impossible for any child earnestly to study the works of God but against its conscience; and the love of nature has become inherently the characteristic of truants and idlers. . . . The art of drawing, which is of . . . real importance to the human race . . . [and] should be taught to every child, just as writing is,—has been so neglected and abused, that there is not one man in a thousand, even of its professed teachers, who knows its first principles: and thus it needs much ill-fortune or obstinacy—much neglect on the part of his teachers, or rebellion on his own—before a boy can get leave to use his eyes or his fingers; so that those who *can* use them are for the most part neglected or rebellious lads—runaways and bad scholars—passionate, erratic, self-willed, and restive against all forms of education; while your well-behaved and amiable scholars are disciplined into blindness and palsy of half their faculties. Wherein there is at once a notable ground for what difference we have observed between the lovers of nature and its despisers. . . .

RICHARD JEFFERIES

The exceeding beauty of the earth, in her splendor of life, yields a new thought with every petal. The hours when the mind is absorbed by beauty are the only hours when we really live. All else is illusion, or mere endurance.

JOSEPH ADDISON

There is something more bold and masterly in the rough careless Strokes of Nature, than in the nice Touches and Embellishments of Art. The Beauties of the most stately Garden or Palace lie in a narrow Compass, the Imagination immediately runs them over, and requires something else to gratify her; but, in the wide Fields of Nature, the Sight wanders up and down without Confinement, and is fed with an infinite variety of Images, without any certain Stint or Number. For this Reason we always find the Poet in Love with a Country-Life, where Nature appears in the greatest Perfection, and furnishes out all those Scenes that are most apt to delight the Imagination.

H. M. Tomlinson

Of all the infernal uses to which a country can be put there is none like development. Let every good savage make incantation against it, or, if to some extent he has been developed, cross himself against the fructification of the evil. As for us whites, we are eternally damned, for we cannot escape the consequences of our past cleverness. The Devil has us on a complexity of strings, and some day will pull the whole lot tight.

HAVELOCK ELLIS

If there is anything anywhere in the world [of Nature] that is rare and wild and wonderful, singular in the perfection of its beauty, Civilised Man sweeps it out of existence. It is the fate everywhere of lyre-birds, of humming-birds, of birds of Paradise, marvellous things that Man may destroy and can never create. They make poor parlour ornaments and but ugly adornments for silly women. The world is the poorer and we none the richer. The same fate is overtaking all the loveliest spots on the earth. There are rare places which Primitive Man only approaches on special occasions, with sacred awe, counting their beauty inviolable and the animals living in them as gods. Such places have existed in the heart of Africa unto to-day. Civilised man arrives, disperses the awe, shoots the animals, if possible turns them into cash. Eventually he turns the scenery into cash, covering it with dear hotels and cheap advertisements. In Europe the process has long been systematised. Lake Leman was once a spot which inspired poets with a new feeling for romantic landscape. What Rousseau or Byron could find inspiration on that lake to-day? The Pacific once hid in its wilderness a multitude of little islands upon which, as the first voyagers and missionaries bore witness, Primitive Man, protected by Nature from the larger world, had developed a rarely beautiful culture, wild and fierce and voluptuous, and yet in the highest degree humane. Civilised man arrived, armed with Alcohol and Syphilis and Trousers and the Bible, and in a few years only a sordid and ridiculous shadow was left of that uniquely wonderful life. People talk with horror of "Sabotage." Naturally enough. Yet they do not see that they themselves are morally supporting, and financially paying for, and even religiously praying for, a gigantic system of world-wide "Sabotage" which for centuries has been recklessly destroying things that are infinitely more lovely and irreparable than any that Syndicalists may have injured.

GASTON BACHELARD

. . . The painter *looks at* what he cannot see: he creates.

— — —

. . . Every creator of forms quite properly claims the power of dwelling within the forms he creates.

— — —

The modeler recognizes the deep meaning of metamorphoses.

— — —

Anterior to the work, the painter, like every creator, knows the contemplative musing, the pondering upon the nature of things. Indeed the painter experiences the revelation of the world through light too intimately not to participate with his whole being in this ceaselessly reiterative birth of a universe.

– – –

The true destiny of the great artist is a *destiny of toil*. There comes a point in his life when toil begins to dominate and guide his fate. Doubts and misfortunes may long torment him. Circumstances may bear him down. He may lose years in obscure preparation. But the will to art, once ensconced in its proper hearth, can never be extinguished. It is the beginning of the *destiny of toil*, ardent, creative toil running right through the artist's life and giving that life a rectilinear quality. Henceforth everything tends toward the goal of a growing body of work. Each day this strange tissue of patience and enthusiasm is woven tighter in the life of toil that turns the artist into a master.

– – –

A botany of the imagination, stemming from an attraction for branches, wood, leaves, roots, bark, flowers and grass, has furnished us with a stock of images of astonishing regularity. We are controlled by *vegetal values*. We would all profit by taking a census of this private herbarium in the depths of our unconscious, where the slow, gentle forces of our life find models of continuity and perseverance. The life of root and bud lie at the heart of our being. We are really very ancient plants.

ANSEL ADAMS

. . . The truth of things simply stated with emotional force gets a terrific response.

– – –

My approach to photography is based on my belief in the vigor and values of the world of nature, in aspects of grandeur and minutiae all about us. I believe in people, in the simpler aspects of human life, in the relation of man to nature. I believe man must be free, both in spirit and society, that he must build strength into himself, affirming the enormous beauty of the world and acquiring the confidence to see and to express his vision. And I believe in photography as one means of expressing this affirmation and of achieving an ultimate happiness and faith.

— — —

How different my life would have been if it were not for these early hikes in the Sierra—if I had not experienced that memorable first trip to Yosemite—if I had not been raised by the ocean—if, if, if! Everything I have done or felt is in some way influenced by the impact of the Natural Scene. It is easy to recount that I camped many times at Merced Lake, but it is difficult to explain the magic: to lie in a small recess of the granite matrix of the Sierra and watch the progress of dusk to night, the incredible brilliance of the stars, the waning of the glittering sky into dawn, and the following sunrise on the peaks and domes around me. And always that cool dawn wind that I believe to be the prime benediction of the Sierra. These qualities to which I still deeply respond were distilled into my pictures over the decades. I *knew* my destiny when I first experienced Yosemite.

George Mallory

Sunrises and sunsets and clouds and thunder are not incidental to mountaineering, but a vital and inseparable part of it; they are not ornamental, but structural.

John Muir

Now, it never seems to occur to these far-seeing teachers that Nature's object in making animals and plants might possibly be first of all the happiness of each one of them, not the creation of all for the happiness of one. Why should man value himself as more than a small part of the one great unit of creation? And what creature of all that the Lord has taken the pains to make is not essential to the completeness of that unit–the cosmos? The universe would be incomplete without man; but it would also be incomplete without the smallest transmicroscopic creature that dwells beyond our conceitful eyes and knowledge.

From the dust of the earth, from the common elementary fund, the Creator has made *Homo sapiens*. From the same material he has made every other creature, however noxious and insignificant to us. They are earth-born companions and our fellow mortals. The fearfully good, the orthodox, of this laborious patch-work of modern civilization cry "Heresy" on every one whose sympathies reach a single hair's breadth beyond the boundary epidermis of our own species. Not content with taking all of earth, they also claim the celestial country as the only ones who possess the kind of souls for which that imponderable empire was planned.

– – –

In God's wildness lies the hope of the world–the great fresh, unblighted, unredeemed wilderness. The galling harness of civilization drops off, and the wounds heal ere we are aware.

The world, we are told, was made especially for man–a presumption not supported by all the facts. A numerous class of men are painfully astonished whenever they find anything, living or dead, in all God's universe, which they cannot eat or render in some way what they call useful to themselves. They have precise dogmatic insight into the intentions of the Creator. . . .

– – –

Music is one of the attributes of matter, into whatever forms it may be organized. Drops and sprays of air are specialized, and made to plash and churn in the bosom of a lark, as infinitesimal portions of air plash and sing about the angles and hollows of sand-grains, as perfectly composed and predestined as the rejoicing anthems of worlds; but our senses are not fine enough to catch the tones. Fancy the waving, pulsing melody of the vast flower-congregations of the Hollow flowing from myriad voices of tuned petal and pistil, and heaps of sculptured pollen. Scarce one note is for us; nevertheless, God be thanked for this blessed instrument hid beneath the feathers of a lark.

– – –

No Sierra landscape that I have seen holds anything truly dead or dull, or any trace of what in manufactories is called rubbish or waste; everything is perfectly clean and pure and full of divine lessons. This quick, inevitable interest attaching to everything seems marvelous until the hand of God becomes visible; then it seems reasonable that what interests Him may well interest us. When we try to pick out anything by itself, we find it hitched to everything else in the universe. One fancies a heart like our own must be beating in every crystal and cell, and we feel like stopping to speak to the plants and animals as friendly fellow mountaineers. Nature as a poet, an enthusiastic workingman, becomes more and more visible the farther and higher we go; for the mountains are fountains– beginning places, however related to sources beyond mortal ken.

– – –

Next to the light of the dawn on high mountain tops, the alpenglow is the most impressive of all the terrestrial manifestations of God.

Now comes the gloaming. The alpenglow is fading into earthy, murky gloom, but do not let your town habits draw you away to the hotel. Stay on this good fire-mountain and spend the night among the stars. Watch their glorious bloom until the dawn, and get one more baptism of light. Then, with fresh heart, go down to your work, and whatever your fate, under whatever ignorance or knowledge you may afterward chance to suffer, you will remember these fine, wild views, and look back with joy to your wanderings in the blessed old Yellowstone Wonderland.

— — —

To let sheep trample so divinely fine a place seems barbarous.

— — —

Butterflies colored like the flowers waver above them in wonderful profusion, and many other beautiful winged people, numbered and known and loved only by the Lord, are waltzing together high over head, seemingly in pure play and hilarious enjoyment of their little sparks of life. How wonderful they are! How do they get a living, and endure the weather? How are their little bodies, with muscles, nerves, organs, kept warm and jolly in such admirable exuberant health? Regarded only as mechanical inventions, how wonderful they are! Compared with these, Godlike man's greatest machines are as nothing.

— — —

Most people are *on* the world, not in it—have no conscious sympathy or relationship to anything about them—undiffused, separate, and rigidly alone like marbles of polished stone, touching but separate.

— — —

These temple-destroyers, devotees of ravaging commercialism, seem to have a perfect contempt for Nature, and, instead of lifting their eyes to the God of the mountains, lift them to the Almighty Dollar.

After dark, when the camp was at rest, I groped my way back to the altar boulder and passed the night on it,–above the water, beneath the leaves and stars,–everything still more impressive than by day, the fall seen dimly white, singing Nature's old love song with solemn enthusiasm, while the stars peering through the leaf-roof seemed to join in the white water's song. Precious night, precious day to abide in me forever. Thanks be to God for this immortal gift.

Any fool can destroy trees. They cannot run away; and if they could, they would still be destroyed,–chased and hunted down as long as fun or a dollar could be got out of their bark hides, branching horns, or magnificent bole backbones. . . . It took more than three thousand years to make some of the trees in these Western woods,–trees that are still standing in perfect strength and beauty, waving and singing in the mighty forests of the Sierra. Through all the wonderful, eventful centuries since Christ's time–and long before that–God has cared for these trees, saved them from drought, disease, avalanches, and a thousand straining, leveling tempests and floods; but he cannot save them from fools. . . .

Nearly all the upper basin of the Merced was displayed, with its sublime domes and cañons, dark upsweeping forests, and glorious array of white peaks deep in the sky, every feature glowing, radiating beauty that pours into our flesh and bones like heat rays from the fire. Sunshine over all; no breath of wind to stir the brooding calm. Never before had I seen so glorious a landscape, so boundless an affluence of sublime mountain beauty. The most extravagant description I might give of this view to any one who has not seen similar landscapes with his own eyes would not so much as hint its grandeur and the spiritual glow that covered it.

— — —

Comprehended in general views, the features of the wildest landscape seem to be as harmoniously related as the features of a human face. Indeed, they look human and radiate spiritual beauty, divine thought, however covered and concealed by rock and snow.

— — —

Freshness and beauty are everywhere; flowers are born every hour; living sunlight is poured over all, and every thing and creature is glad. Our world is indeed a beautiful one, and I was thinking, on going to church last Sabbath, that I would hardly accept of a free ticket to the moon or to Venus, or any other world, for fear it might not be so good and so fraught with the glory of the Creator as our own.

— — —

How infinitely superior to our physical senses are those of the mind! The spiritual eye sees not only rivers of water but of air. It sees the crystals of the rock in rapid sympathetic motion, giving enthusiastic obedience to the sun's rays, then sinking back to rest in the night. The whole world is in motion to the center. So also sounds. We hear only woodpeckers and squirrels and the rush of turbulent streams. But imagination gives us the sweet music of tiniest insect wings, enables us to hear, all around the world, the vibration of every needle, the waving of every bole and branch, the sound of stars in circulation like particles in the blood. The Sierra canyons are full of avalanche débris—we hear them boom again, and we read the past sounds from present conditions. Again we hear the earthquake rock-falls. Imagination is usually regarded as a synonym for the unreal. Yet is true imagination healthful and real, no more likely to mislead than the coarse senses. Indeed, the power of imagination makes us infinite.

— — —

No synonym for God is so perfect as Beauty. Whether as seen carving the lines of the mountains with glaciers, or gathering matter into stars, or planning the movements of water, or gardening–still all is Beauty.

— — —

Yet this glorious valley might well be called a church, for every lover of the great Creator who comes within the broad overwhelming influences of the place fails not to worship as he never did before. The glory of the Lord is upon all his works; it is written plainly upon all the fields of every clime, and upon every sky, but here in this place of surpassing glory the Lord has written in capitals.

— — —

Walk away quietly in any direction and taste the freedom of the mountaineer. Camp out among the grass and gentians of glacier meadows, in craggy garden nooks full of Nature's darlings. Climb the mountains and get their good tidings. Nature's peace will flow into you as sunshine flows into trees. The winds will blow their own freshness into you, and the storms their energy, while cares will drop off like autumn leaves. As age comes on, one source of enjoyment after another is closed, but Nature's sources never fail.

— — —

Only by going alone in silence, without baggage, can one truly get into the heart of the wilderness. All other travel is mere dust and hotels and baggage and chatter.

— — —

The clearest way into the Universe is through a forest wilderness.

WILLIAM BLAKE

A Robin Red breast in a Cage
Puts all heaven in a Rage.
A dove house fill'd with doves & Pigeons
Shudders Hell thro' all its regions.
A dog starv'd at his Master's Gate
Predicts the ruin of the State.
A Horse misus'd upon the Road
Calls to Heaven for Human blood.
Each outcry of the hunted Hare
A fibre from the Brain does tear.
A Skylark wounded in the wing,
A Cherubim does cease to sing. . . .

— — —

For every thing that lives is Holy.

— — —

To Generalize is to be an Idiot. To Particularize is the Alone Distinction of Merit. General Knowledges are those Knowledges that Idiots possess.

– – –

Sacrifice the Parts, What becomes of the Whole?

– – –

Without Unceasing Practice nothing can be done. Practise is Art. If you leave off you are Lost.

– – –

Commerce is so far from being beneficial to Arts, or to Empires, that it is destructive of both. . . . Empires flourish till they become Commercial. . . .

– – –

Let us teach Buonaparte, & whomsoever else it may concern, That it is not Arts that follow & attend upon Empire, but Empire that attends upon & follows The Arts.

– – –

No Man of Sense ever supposes that copying from Nature is the Art of Painting; if Art is no more than this, it is no better than any other Manual Labour; anybody may do it & the fool often will do it best as it is the work of no Mind.

– – –

To learn the Language of Art, "Copy for Ever" is My Rule.

– – –

Minute Discrimination is Not Accidental. All Sublimity is founded on Minute Discrimination.

— — —

Without Minute Neatness of Execution The Sublime cannot Exist! Grandeur of Ideas is founded on Precision of Ideas.

— — —

How ridiculous it would be to see the Sheep Endeavouring to walk like the Dog, or the Ox striving to trot like the Horse; just as Ridiculous it is to see One Man Striving to Imitate Another.

— — —

Obscurity is Neither the Source of the Sublime nor of any Thing Else.

— — —

God forbid that Truth should be Confined to mathematical Demonstration!

— — —

I must Create a System or be enslav'd by another Man's.
I will not Reason & Compare: my business is to Create.

ARTUR SCHNABEL

. . . The more one is inclined, or seduced, to possess, conserve and enjoy material things, the less one may have to give in the personal exchange of souls, minds and brains. By machines man's toil has been eased. He has, theoretically, more time—free time—than before. The trouble seems to be that he has to devote this free time to what the machines produce.

— — —

Talent is the premise. It may be released, but cannot be supplied by a teacher. Neither can he guarantee world fame to his students. He is no magician; the student is more important than he. What can a teacher do? At the best open a door; but the student has to pass through it.

— — —

I would say that many of the questions asked [me by students] point to a belief in the existence of what I would call *a safe conduct to wisdom*, a trust in methods and books and rules to lead to the solution of problems, to settle everything. Also a belief that there is only one solution, one way, one type of experience.

— — —

It is important to be aware of different levels of happiness. It depends upon how many regions of receptivity we have in our system. It is quite a legitimate pleasure to be tickled on the surface; it is a deeper satisfaction and help to be struck or touched in your innermost region.

I can enjoy strolling along Fifth Avenue and looking at the window displays. I may be perfectly happy. I can also be perfectly happy after climbing for hours to arrive at the peak of a mountain. Only he who has derived happiness from both, the climbing and the strolling, knows that they are incommensurable and will, asked to choose, certainly decide for the mountain.

— — —

. . . Time and distance, posterity, longevity, acknowledgment through generations, are criteria of distinction which cannot be matched by our personal opinion and which we should not refute, even if we prefer contemporary, ephemeral, familiar output to the small *elite* of creations strong enough to satisfy and to ennoble human beings for ever.

Gustav Mahler

Composing is like playing with bricks, continually making new buildings from the same old stones.

— — —

We know that our second self is active while we sleep, that it grows and becomes and produces what the real self sought and wanted in vain. The creative artist, in particular, has countless proofs of this. But that this second self should have worked on my Fourth Symphony throughout the ten months of winter sleep (with all the frightful nightmares of the theatre business) is unbelievable!

— — —

How I lose through not being able to try out my things in live performance! How much I could learn from that! . . . I am deprived of all living interaction between the external world and my inner world, between the work and the ultimate effect of this work. You can't imagine how that paralyses me!

— — —

. . . Spiritual conception is very like physical birth. What struggles, what agony, what terror accompany it—but what rejoicing when the child turns out to be fit and strong!

– – –

How can people forever think that Nature lies on the surface! Of course it does, in its most superficial aspect. But those who, in the face of Nature, are not overwhelmed with awe at its infinite mystery, its divinity (we can only sense it, not comprehend or penetrate it)–these people have not come close to it. . . . And in every work of art, which should be a reflection of Nature, there must be a trace of this infinity.

RENE DUBOS

A relationship to the earth based only on its use for economic enrichment is bound to result not only in its degradation but also in the devaluation of human life. This is a perversion which, if not soon corrected, will become a fatal disease of technological societies.

– – –

Early man possessed extensive knowledge of the sky and clouds, the plants and animals, the rocks, springs, and rivers, among which he lived. He derived from his senses much factual information about nature around him, which enabled him to cope effectively with the external world. Very soon in his social evolution, however, perhaps at the time of becoming *Homo sapiens*, he began to search for a reality different in kind from that which he could see, touch, hear, smell, or otherwise apprehend directly. His awareness of the external world came to transcend his concrete experiences of the objects and creatures he dealt with–as if he perceived in them a form of existence deeper than that revealed by outward appearances. He imagined, though probably not consciously, a Thing behind or within the thing, a Force responsible for the visible movement. This immaterial Thing or Force he regarded as a god–calling it by whatever name he used to denote the principle he thought to be hidden within external reality.

– – –

The very word "desecration," now often used to lament the damage men are causing to the earth, implies belief in the sanctity of nature—as if its relation to human life had a sacred quality.

Rachel Carson

Is it the right of . . . our generation, in its selfish materialism, to destroy . . . [nature] because we are blinded by the dollar sign? Beauty—and all the values that derive from beauty—are not measured and evaluated in terms of the dollar.

– – –

Mankind has gone very far into an artificial world of his own creation. He has sought to insulate himself, with steel and concrete, from the realities of earth and water. Perhaps he is intoxicated with his own power, as he goes farther and farther into experiments for the destruction of himself and his world. For this unhappy trend there is no single remedy—no panacea. But I believe that the more clearly we can focus our attention on the wonders and realities of the universe about us, the less taste we shall have for destruction.

– – –

. . . [Concerning] my feeling for whatever beautiful and untouched oases of natural beauty remain in the world, my belief [is] that such places can bring those who visit them the peace and spiritual refreshment that our "civilization" makes so difficult to achieve, and consequently my conviction that whenever and wherever possible, such places must be preserved.

ALDO LEOPOLD

... Our appreciation of the crane grows with the slow unraveling of earthly history. His tribe, we now know, stems out of the remote Eocene. The other members of the fauna in which he originated are long since entombed within the hills. When we hear his call we hear no mere bird. We hear the trumpet in the orchestra of evolution. He is the symbol of our untamable past, of that incredible sweep of millennia which underlies and conditions the daily affairs of birds and men.

H. E. BATES

[The wood] is a contrast of power and delicacy, space and littleness. Yet all the time, throughout the year, it has its own special atmosphere. You have only to walk a yard under the trees in order to become under its spell, to sense the change, the sometimes startling, sometimes soothing difference in the spirit of the air. There is some precious quality brought about by the close gathering together of trees into a wood that defies analysis. The mere planting together of trees will not create it. An avenue will not do it, nor a park, nor an orchard. There must, it seems, be a closeness, an untidiness, a wildness. There must be all kinds of trees, all kinds of flowers and creatures, a conflicting and yet harmonious pooling of life. A wood planted, as fox-coverts often are, with one kind of tree, has no life at all. It stands dead as a wood of hop-poles. It is the wood of little and great trees, of flowers and water, of squirrel and fox, bird and badger, of light and shadowiness, that has the everlasting vibration of life in it, that special rare atmosphere, at once soothing and refreshing and somehow elevating, that only the best of woods can give.

HENRY BESTON

Poetry is as necessary to comprehension as science.

— — —

It is impossible to live without reverence as it is without joy.

— — —

Nature is a part of our humanity, and without some awareness and experience of that divine mystery, man ceases to be man.

— — —

What has come over our age is an alienation from Nature unexampled in human history. It has cost us our sense of reality and all but cost us our humanity. With the passing of a relation to Nature worthy both of Nature and the human spirit, with the slow burning down of the poetic sense together with the noble sense of religious reverence to which it is allied, man has almost ceased to be man. Torn from earth and unaware, having neither the inheritance and awareness of man nor the other sureness and integrity of the animal, we have become vagrants in space, desperate for the meaninglessness which has closed about us. True humanity is no inherent and abstract right but an achievement, and only through the fullness of human experience may we be as one with all who have been and all who are yet to be, sharers and brethren and partakers of the mystery of living, reaching to the full of human peace and the full of human joy.

— — —

Whatever attitude to human existence you fashion for yourself, know that it is valid only if it be the shadow of an attitude to Nature.

— — —

Touch the earth, love the earth, honour the earth, her plains, her valleys, her hills, and her seas; rest your spirit in her solitary places. For the gifts of life are the earth's and they are given to all, and they are the songs of birds at daybreak, Orion and the Bear, and dawn seen over ocean from the beach.

ANTOINE DE SAINT-EXUPÉRY

When the wild ducks or the wild geese migrate in their season, a strange tide rises in the territories over which they sweep. As if magnetized by the great triangular flight, the barnyard fowl leap a foot or two into the air and try to fly. The call of the wild strikes them with the force of a harpoon and a vestige of savagery quickens their blood. All the ducks on the farm are transformed for an instant into migrant birds, and into those hard little heads, till now filled with humble images of pools and worms and barnyards, there swims a sense of continental expanse, of the breadth of seas and the salt taste of the ocean wind. The duck totters to right and left in its wire enclosure, gripped by a sudden passion to perform the impossible and a sudden love whose object is a mystery.

— — —

But I refuse to consider the fact that people are satisfied with what they have as a proof that they lack nothing. There is no absolute instinct that makes one demand something as yet unconceived. But if one makes people aware of an inner impulse that exalts them, then they will demand to know what the conditions for it are.

— — —

I reject non-being. My purpose is to be. And if I am to be, I must begin by assuming responsibility.

Index

(Below is the index to Parts One, Two, and Three, followed by an unconventional index to select ideas in the credos of Part Four.)

Important problems:
  compared to intellectual stunts, 50, 112
Integrity:
  how to instill, 94
Intuition:
  feeding of, 111
  in recursion, 25
John Muir naturalists:
  attitudes,
        on developers, 156
        on gradualism, 159
        on nature's interrelated variety, 153
        on public support for preserving nature, 163
        on recreational machines in wilderness, 155
        on rights for natural places, 153
        on spiritual vs. mercantile prosperity, 152
        on the one-person-one-vote principle, 158
        on the size of the human population, 154
        on the term "natural resources," 157
        on the term "rational man," 157
        on the training of elected officials, 159
        on the use of benefit-to-cost ratios, 156
        on the value of the human race vs. its people, 154
        on the willingness-to-pay method, 158
        on wild animals and property rights, 155
  benefits of raising children to be,
        arms them against impiety, 160
        lifts their creative standards, 160
        sensitizes their spirits, 160
        swells the ranks of future preservationists, 161
  definition of, 151
  means of raising children to be,
        instilling attention to nature, 161-162
        learning natural science that excites wonder, 163
        reading nature poets and writers, 162

(Examples of using the following index to select ideas in the credos of Part Four: The entry 198 JR denotes the sole quotation of Jean Rhys, page 198. The entry 204 SA (3) denotes the third quotation of Sherwood Anderson, under his name on page 204. The entry 239 CD (2,5) denotes the second and fifth quotations of Claude Debussy, under his name on page 239.)

Altruism:

Those who claim that self-interest is necessarily the motive behind altruism have it wrong. 196 LC

The charitably drawn are above the selfishly driven. 263 SB (2)

Art and artists:

The one common feature of great artists is they constantly toil. 170 JM (1), 215 DT (2), 337 GB (5)

Great artists are never satisfied with their work. 170 JM (2), 264 PP (6)

Artists do not create by values that are purely economic. 171 DLS (4)

Art shows and refines the human soul and the meaning of life. 182 AR, 247 OW, 248 MB (1), 291 WK (1)

Through art we may construct a life of wonder and serenity. 206 GG

The painter's duty is to be absorbed by nature and express sentiment. 232 VVG

Scientific knowledge is important to the artist, for broadening the range and significance of expression. 253 RJ (1)

Artists are givers of new forms of expression. 266 KAP

Commercial artists put their talents to unworthy use. 281 GOK (3)

Artists strive to make the unknown known. 281 GOK (4)

Art is a medium for communicating emotions. 291 WK (4)

Painting is leading to the spiritually purposeful. 291 WK (7)

The artist's duty is to make society better at its core. 334 MVD

Benefit-to-cost analysis:

In certain cases, great enterprises have been carried out successfully only because those who undertook them did not count the cost. 302 THH (7)

Choosing one's career:

Use the talent you have, not the talent you have only a taste for. 212 BS (1)

In realizing your talent, learn from doing things you have no taste for. 219 FSF

Collaborative work:

The creative power of a group compounds from that of its members. 300 ASP (2)

Collaborative work creates a reality more durable and valuable than oneself. 173 PTDC (3)

Commercialism and materialism:

The industrial world has become our master. 180 MRR (5)

Capitalism tempts students into a disabling course of life. 225 AE (7, 8)

Commercial and poetical minds share a core of similarities. 258 MCE (1)

Endless material progress is no index of human welfare. 230 EAR, 302 THH (4), 310 KL (3), 330 JWK (2)

The modern age suppresses creativity. 326 FH (2)

The spread of the machine has de-romanticized the world. 333 AW

Development is making the world poorer. 336 HMT, 336 HE

God created nature but God cannot save it from those blinded by the dollar sign. 339 JM (9, 11), 352 RC (1)

Commercialism is destructive of the arts. 346 WB (6)

Materialism hinders soulful communication. 348 AS (1)

Use of nature for economic enrichment impoverishes human life. 351 RD (1)

Courage:

True courage is that which is without witnesses and accomplices. 175 AG (6)

Creativity:

The genuinely creative develop their work in accordance with its own nature and not theirs. 171 DLS (1)

Two enemies of creating great works: trying to impress people by it, and intending to make a living by it. 174 TW

Create only those things that are in no one but you. 175 AG (2), 228 IBS, 247 CC, 290 JJ (2), 291 WK (2), 300 VH

To create really great works, break free of precedent. 213 EOW, 237 PC (4), 239 CD (2,4)

Creating creates the creator. 175 AG (3)

We stay young as long as we create. 177 IA, 194 RC

If your work pleases everyone, consider it a total failure. 178 VEM

The method of getting great ideas is to persevere to the point of madness. 211 CC (2)

Creativeness may wait to appear until one ages. 219 LWA (1)

Accepting prizes and awards can endanger creative freedom. 233 SL

The most crucial part of human character is the creative spirit. 243 NN

Artists should conserve their emotions for creating the big things in life rather than dissipating them on the little things. 281 GOK (1)

Detaching your emotions from the thing you are creating makes you more capable of expressing the thing as it is. 285 GF (5), 286 GB (3, 4)

Creating makes troubles vanish. 289 MT (1,2)

The answer to criticism is to create better. 296 LB

An unsuccessful vision is like a meteor that falls to earth. 193 JRL (2)

Often the fallen meteor is resurrected as part of new successful comet. 264 PP (4)

To become a decent writer takes great fortitude. 282 SS (2)

The creative spirit is the binding of our creative individuality with the creators of all time. 322 JCP (2)

Creators live in their creations. 337 GB (2)

Envisioning is like conceiving one's child. 350 GM (4)

Dedication:

Dedication is necessary for life to be worth living. 184 PH

Essential to personal success and fulfilment are total dedication and a tendency to underestimate difficulties. 189 RLM

Discipline:

Because excellence relies on disciplined and patient recursive work, the creations of drug users are pap. 235 JC

If discipline is less than total it is nothing. 243 VS

Through discipline we can attain personal peace. 243 RO

Education:

Education should help and enthuse a child to find and release its greatest talent. 207 PL, 211 CC (1)

Self-education is more valuable than formal education. 238 EG (2)

The most precious gifts for parents to give their children are perfectionism and enthusiasm. 241 CM (2)

To do great things, learn what great things are. 263 SB (3)

Schools and colleges suppress genius in students. 263 SB (4)

The heart is educated by using it. 284 ED (1)

Teach students pleasure and pride in setting standards and living up to them. 300 JG (1)

Schools should direct themselves to solving intellectual, aesthetic, and spiritual starvation. 301 JBSH (2)

Every child should be given a panoramic view of nature. 302 THH (8)

Great teachers teach how to get at the depth of things. 331 VFW (1)

The teacher's responsibility is to open a door, and the student's is to pass through it. 212 LCG, 348 AS (2)

There is no single way to the truths of the world; the partial truths from the various ways must be joined. 331 VFW (2), 348 AS (3), 354 HB (1)

Effort:

    In following the line of least resistance, we make ourselves least. 173 PTDC (2)

    The conviction of the necessary effort is the effort without which some part of being will never be achieved. 173 PTDC (4)

    What thwarts us and demands our greatest effort can teach us most. 175 AG (5)

    Moral failure can only be asserted when our efforts fall short of our limits. 205 CD (1), 206 JRRT

    The effort to understand increases the capacity to understand. 269 ER (2)

    Inactivity brings spiritual death. 298 TM (1)

Excellence:

    Congeniality is no substitute for competence. 216 PL (1)

    By doing things badly we make ourselves less real. 298 TM (3)

    Excellence is the lifeblood of democratic societies. 300 JG (2)

    Classic excellence is objectively absolute, independent of the times and our personal opinion. 348 AS (5)

Family size:

    Having n children means giving each 1/n of what they need to be best prepared for an intellectually creative life. 300 ASP (3), 306 JR (1, 2)

Freedom:

    Voluntary bondage to passionate interest gives freedom. 238 EG (1)

    Factory work enslaves. 249 PAR (6, 7)

    Imitating another enslaves the imitator. 346 WB (12, 15)

Happiness:

    Ultimate happiness is infinitely above proximate happiness. 209 JL (1, 2, 3)

    The saddest and most jaded person is the professional pleasure-seeker. 298 JWH (1, 2)

    For life to be happy, tie it not to people or perishable things but to striving to create great goodness for the world. 225 AE (10), 244 KH (2)

Creators hate the idea of an afterlife in which all desires are automatically satisfied. 187 GG

Suffering is good because it purifies, sanctifies, enlarges, elevates. 297 LDP (1)

Happiness comes in absolute grades. 348 AS (4)

That people are materially satisfied with what they have is no proof they do not lack a spiritual necessity. 355 ADSE (2)

Imagination:

Imagination acts as stimulus to the senses. 199 MW

The more we know, the better we are able to imagine. 231 RF

The power of imagination makes us infinite. 339 JM (15)

Intuition:

Intuition may be readied to speak by force feeding it. 232 JJ, 255 MF (1)

Intuition suggests, and reasoning checks on what it suggests. 281 GOK (2)

Leisure:

If leisure is to be joyful, it must follow work that raises you in your own eyes. 175 AG (7), 293 ED (3)

Life goal:

The life goal (in answer to Mr. Murnen) is to be responsible for one's own being – a being in the sense of always learning, and always becoming a better creator, conceiving and making works of great goodness, serving society and the species, vivifying the creative spirit. 169 THW, 173 PTDC (1), 174 JPS (1, 2), 175 AG (1), 178 JR, 180 MRR (2, 6), 181 KM (1, 2), 182 JPP (1, 2), 185 AS, 185 ML, 187 GG, 187 WF, 188 JC, 188 IB, 188 HGR, 189 EH, 190 KW, 190 AF, 191 JK (2), 191 STC (1), 193 JRL (1), 193 MBE, 193 GHH, 194 RC, 195 JA, 198 JR, 198 OWH, 200 LB, 200 MHB, 201 AC (1), 202 HJ, 204 N, 204 SA (4), 204 JJR (2), 205 HGW, 209 JL (1, 2, 3), 210 WSC, 214 AT, 217 WO, 217 MCT, 222 AK, 223 G, 225 AE (2,11), 251 LDV (1), 258 MCE (4), 264 PP (1), 266 TC, 268 PSB (2, 3), 283 RH, 286 GB (2), 287 BR (1), 294 BDV (1,2), 296 WS (2), 299 AT, 320 HDT (1), 355 ADSE (3)

Foolish ideas of success are founded on advancement, power, recognition, wealth, commercial gain, good looks, fame, etc. 169 AS, 203 AC (2), 222 TEL (2), 279 VB (2, 3, 4), 285 GF (2), 310 KL (3), 320 HDT (3)

Follow your true nature. 177 RH, 189 GO, 195 HA, 217 WO

Aim life toward simplicity not complications, and appreciation not possessions. 179 CL (1, 2)

Setting yourself a new purpose sets yourself a new existence. 183 FJ

Life is a trap for logicians. 191 GKC

Most people live at a small fraction of their potential capacities. 199 AH, 293 ED (1)

The young's chief zero hour is in believing and acting on "I must now start making my life in improving the world." 207 JK, 210 EA

We should live for, and in, humanity, and not for, or in, ourselves. 263 SB (1)

People need a great cause whose value is never questioned. 184 PH, 331 VFW (4)

Limitation of means:

Limitation of means develops patience, style, and engenders new form. 216 PL (2), 286 GB (1)

Modeling:

Modeling gives different ways of sensing. 337 GB (3)

A lack of the ultimate form of modeling hinders musical composers: trying designs out in live performance. 350 GM (3)

Motivation:

Love and obsession to create override all pain of toil and exasperation. 171 DLS (2, 3)

Doubts rise soon after envisioning a work, and mainly determination and a trusting sense of impending shape and that something of value will be found in the end keep one at it. 172 VW (3, 5), 258 MCE (3), 259 MS (5)

Essential to everything the creator does are choice, love, and passion. 174 NB

The joy of rock climbing is to stretch one's powers. 205 CB

Nature:

Nature gives new life to artists who study in its presence. 237 PC (2)

Nature stimulates the imagination. 249 PAR (5), 285 GF (8), 335 JA

Nature is the source of all inspiration and creative impulse. 252 HH, 253 OR, 318 RWE (5)

Only *large* tracts of wilderness refresh the creative spirit. 255 MF (4)

Nature is a pacifier. 270 EH (1), 297 LDP (2), 307 RB (2), 313 WH (2), 339 JM (5, 18), 352 RC (3)

Nature teaches obedience, patience, peace. 328 JCVD (5)

For nature to fill us with peace, it must contain no trace of our species. 308 TG (2)

Nature is an inexhaustible source of ideas. 293 ED (5), 313 WH (3), 335 RJ

Nature is an inexhaustible source of strength. 315 BW (2)

Nature increases us. 307 HN (2)

Nature is the only thing that is pure and beautiful in this world. 317 AN (1, 2)

Nature reveals truths that are hidden from political economists. 325 RLS

Nature radiates spiritual beauty, divine quality. 339 JM (12, 13)

Even to the deaf, nature has much to teach of music. 239 CD (5), 339 JM (3)

Nature has other-worldly serenity. 307 RB (1)

Nature is reflected in the human soul. 239 CD (6)

Nature is anciently imprinted on our brains. 327 WW (2), 331 VFW (5), 337 GB (6)

Love of nature rests on its airy abstraction that is its spirituality. 313 WH (1)

To be in kinship with every part of nature is to gain its spirit. 315 BW (1)

The call of the wild is the call of the creative spirit of nature. 355 ADSE (1)

Nature is the infinity below the surface of what we falsely think of as nature. 350 GM (5)

To behold the creative spirit of nature is to behold the Thing behind the thing. 351 RD (2), 353 AL

Sublimeness in art and nature rests on minute discrimination. 346 WB (3, 4, 10, 11, 13)

Nature has places that would awe an atheist into belief. 308 TG (1)

Nature possesses the power to hypnotize. 315 HI

Nature is the expression of God's face. 279 GMD (2)

Nature is essential for loving God. 316 CSL (2)

To connect to the creative spirit of God, learn to feel the beauty of all things. 231 IG

The beauty of nature reveals the beauty of God. 339 JM (5, 17)

The beauty of nature in our world is unique in the solar system and maybe beyond. 339 JM (14)

To sense nature in solitude is to be on the highway leading to God. 318 RWE (1)

We are no more marvelous than the least part of nature. 205 ·CD (2)

Next to animals, considered as machines, our machines are nothing. 339 JM (7)

Nature is more wonderful than human beings. 281 GOK (5)

More rewarding than contemplating oneself and human affairs is contemplating the universe. 253 RJ (3, 4)

Nature proves there is no such thing as spiritual evil. 272 EMF (2), 328 JCVD (2)

To learn where you have come from, where you are, and where you should go, go alone into wilderness. 327 WW (3)

Our experiences in nature remain within us to be forever re-lived. 339 JM (10)

Mountaineering sharpens attention to nature. 255 MF (2)

That mountaineers have no interest in climbing slag heaps proves the connection between the beauty of nature and the creative challenges of climbing. 339 GM

Injure, destroy, develop a part of nature, and there goes its unified whole, and thus its beauty, its quality, its sublimity, its majesty. 175 AG (9), 191 STC (5), 334 JR (2), 346 WB (4)

Replacing nature with development has gone too far. 255 JSM, 277 WM (1)

Scenes in nature are injured less by what is removed from them than by what is added. 327 WW (4), 339 JM (6)

In tallying how much nature remains, don't include fields, as they are as much a human product as a street. 301 JBSH (3)

Planted woods have no spiritual life at all. 353 HEB

The price of divorcing ourselves from nature is separation from our humanity. 354 HB (3, 4)

For the sake of money, certain males have always tried to cut nature's beautiful and irreplaceable throat. 328 JCVD (3)

Only limited power to destroy all of nature has so far saved society from doing so. 320 HDT (4), 328 JCVD (4)

If we are to stop destroying nature we must learn to sense its wonders and realities. 352 RC (2)

Every child should grow up well acquainted with nature. 301 JBSH (4)

For children, bonding with nature promotes good mental health. 287 BR (3)

Teach children the practice of drawing nature, and there will be more lovers of nature. 334 JR (3)

Experiencing nature in earliest childhood may set a regret-free course in life. 338 AA (3)

When the day comes that music composers snorkel in the living beauty of the seas, excellence in music will rise. 324 RT (2)

What little remains of nature should be defended with all vehemence. 310 KL (7)

Over-population:

To master the threat of our own numbers is our greatest need.
307 JH, 312 JRA (1)

Patience:

Without patience there can be no genius. 174 TW, 175 AG (4),
224 CSDSE, 237 PC (1), 284 ED (3)

Hustle and rush in work are the allies of superficiality. 307 HN
(1)

Quality vs. quantity:

Rather than make many inconsiderable works, make a few of
great goodness causing the goodness of quality to appear.
182 JPP (1), 282 SS (2), 298 TM (3), 330 JWK (1)

Religion:

The ethical codes of churches today are half complete, suited
only to the simpler social organization of bygone times. 301
JBSH (1)

Some churches preach for obedience to the commandment "increase and multiply," which on the other hand is the cause
of violence and war they preach against. 302 THH (9), 306
GMC, 310 KL (4)

Some churches preach for obedience to the commandment "increase and multiply,"which on the other hand results in devastation of nature, cutting us off from God, the very condition
they seek to avoid. 310 KL (4)

Responsibility:

Our duty is to do not what is best for us but best for the work.
197 FN

Only by assuming responsibility do we become important for
ourselves and for the world. 214 VH (1, 2)

Most people are on the world but have yet to assume the duty
of putting themselves in it. 339 JM (8)

Reverence for life:

Children feel the equality of animals and people. 241 CM (1)

Betraying the confidence of an animal is criminal. 312 JRA (2)

Animals' feats and humans' intellectual feats reflect God equally.
326 FH (1)

Animals are more interesting alive than dead. 326 FH (4)

Our species is no more valuable than any of nature's others. 339 JM (1, 2)

We cannot boast of humanity as long as animals are killed for pleasure. 275 MS (3)

Mercy to animals should be taught as part of religion. 275 MS (4)

Cruelty is the deepest and longest affecting of crimes. 276 TP

Holding profits above kindness to animals makes human ethics a sham. 310 KL (6)

Vivisection cancels the single advantage of our race. 322 JCP (1)

The power of the creative spirit will come to defeat the atrocities of cruelty. 322 JCP (3)

Reverence for all life puts us in a spiritual relationship with the entire universe. 323 AS (4)

Curiosity without compassion is inhuman. 331 VFW (3)

Cruelty to animals is ungodly. 346 WB (1, 2)

It is virtually impossible for an artist to be a killer. 203 AC (3)

The artist is obliged to fight for moral justice. 234 ESVM (1)

The aesthetic and the humane are indivisible. 257 VWB (3)

The aesthetic and the moral are all one. 309 HM, 310 KL (1)

Troubles of the world (including inhumane acts) depress the creative spirit and impede the creation of artistic excellence. 285 GF (7)

Cruelty mutes our sense of beauty. 299 OS

Kindness will pervade society only when we teach the very young to imagine with the heart the pain that harassed and cruelly-treated creatures feel. 310 KL (5)

Self-confidence:

To generate self-confidence, concentrate on realistic tasks. 185 SEL

Feeling inferior to the task makes progress possible. 284 ED (6)

Self-criticism:

Be prepared to recognize one's false positions in order to evolve beyond them. 198 LS, 300 ASP (1)

Self-denial:

Chastity gives the world a meaning. 203 AC (1)

Self-respect:

To generate self-respect, become needed by joining others in an important cause. 186 AM

Self-respect derives from creative work. 287 BR (2), 293 ED (3)

Sensualism:

All sensual appetites are one and the same. 320 HDT (7)

Solitude:

Solitude, by pacifying the conscious mind, allows the subconscious mind to open its door. 257 VWB (1)

Constant immersion in solitude is essential for the artist to create. 284 ED (4)

Being alone in one's youth develops imagination and self-reliance. 308 RK (1, 2)

Subconscious:

The subconscious is our tirelessly working second self. 221 LP (2), 350 GM (2)

Truth:

Mathematics but scratches the surface of truth. 346 WB (14)

Women creators:

A woman's desire to bear creative works into the world may equal or exceed her desire to have children or domestic life. 172 VW (4), 229 VT, 259 MS (8), 288 SP (1)

For a woman to be free of sensuality means greater power to create excellent works. 244 KH (1)

Printed in the United States
3623